The
Berry Grower's
Companion

The
Berry Grower's Companion

Barbara L. Bowling

TIMBER PRESS
PORTLAND • LONDON

Paperback edition published in 2005 by Timber Press, Inc.

The Haseltine Building
133 S.W. Second Avenue, Suite 450
Portland, Oregon 97204
www.timberpress.com

2 The Quadrant
135 Salusbury Road
London NW6 6RJ
www.timberpress.co.uk

Fourth printing 2009

Printed in China

Mention of particular pesticide brands, products, or vendors does not constitute a guarantee or warranty of the product by the publisher or authors. No endorsement is intended by the inclusion of trade names, nor is criticism implied of products not mentioned.

Library of Congress Cataloging-in-Publication Data

Bowling, Barbara L.
    The berry grower's companion / Barbara L. Bowling.
        p.   cm.
    Includes bibliographical references (p.   ).
    ISBN-13: 978-0-88192-726-9 pbk.
    1. Berries. 2. Ornamental berries. I. Title.

  SB381.B68   2000
  634'.7—dc21

                                                    00-026907

To my wonderful family:
John, my illustrious consort and spouse
Beth, the elder daughter
Sarah, the younger daughter
Cassie, the noble beast, and
Calico, the bad dog

Contents

Color plates follow page 144

Preface

Berries! Even the word sounds light and delicious, full of promise and exuberance. At a time when raspberries, strawberries, and blueberries may come from increasingly distant locations, the appeal of these fruits remains constant. And because the plants that bear them require minimal space, there are few plots of soil that cannot support enough to satisfy our longing for their succulent sweetness.

Early in my career, I was harvesting raspberries for a cultivar trial. The rule for researchers, and those who harvest for them, was that you can't eat anything until it has all been weighed and counted. After that, the data (that is, the fruits) were dealt with in a variety of ways, but I often ended up with a flat of red raspberries that I was supposed to "get rid of." One time when I took the extra berries to a colleague's house (she worked with potatoes), we got out the whipped cream and sat and ate raspberries and cream until we could eat no more. "You know," she said, "that's the first time I've ever had *enough* red raspberries." Can anyone imagine a more delectable fruit? The fact that raspberries are relatively scarce and ephemeral makes them, like their cousins the roses, that much more appealing.

As our population continues to migrate from farms to urban and suburban settings, we are losing a knowledge that was once common, even assumed. We no longer know exactly where our food comes from and how it is produced, and this has created a general sense of alienation between consumers and producers. The good news is that gardening remains the number one hobby in the United States, its popularity a reflection of the fundamental attraction between humans and plants. Few gardeners can resist growing the edible kinds of plants, and many try their hand at growing berry crops. Sometimes good culture, or good luck, brings success. Often, however, seemingly inexplicable problems hobble the most well-intentioned efforts.

This book provides insight into the background, history, and nature of these delightful plants, addresses some problems that berry growers can expect to encounter, and illuminates less obvious philosophical and strategic issues related to growing perennial berry crops. It is intended as a practical introductory guide to the art and science of growing berries in the garden and home landscape, as well as a source of inspiration for considering the deeper issues associated with the production of plants and food. It also provides essential reminders and information of interest to established large-scale growers.

My original working title for this book was *Berry My Heart: A Small-Fruit Specialist Tells the Truth About the Art, Science, and Philosophy of Growing Berries in the Garden,* and though since abandoned, this first title reveals much about my motivation for writing the book. I put "my heart" in the title because it conveyed, through a play on words, the passion that I have for these plants. (To avoid running the risk of offending Native Americans by potentially appearing to make light of a profound event in their history, that part of the title was eliminated early in the editorial process.) The idea of "telling the truth" seemed appropriate, given that so much of the existing literature does not tell the whole truth. For example, cultivars that are often called "bland" in actuality taste terrible; and controlling deer with soap rarely works. As for the "art," anyone who gardens knows that this is part of all gardening. Berries and small fruits elevate that art by what they are: beautiful jewels grown on plant structures that we shape through pruning and training. The "science" provides the basis for most of our cultural strategies, and it is also what I've been doing for most of my academic career in an attempt to elucidate truths about growing these crops. "Philosophy"? What philosophical issues are raised by growing berries? Here are a few: How do we, as a culture, grapple with the fact that so few people know what it takes to produce food and fiber? How

DIGRESSION

On the Depth and Breadth
of the Seemingly Minor

I remember when I first met my father-in-law. He was, by vocation, a plant manager and part-owner of a company that made wire brushes. When I told him I was working on a doctorate in horticulture, specifically on the effect of growing strawberries on raised beds, he asked, without any intention of offense, "How did you get into that?" His tone was incredulous, and the emphasis was on the word *that*. He was, after all, a gardener. Not the well-read sort likely to read Timber Press books, but someone who just loved to mess around in the soil. It had never occurred to him that there would be much to know about an area as seemingly narrow, perhaps arcane, as berry culture, let alone that one might make a living at it.

I have told that story to many people, including the undergraduate students who take my small-fruit culture class. Few, if any, of them have ever given much thought to berry crops, but they like plants, and they think the class might be "neat." The point I try to make to them is that there is a lot to know about berry crops. Each crop has a story. This story involves not only the crop's history, but a lifestyle of sorts, a means of propagating, and a series of requirements that must be met if it is to thrive. These plants are as individual and complicated as we are.

does the production of edible crops fit into our local communities? What issues confront a perennial plant grower as compared to an annual plant grower? How does one go about developing a philosophy about pesticide use?

Anyone who is interested in the horticultural aspects of berry production will, I hope, find this book useful. Nothing makes me happier than to see a production guide I've written that has obviously been thumbed through and is dog-earred and dirty with use. For those who have developed, as I have, a passion for berries, I hope the insights offered here will be thought about, gone back to, and considered and reconsidered. And for those who have yet to be fully captivated by the allure of the berries, hopefully you will look to this guide often as you head off and explore the world of berry culture. OK—you don't have to get it dirty.

Acknowledgments

First and foremost, I want to thank my family for putting up with me for the last month or so of writing this book. Special thanks to John, Illustrious Consort and Spouse, who helped me enormously with computer support and advice.

Thanks also to Kathy Demchak, the "other half" of the small-fruit program as it used to exist at Penn State University. Not only did she read sections of the book and make suggestions, but Kathy also did the tedious work of updating valuable information like the list of nurseries, and she took several of the photographs contained herein.

Speaking of photographs, my sincerest thanks to David Handley and Jim Dill at the University of Maine, and Kim Hummer of the USDA/ARS in Corvallis, Oregon, for generously sharing their excellent photographs for use in this book.

Thanks also to John Clark, University of Arkansas; David Handley, University of Maine; Bernadine Strik, Oregon State University; and Rebecca Darnell, University of Florida, for supplying cultivar information for their particular regions of the United States.

Special thanks to Jim Hancock of Michigan State University. His unswerving enthusiasm and belief in my ability to conduct mycorrhizal research *and* write a book for the passionate berry grower gave me the inspiration I needed when it all seemed impossible.

Thanks to Josh Leventhal, editor of this book. His excellent and provocative questioning made this book more readable and sane than it would have been otherwise. Thanks also to Timber Press for supporting this project.

Finally, I'd like to take a deep breath and thank the community of small-fruit researchers, extension workers, and teachers across the United States and the world. They are the most supportive, interesting, eccentric, and unselfish group of professionals I've ever had the privilege of working with. Good growing.

Introduction

WHAT ARE BERRY CROPS?

The fruits that are commonly referred to as "berries" include straw-berries, brambles (raspberries, blackberries, and various hybrids), blueberries, cranberries, currants, grapes, gooseberries, and elder-berries. Technically, most of these fruits are not berries, since in botanical terminology a berry is defined as a fruit that is multiseeded and derived from a single ovary. Among those fruits mentioned, only blueberries and grapes are true berries.

The plants discussed in this book are also often referred to as "small fruit," but this can be confusing since the word *small* refers not to the size of the fruit but to the size of the plant upon which the fruit is borne. For example, the cherry is not called a small fruit, even though the individual fruits are diminutive, because cherries are borne on trees. The two major groups of fruit are, therefore, small fruit and tree fruit. The term "cane fruit" is sometimes used in the literature to refer to certain classes of small fruit. Canes are the stems of such fruit plants as brambles, blueberries, and grapes. This category does not include strawberries, cranberries, currants, or gooseberries, however, so for the purposes of this book, the com-mon term "berries" will be employed.

This diverse group of fruits has been a source of sustenance throughout written history, and berries most certainly were sought by the earliest hunting-and-gathering peoples. They are often con-sumed as a fresh product, but they are also extensively processed into juices, jams, dairy products, and pastries. Berries offer a remarkable collection of flavors and colors, and they are high in nutrition and fiber and low in fat; recent evidence suggests that many species have high levels of numerous antioxidants and anti-tumor compounds. Berry growing is attractive to both the home and commercial producer since it requires relatively little space and most species begin fruiting within 2 to 3 years of planting. Because many berries have a short shelf-life, it is often difficult to find good quality fruit at the local grocery store, making home growing an appealing option.

THE PHILOSOPHY OF
PERENNIAL CROP PRODUCTION

The growth habits of berry plants range from trailing vines (cranberries) to vines that require support (thornless blackberries) to upright, freestanding shrubs (highbush blueberries). Some berries, such as grapes, have been cultivated for centuries, whereas others, such as blueberries, are relatively recent additions to the commercial fruit industry and the garden landscape. All are perennial, dicotyledonous (broadleaf) angiosperms (flowering plants), and with the exception of the strawberry, all are woody plants.

The perennial nature of these plants is highly significant. Due to the long-term nature of perennial crop production, the grower must simultaneously consider this year's crop, next year's crop, and the continued overall health of the plants. Individual specimens of some species, such as blueberries or grapes, may successfully yield fruit for 50 years or more. Maintaining the longevity of any berry planting requires vigilant care that includes controlling pests, attention to cultural tasks such as pruning and weed removal, and controlling crop size. A little good luck doesn't hurt either. Berries are among the most intensively cultivated crops. Whether grown on a commercial or garden scale, they require a high initial investment and a lot of hand labor. If managed well, though, berry crops produce high profits per unit land area—or just a lot of great fruit to eat, process, and share.

I have spent most of my professional horticultural career working with commercial producers of berry crops. Although it is often quoted in agricultural circles that berries bring some of the highest profits per acre, what is not often mentioned is that it is easier to lose a fortune than to make one in berry crops. Even with the advantages of farm machinery, fertilizers, and pesticides to help manage the many obstacles that nature may throw in the path of the commercial grower, berry production is not an easy business in which to survive. Like investing in the stock market, the key to success is long-term investment. Save during good years so that you can absorb the losses in the bad years, and in the end hopefully you will realize a profit, not only fiscally but in the satisfaction of producing beautiful food that is delicious and good for your family and the extended family of fellow humans. (In my case I have to include my raspberry-eating bad dog in that equation.)

Even with the aid of all that is modern, growing berry crops still requires that the grower get off of his or her tractor seat, walk amid the plants, look for pests, prune, touch the leaves—just as any gardener must do in the backyard. There is a certain fairness about this, not true of so many vegetable crops that are grown on a massive scale in a manner such that an individual plant (particularly one in the middle of a field) is never touched, never looked at, never embraced, never thanked specifically for its generous offering. The importance of careful, timely management based on close, hands-on observation and attention to detail cannot be overstated, whether you are growing a few plants in your backyard or thousands of plants on many acres.

Before launching head-on into the world of berry growing, I offer one important caveat. The berry crops discussed in this book are all, albeit to varying degrees, extremely sensitive to local growing conditions. Because my experience in berry production has been in the eastern and midwestern United States, my comments will be of most practical use for gardeners in or near those regions, or in regions throughout the world that have similar growing conditions. I encourage you to consult with other growers in your area and with your local extension office to learn more about growing berries in your particular location.

The Bramble Bush.

CHAPTER 1

General Principles for Growing Berries

Chapters like this one are sometimes difficult to read. You think you know most of what you need to know in order to get started, and you just want to get to the good stuff, the information specific to your favorite berry crop or crops. Bear with me: this information *will* be useful.

LOCATION, LOCATION, LOCATION

The real estate people always say that the three most important considerations about a property's value are location, location, and location. I suspect they borrowed that notion from early agriculturists, because it could not be more true for selecting a site for berry production. Location refers to what many books, particularly agricultural production guides, call "site selection." Where do you intend to plant your future delectables?

Macroclimate

The first location is the large-scale macroclimate. The hardiness zone of your garden is a primary concern. If you are able to choose where you live based on where raspberries grow best, you are certainly a lucky gardener. But if you are like most of us, you already live somewhere and have to work within the constraints of local conditions. You first need to find out if it is even possible to produce a particular crop in your current location. In many cases you may be able to grow certain cultivars of a plant but not others. For example, gardeners in the Pacific Northwest can grow 'Tulameen' and 'Willamette' red raspberries; move to central Pennsylvania, however, and those cultivars will not make it through the first winter. The good news is that the 'Sentry', 'Amos', and 'Canby' red raspberries all can be grown in this region. Fortunately, information about what grows best in your location is usually readily available. The local extension service and other growers in your area are the best resources. This book provides some general information on cultivar selection within each crop group, but be sure to check out the local sources.

Mesoclimate

A site's mesoclimate depends on the mitigating effects of topology, such as proximity to a mountain or a large body of water. For example, the south side of Lake Erie would be a mesoclimate. It is an area larger than the average farm but has particular climatic characteristics that set it apart from other areas nearby. The moderating effect of the lake makes it possible to produce species of cold-tender grapes, for example, and other fruits that could not otherwise be grown at this northern latitude. Another example of a mesoclimate is the north slope of a mountain, which imposes colder absolute temperatures and less warming temperatures early in the season compared to a southern exposure. This difference might determine whether or not certain cultivars or even species could reliably be grown.

Microclimate

The microclimate is the last and smallest of the locations. Technically, the term *microclimate* is used to describe very local conditions, such as the temperature or relative humidity within a canopy of a plant, but it is often used more broadly to describe the conditions at an individual site. A great deal of research is being conducted toward using the Global Positioning System (GPS) to pinpoint weather conditions down to a square foot, but the best knowledge is that gained by careful observation of a plot of soil over time. In most of the United States, weather is monitored in several locations throughout a state, usually through the department of agriculture. Universities may also supply such information to the public. Such data are useful for making a first cut at characterizing the climate of your garden, but nothing beats measuring the conditions of the specific site yourself. Maximum/minimum thermometers, which have two columns of mercury to show the lowest and highest (as well as current) temperatures, are inexpensive and readily available from most garden or farm supply centers (they're quite cool and clever, too). Rain gauges are also useful and easy-to-find tools for assessing the conditions of your site. You may be surprised to find differences between your observations and those made on a site only a few miles away.

Other Factors Related to Site

Climate is important, but other factors must be considered before planting any berry plant.

Soil drainage. Before planting, you should make sure that your intended site has good internal soil drainage. If the area puddles and holds water for more than a few hours after a rain storm, it probably is not suited for any of the berry crops. If you are not certain whether your soil is well drained, get the shovel out. Dig a hole 1 to 2 feet (30–60 cm) deep and look for any yellow or gray mottling in the soil. If you see such mottling anywhere less than 18 inches (45 cm) deep, the site is probably marginal. If possible, leave the hole open and observe how quickly water drains after a rainstorm. If the water sits there for more than 12 hours, the site is not appropriate for small fruits.

One way to improve marginally drained soils is to lay ceramic pipes below the frost line to drain off excess soil water, but this procedure, known as tile draining, is expensive. Heavy clay soils with poor drainage are often beyond hope and help, but they can be amended with organic matter to increase friability. Other options include bringing in good soil for your plot, or creating beds mounded 18 to 24 inches (45–60 cm) high.

DIGRESSION

Regarding Cold Hardiness

Because the ability of a given species to survive in a particular
location is so often limited by its ability to withstand cold temperatures, a word about our use of the term *cold hardiness* is
in order. Throughout this book you will find discussions of
the relative cold hardiness of cultivars for each crop. These
cold-hardiness ratings refer to how well a plant withstands
winter temperatures when completely dormant—but this is
not a perfect system. For one thing, these ratings may be, and
often are, determined at times when the researcher's plot is
experiencing atypical conditions, such as exceptionally cold
weather, so the information often is not based on tightly controlled experimental data.

In addition, some plants may lose dormancy more quickly
(meaning they require less chilling) than others as the winter
drags on. Once they have lost some of that dormancy, the
plants are more active metabolically (even though they still
look dormant) and may be injured at considerably higher temperatures than that at which they were completely dormant.
Furthermore, these cold-hardiness ratings do not take into ac-
count injury from frosts in the spring. As an example, hardy
kiwis *(Actinidia arguta)* are extraordinarily cold hardy when
dormant, tolerating temperatures into the −40°F (−40°C) range,
so we call them "hardy." Once they have lost dormancy in the
spring, however, the plants leaf out extremely early, and the
tender shoots are often injured by late frosts. A dormant plant
can withstand temperatures of 25°F (−4°C) fairly easily, but
consider how that plant would handle the same temperature
in the middle of summer.

The bottom line? View hardiness ratings as guides, not
absolute measures.

Sunlight. The most frequently asked question by people with small plots of land is "Can I grow berries in shade?" The answer: Not if you want fruit, and probably not if you want healthy foliage, either. There are a few exceptions, however. Gooseberries will produce fruit and usually survive if planted in areas with filtered shade. The fruit will not be abundant, and the quality may not be quite as good, but the plants do give you something back for your hard work. Blueberries also tolerate shade quite well, but they usually produce little or no fruit under these conditions. They make wonderful ornamentals, however, turning lovely shades of red and yellow in the fall, and many cultivars have beautiful red stems. So, if you do not require fruit, blueberries are still useful even in shade.

Water. Most plants require irrigation, but particularly shallow-rooted crops such as strawberries and blueberries. In fact, irrigating these plants is a necessity in most locations. For all small-fruit crops, irrigation may be essential at planting and during fruit swell, since natural rainfall is often not adequate.

Trickle irrigation is the application of small amounts of water to the soil surface using hoses or emitters specially designed for this purpose. It works extremely well for berry crops, particularly for irrigating raspberries, blueberries, and strawberries during fruiting because it allows the grower to apply water at the critical period of fruit development but avoids wetting the fruit. Wet fruit is more susceptible to disease infections that cause rot.

SOIL FERTILITY: PLANNING FOR HUNGRY PLANTS

Soil wins the prize as our most underappreciated resource, perhaps due to the increasingly nonagrarian nature of our culture. Soil takes millions of years to form and to build up the rich reservoir of nutrients so essential to the growth of our plants—yet soil can be lost in a single downpour. Treat it as the precious commodity that it is. It is only correctly called "dirt" if you find it on your kitchen floor.

Regarding Sunlight and Fruit

Making fruit is a plant's way of producing tasty, transportable progeny for the continuation of its species. Reproduction, across both the animal and plant kingdoms, is an energy-intensive process. Plants acquire their energy directly from the sun via a process called photosynthesis. This is no minor miracle, and it allows the rest of us on earth to exist. Leaves can be thought of as the factories that provide housing for the process of changing the energy in the light to the chemical energy that they (and we) can use. Leaf exposure to sunlight is directly linked to the plant's ability to acquire energy for all its life processes, including reproduction. This information begs the question, "Why do some plants flower in the shade?" The plants that flower in shade have adapted to this role over the course of millions of years of evolution. None, however, produces edible fruit in what we would consider reasonable quantities. The production of the fruit itself, full of sugars, vitamins, and other useful compounds, is a further burden on the plant. Why does the plant bother to make fruit when it could just as well produce only seeds, as many plants do? We can't know for sure, but it's a good guess that the fruit is produced so that birds and animals will eat it and distribute the seeds, vastly increasing the geographic range of the plant. Many evolutionary strategies for reproduction are successful in nature; the production of fruit is one of the more successful.

A commercial grower recently complained bitterly to me that his soil was "more suited to making bricks than growing plants," and he wanted to know what "The University" was doing about that. My response was that we *never* recommend growing small fruits on poor soils. The plants are expensive to establish, they are labor intensive, and on a commercial scale, they are a high-risk crop. Many soils can be helped, though.

The first thing to remember about soil fertility is that berries are perennial plants. The expected life spans of these plants range from a few years (strawberries) to decades (blueberries, grapes). The level of nutrients and organic matter in the soil before you plant is critical—think of it as preventative nutrition.

Soil Testing and Preparation

The first step toward optimizing the condition of the soil is soil testing. You have heard this before, and it's still important. All county extension offices across the United States can provide information on how to conduct a soil test. Some will conduct a soil pH test on site. You probably will have to pay for the test, but it is worth it for both the valuable information and the peace of mind.

Soil tests should be conducted in the late summer (August or September) prior to the spring when you intend to plant. For the test, gather soil from several spots within the planting area. The samples should be taken from the top 12 inches (30 cm) of soil. Thoroughly mix all the soil from these various areas in a bucket, and then put a small (about 1 cup) subsample in the sampling bag provided by the extension office. Be sure to fill out the forms that come with the soil sampling kit. Based on the sample, the soil test will offer recommendations for optimizing the soil for your particular crop.

The soil test recommendations are essential for meeting the following important soil needs:

pH. Soil pH is a measure of how acidic or alkaline the soil is. Old timers used to refer to this as the "sourness" or "sweetness" of the soil, because they would literally taste the soil to make an assessment. (I haven't tried this method and am grateful for the invention of pH meters.) The pH is a measure of the concentration of hydrogen ions, which is a reflection of acidity. A pH of 7 is neutral, and anything higher than 7 indicates alkalinity whereas a pH lower than 7 indicates acidity. The main thing that gardeners should know is that most garden plants thrive in soils with a pH of 5.5–6.5. Such a pH level is optimal because it provides a soil solution in which the nutrients can be readily acquired by the plant. For example, although most soils contain plenty of iron, iron deficiency is a common problem in high pH soils because the chemical form of the iron in the alkaline soil solution cannot be taken up by the plant. By altering the soil pH (as opposed to adding iron), you eliminate the iron deficiency because the existing iron is now in a form that is available to the plant. Adding iron would, in fact, be useless without changing the soil pH, since it would immediately change to the unavailable form.

If the soil is too acidic, the soil test will recommend adding lime. If the soil is too alkaline, sulfur may be recommended. Each of these amendments takes a long time to move through the soil, so if required, they should be applied as soon as possible, usually the fall before you intend to plant. Note, too, that though most plants prefer a pH of 5.5–6.5, certain berry plants prefer more acidic soil, including blueberry, lingonberry, and other plants in the family Ericaceae. It is therefore important to specify on the soil-test form which plants will reside in the intended site.

Phosphorus. Phosphorus is the element that is responsible for energy transfer in the plant. It is also found in numerous enzymes and in protein synthesis. Common symptoms of phosphorus deficiency are a general stunting and a darkening and/or reddening of older leaves, as well as poor flower and fruit formation. Because phosphorus is not very water-soluble, like lime and sulfur, it moves slowly in the soil and should be added to the soil the fall before planting.

Potassium. Potassium is involved in many biochemical reactions in plants, including drought resistance. Deficiency often results in small root systems as well as increased likelihood of lodging (falling over). Potassium is intermediate in water solubility, so it can be added either in the fall or the spring before planting.

Magnesium. Magnesium is a nutrient that is needed in smaller quantities than the previously mentioned one. It is often found lacking in small-fruit crops, so soil test results regarding this nutrient are particularly valuable. Like potassium, it is intermediate in mobility in the soil and can be applied in either fall or spring.

What the soil test *won't* tell you:

Nitrogen. Nitrogen is the element most often needed by plants in the garden and in commercial situations. It is the basic element in proteins, which are fundamental components of both plants and animals. It is also an essential element in the pigment chlorophyll, which gives the plants their green color, hence inadequate nitrogen will result in pale green leaves. Nitrogen does not occur in the geologic materials that make up soil but is present only in organic matter (applied or naturally occurring) or via rainwater through fixation by lightning. Nitrogen is also very ephemeral and changes forms rapidly, so it is the only major nutrient *not* included in soil tests. I and other experts make general nitrogen recommendations for each crop, based on experience and extensive experimentation. Because it is very soluble in water, nitrogen moves readily in the soil. It should be applied just before or after planting or in the spring when the plants resume growth. The recommended amount of nitrogen can also be divided and apportioned out in several smaller applications throughout the growing season to provide a continuous supply. This method may be particularly useful for growers in sandy soils, where nitrogen leaches through the soil readily.

Micronutrients. Micronutrients are elements that plants need in minute quantities (measured in parts per million). Soil tests rarely include a micronutrient analysis because micronutrients are much more accurately measured from the leaves of the plants, rather than from the soil. Unless you know in advance that your soil lacks a particular micronutrient, you will not correct for micronutrient deficiencies before planting. If you suspect a deficiency in an established plant, you can get information on leaf analysis (also referred to as "tissue analysis") from local extension personnel. The good news is that most soils have plenty of micronutrients, and a deficiency in home gardens is unusual.

When adding nutrient amendments to the soil, a spade or rototiller should be used to mix in any of the relatively immobile nutrients (such as phosphorus, lime, or sulfur) as much as possible. The more water-soluble nutrients, such as nitrogen and potassium, should be worked into the top 6 to 12 inches (15–30 cm) of soil for best results. Nitrogen can also be top-dressed later in the season if your crop requires it.

Cover crops can also be incorporated to the site in the fall, after any necessary nutrient amendments have been added to the soil, if it is early enough in the season. Cover crops offer two advantages. First, they hold the soil in place over the winter, which is particularly important if the site is sloped or if your area is prone to heavy rains in the winter and early spring months. The other benefit is that the cover crop can be tilled back into the soil before planting to provide additional organic matter. Rye or oats work particularly well as cover crops.

Organic Matter

Organic matter in the soil is the Holy Grail of horticulturists the world over. It offers a slow-release reservoir of nutrients. As microbes in the soil break down the organic matter, nutrients are released. Along with the clay component of the soil, the organic matter also provides a chemically charged surface that attracts nutrients and holds onto them, preventing them from washing through the soil to the ground water. Finally, it contributes to a soil characteristic known as tilth, or friability. These terms are used to describe how easily the soil breaks up into smaller pieces. Soils with a lot of heavy clay tend to form clumps in your hands and do not break up into smaller pieces easily. This trait is great for building bricks or pots, but not one that is conducive to the growth of root systems. By adding organic matter to the soil, either by growing and turning under a cover crop or by amending the soil with materials such as rotted sawdust, manure, spent mushroom compost, or leaf compost, the clay aggregates are broken apart, and the soil environment is made more hospitable to plant roots.

We have a tendency to think that all organic matter is alike, but this could not be further from the truth. Some have higher levels of nitrogen, some have more carbon. All are broken down by organisms that consume nitrogen, so be aware that even though organic matter is a long-term, slow-release source of nitrogen, the plants may require more nitrogen to "get started."

Fertilizer Application

Throughout this book and many others, fertilizer recommendations are based on how much of the "actual" element should be applied. "Actual nitrogen" (or potassium or phosphorus) refers to the percentage of nitrogen in the material you are using. If a crop requires 0.5 pounds of actual nitrogen, you will need to calculate this amount based on how much nitrogen is in your fertilizer. To determine how much fertilizer is needed, divide the required rate by the percentage of nitrogen in the material being used. For example, urea has 45 percent nitrogen, and if you want to apply 0.5 pounds of actual nitrogen, divide 0.5 by 0.45: 0.5 lb./0.45 = 1.1 lbs. urea.

CHOOSING A CROP

What berries do you like? It would be silly to grow a crop that does not make your eyes sparkle and your mouth water at its very mention. It amazes me that there are people who don't like certain berries, but it happens. (I once worked with a graduate student who actually disliked raspberries—an incomprehensible concept to a raspberry-phile such as myself.) Start with what you like, then narrow it down by considering what crops can be grown easily on your site. You may also want to consider whether you want to grow crops that require processing. Few of us have a palate for raw black currants, but this fruit makes wonderful juice. Elderberries, likewise, are not for the timid if fresh consumption is the goal, but they work beautifully for pies and jams, and they have few serious pests.

SELECTING CULTIVARS FOR YOUR REGION

For each berry crop treated in this book, recommended cultivars are given for different regions of the United States, according to the recommendations of extension personnel around the country. These regional divisions are based on similarities in climatic and soil conditions. The regions cover broad geographical areas and thus should be used as guidelines rather than absolutes. If, for example, you live and garden in northern Maine, you will want to select the hardiest of the selections recommended for New England. In the Midwest, a Minnesotan might opt for the half-high blueberries developed for that region, whereas a grower in southern Ohio may choose the more tender highbush blueberries. As always, consult local sources such as extension personnel and other growers. Their experience is invaluable.

Recommended cultivars are not provided for California and some of the adjoining desert states. The reason for this exclusion is that the plants in this book are all temperate-zone crops and do not perform well in non-temperate climates. California is an obvious exception, as that state is a major producer of strawberries and also has some raspberry production. The production systems in California are somewhat different, however, and many of the cultivars grown there are proprietary. It is also strictly large-scale farming, primarily for an export market, so the principles do not translate well to the home garden.

ACQUIRING PLANTS:
A CRAZY PLACE TO SKIMP

Purchasing plants that are certified and virus tested, as opposed to digging up some of your neighbors' plants and transplanting them to your site, is like buying an insurance policy. If it turns out that you need the insurance, you'll be glad that you invested in it. My advice to commercial growers is, "Always buy the insurance policy." Their livelihood and the success of the commercial operation depend on the quality and the trueness to name of the cultivars they buy. My advice to gardeners: "Know what you're getting into"—that is, familiarize yourself ahead of time with the specific problems you are likely to run into, and weigh the risks. Unlike getting seeds from a fellow gardener, taking some of their plants can invite big problems. So, what's the worst that can happen?

Bad, but not terrible. The plants are infected with a virus. Viruses are forever, at least with the current technology. They will deplete the plants' resources, the plants will decline for no apparent reason—either quickly (if the infection is major) or more slowly, over 3 or 4 years—and within a few years you'll be claiming that you just can't grow raspberries/blueberries/strawberries, and you'll deprive yourself of the joy of great fruit.

Very bad, still not terrible. The plants are infected with a virus, and the soil has nematodes (naturally occurring microscopic worms, most prevalent on sandy sites). The virus causes the plants to decline and eventually die, so you dig them out and start over with virus-tested, high-quality plants from a nursery. Unfortunately, the nematodes in your soil had been dining on the virus-infected roots—they can do this without hurting the plant, unless the numbers get too high—and now they carry the virus in their gut. The nematodes are more than happy to dine on your new virus-tested plant, thus infecting it with the virus they are carrying. This site is now useless, unless you use soil sterilants to clean it up, which is an unlikely and unattractive option, particularly as regulations restrict use of these chemicals.

Truly terrible. Your raspberry or blackberry plants are infected with crown gall bacteria *(Agrobacterium tumafaciens)*. Not only will the galls slow the growth of your raspberry planting, eventually to the point that it won't be worth keeping, but they will pollute your soil. Now you have a serious problem. There are no fumigants available to get rid of the galls (which are hard coated, often too small to see, and blend into the soil), and crown gall infects a wide range of plants. Any plant in the family Rosaceae, which includes roses, raspberries, strawberries, and many other ornamentals, is highly susceptible to crown gall, and few ornamental plants are immune.

How do you avoid such unfortunate outcomes? The first consideration is to know the crop well and to make sure, to the best of your ability, that the plants are healthy. Examine them for disease symptoms, and gauge the level of vigor and productivity of the planting in its current environment. Even well-intentioned and kind people can be "Typhoid Marys," so if you decide to obtain plants from someone else's garden, be aware that you are taking a risk that may develop into a liability. Knowing the name of the cultivar you have acquired will also be useful if you run into any problems with the plant.

The alternative, and the route of the more cautious or thoughtful, is to purchase plants from a reputable nursery. A listing of nurseries and the small-fruit crops they carry is provided in the Appendix at the back of this book; your local extension office may have additional sources as well. Avoid purchasing plants from nurseries where the plants are not clearly identified. Nursery catalogs that carry small fruit only as a sideline should also be avoided. The best strategy is to buy directly from a nursery that propagates the plants itself. All plant labels should provide the species or cultivar name and indicate somewhere that the plants are virus tested and certified.

DEALING WITH DRAGONS AND OTHER PESTS

Oh, that dragons were the only pests we had to contend with in berry production. They are not, of course, and being forewarned is indeed being forearmed. Specific pest problems are described in the subsequent chapters on individual berry crops, but some general concepts and philosophical issues need to be addressed.

Pests are any living organisms that either injure your crop plants or injure your crop. There are four major pest groups: weeds, insects, diseases, and vertebrates.

Weeds. Weeds are simply plants that are out of place, at least by the grower's definition. (I expect that the weeds would hold an altogether different opinion.) When they are growing next to your crop plant, weeds are competing directly with that plant for resources such as sunlight, water, nutrients, and space. Reducing these resources will limit the growth and productivity of the crop plants. Weeds also limit air circulation around the plants, which prevents moisture from dew or rain from drying off as quickly. Many fungal diseases that infect berry plants thrive in wet environments, so the weeds tip the balance in favor of the disease against your plants. Weeds can harbor insects or, worse, viruses that can infect and harm your fruit plants. For example, dandelions are widely infected with tobacco ring spot virus. If a nematode takes a bite out of the infected dandelion and then feeds on your raspberry roots, the raspberries will become infected with the virus, producing a symptom called crumbly berry that ruins fruit quality. The only cure at this point is to remove the raspberries—hardly an appealing "control."

Insects, mites, and slugs. Of the hundreds of thousands of insect species in nature, a small percentage are pests, but those few can cause a lot of damage. Some injure the fruit directly by feeding or laying eggs on them; others damage the plant by sucking sugars from the leaves or by consuming the leaves and roots, thus indirectly affecting fruit yield. Some insect pests also transmit viruses, which tend to debilitate the plant over time. Mites are tiny insectlike creatures often found on the undersides of leaves. They are mentioned separately because technically mites are not insects but are more closely related to spiders. Chemicals that control insects often have no effect on mites, and vice versa. Likewise, slugs are not insects but still can exact a toll on a strawberry planting, particularly in wet years.

Diseases. Diseases in plants, like those in humans, are caused by microorganisms. Most plant diseases are caused by fungi or viruses, though a few bacterial diseases also affect plants. Fungal diseases are usually instigated by spores that are ubiquitous in the atmosphere. Once these spores come into contact with the plant, they grow and develop on the plant. In the case of a pathogen (a disease-causing agent), this is always to the detriment of the plant. As with insect pests, some diseases affect the fruit directly (such as gray mold caused by *Botrytis cinerea*), and others grow on foliage or invade the root system. In general, wet conditions exacerbate disease problems. Extended periods of rainy weather, over-irrigation, or conditions that hamper the drying of dew, such as shady conditions in the morning hours, all can increase the likelihood of disease. In addition, careful cultural management, such as pruning and thinning overly dense foliage and eliminating weed populations, can reduce the threat of disease.

Vertebrates. Vertebrates are animals with backbones—deer, mice, rabbits, birds, and so forth. They can cause problems and even considerable injury to small-fruit plantings. Deer feed directly on leaves and shoots, most problematically in grape and raspberry plantings. In times of desperation they may even feed on the bark of grapevines. Mice and rabbits can eat away the base of fruit plants. Sometimes mice or rabbit populations become so dense that they damage the plants' root systems by their burrowing.

Do Pests Need to be Controlled?

Each grower of berries has to determine how aggressive he or she wants to be in managing pest populations. Being armed with a few facts will help you make the best decisions.

FACT 1. Viruses will drain and ultimately kill your berry planting and therefore must be controlled. You should learn which viruses might damage your crops. Few viruses affect strawberries, for example, and so you do not need to worry too much about your strawberry planting. Raspberries, on the other hand, are susceptible to several viruses, so you should become familiar with and implement the control measures available to you.

FACT 2. Pests that cause direct damage to the berries, such as slugs or sap beetles, pose more immediate threats than indirect pests such as aphids or mites. Many of these pests can be controlled with cultural (pesticide-free) methods. Once you start seeing excessive injury to the plants, however (such as leaf discoloration from mites, leaf deformation by aphids, or leaf removal by Japanese beetles), it's probably time to exert some stronger control methods.

FACT 3. A healthy plant is a pest-resistant plant. For reasons that have not been clearly elucidated, plants that are struggling due to poor location, excessive shade, excessive cold, drought, overwatering, or nutrient deficiencies are much more likely to become afflicted with insects and diseases. (It seems a grave injustice that some poor plant that already has its share of troubles keeps getting more.) Establish a healthy planting, maintain it well, and you won't see many problems. Good site selection and preparation and attention to the water and nutrient needs of the plants are especially important. Even weeds do not grow well in a healthy, well-filled-out canopy of berry plants. I should add that plants do not have immune systems like mammals do, though they do have mechanisms for dealing with attack.

The extent to which you need to control pests in your planting also depends on how much you can tolerate losses of fruit and plants. I always recommend that commercial growers control tarnished plant bug *(Lygus)* since consumers will not buy deformed fruit, but I never bother to control them in my home planting. The slightly deformed berries taste just as good, and I do not have many deformed fruit, so I can tolerate that level of pest infestation. If every berry were affected, however, I might be more inclined to treat the pest chemically. If you prefer to have every berry as perfect as possible, you can exert more control (as described in Chapter 3, "Strawberries").

What Are Pesticides?

A pesticide is any chemical that is applied to a crop or an area with the intent of killing a pest. Although the word *chemical* has come to have a negative connotation in our culture, the darkness that surrounds the word is undeserved. Chemicals are simply the components of the physical world.

Pesticides are classified according to the pest they are supposed to kill: fungicides kill fungi, insecticides kill insects, miticides kill mites, and herbicides kill herbs, or plants such as weeds. Whether naturally occurring or synthesized by humans, pesticides are by definition toxic.

Controlling Pests with Integrated Crop Management

The concept of integrated crop management (sometimes called integrated pest management) is based on substituting knowledge for rote application of chemical pesticides. Some of the best pest-management techniques require no chemicals. Remember, establishing a healthy plant stand in an appropriate site with an optimal density and maintaining it in good health goes a long way toward controlling pests. The following are some strategies for controlling pests without the use of pesticides.

Site selection. Although it has already been stated, the importance of appropriate site selection bears repeating. The conditions of the site will have a profound affect on pest problems throughout the life of a planting. Well-drained soil will eliminate most root rots. Exposure to sunlight will speed the drying time of the leaves, thus reducing fungal leaf and fruit rots. Planting in an area that has not been exposed to a *Verticillium*-susceptible crop will likely eliminate any problems with that fungal pathogen.

Cultivar selection. Finding out which cultivars recommended in your area are resistant to pests or diseases is an important step. Certain strawberry cultivars offer excellent resistance to root rots, and others have marginal resistance to fruit and leaf fungal diseases. Some raspberries are resistant to the raspberry aphid, a pest that transmits lethal viruses. Not only is resistance a factor, but cultivars that are well adapted to your area will grow better and will resist disease and insect infestation by virtue of their good health.

Keep plants free from weeds. Weeds not only weaken the planting by competing for water, nutrients, and sunlight, but they can slow the drying of moisture within the berry plant canopy, thus encouraging the proliferation of fungal diseases.

Maintain appropriate plant density. Keeping rows narrow, shoots thinned out, and vines well trained fosters good air circulation around your plants. Such thinning not only allows the plants to dry more quickly following a rain or watering, but it can also prevent fungal spores from settling or germinating on the leaves. Maintaining the appropriate plant density is done by renovation in strawberries (see Chapter 3) and by pruning in all other berry crops.

Harvest ripe fruit and remove decaying fruit. If the ripe berries are not going to be consumed right away, they can be picked as they ripen on the plants and then stored in a freezer container. In most cases I process the frozen fruit later, when the garden is not demanding my immediate attention. If freezer space is limited, fruit can also be processed into jam or canned in some other way.

   When fruit rots are present, be sure to remove the rotted fruit from the planting. Although pulling a rotted raspberry or strawberry off a plant is not a pleasant prospect (sometimes you have to sort of squish them off), leaving it on the plant creates a source of infection for all the ripening fruit.

Controlling Pests with Pesticides

Although I always recommend using the above-mentioned non-chemical methods for pest control, for certain insects and diseases and in certain years pesticides are the only option. For the home grower, some general rules of pesticide use should be remembered.

1. Use only pesticides that are labeled for the crop to which they are being applied.
2. Do not apply more than the recommended dosage indicated on the label, but do not apply less, either. Too-low dosages can encourage the gradual buildup of resistance in a population of pests.
3. Do not use the same pesticide continually. Although many

DIGRESSION

A Brief History of Pest Control

People have a tendency to wax nostalgic about the "good old days" when people didn't use pesticides and the food was pure and the air was clear. The truth, at least as far as pesticides are concerned, is that we have never had it so good. The earliest humans were hunter-gatherers. They took what nature had to offer, spending most of their time foraging for food or going without food in the event of environmental disaster. As humankind developed agriculture, they found that when they planted large amounts of a single crop in one spot, a lot of pests showed up for the party. Thus, they tried to plant enough to supply both the pest and themselves, and they dealt with the consequences of hunger. At the time, prayer was the most common technique of pest control. It is documented that the Roman Catholic Church even tried excommunicating the locusts in a desperate but ineffective attempt at control.

The applying of a substance on a crop to kill pests is a relatively new concept. It began around 1900, when it was discovered that certain natural products, when applied to plants, controlled pests. "Natural products" included lime and sulfur, both fairly caustic compounds, as well as a number of heavy metals. Paris green, for example, a compound used to control diseases in grapes, was composed of 40 percent arsenic by weight. Most of these chemicals worked because they were general biocides—that is, toxic to all life forms. It just took less to kill a fungus than it did to kill the plants or the humans. Natural products and heavy metals might have been our only chemical defenses had it not been for the need to develop more sophisticated alternatives during World War II.

Just after the war, there began an era of optimism in insect control. Crop yields rose dramatically. For the first time, we were able to control mosquito populations, which carry diseases so devastating to humans.

When discussing pesticides with my students, I always like to pause a minute to reflect on what motivated people to develop these early pesticides. It is particularly instructive since the word *pesticide* has come to have such a negative connotation in recent years. The primary motivation behind the development of organo-chlorine compounds, typified by DDT, was purely humanitarian. In fact, two Nobel Peace Prizes were awarded for the development and testing of DDT, the first to Alfred Von Baeyer and the second to Paul Muller. DDT did an excellent job controlling insects at relatively low rates.

The era of optimism came to an abrupt and crashing halt with the publication of Rachel Carson's *Silent Spring* in 1962. By most accounts, the book was not a scientifically sound publication, with primarily anecdotal evidence of the perils of wanton use of pesticides. However, it struck a nerve that, in hindsight, needed to be struck. The scientific community was thrown into an uproar, and divisions among scientists on the controversy surrounding pesticides persisted for decades. Two major issues were of concern. The first was the alarmingly high levels of DDT that were found in everything from fish to human breast milk, and the clear natural consequences that were being manifested in higher order animals, such as thinner shells in certain bird eggs. The second issue was pest resistance to pesticides. Initially, low concentrations of materials like DDT had good results. As the pesticide continued to be used, however, more and more was needed to obtain

the same results until, eventually, it had no effect at all.
The build-up of resistance to pesticides in populations,
particularly insect or fungal populations that multiply
rapidly, has been and will continue to be the subject of
much research and study.

After *Silent Spring,* the mood in pesticide research
could be dubbed the era of doubt. Scientists researched
the mechanisms of resistance. Pesticide spills and the
resulting fish kills became common stories in the newspaper. The consequences of using chlorinated hydrocarbons
were illuminated. These were all alarming developments.
Somehow, middle ground had to be plowed. We could
not produce enough food to feed the people of the world
without these chemicals, but we had to find a way to
minimize the consequences of using them.

By 1976, the concept of integrated crop management
(ICM) began to evolve, and with it came a return to
understanding the complexities of biological interactions
in our cropping systems. Researchers reinstituted the
study of pests and their interactions with other organisms
and their environment. In a sense, we picked up where
we had left off when pesticides were first introduced as a
"silver bullet" solution for pest control. It was clear that
chemical pesticides could not substitute for understanding the biology of our plantings and their pests. Whereas
growers in the 1960s followed fixed time schedules for
applying pesticides, with ICM the growers went into
their plantings, be they orchards or corn fields or berry
patches, to observe the species of life there. They monitored the periods of leaf wetness to schedule the applica-

tion of fungicides. They learned to identify which insects caused damage, to estimate their numbers, to learn their life cycles, and to make informed decisions about whether or not a given insecticide needed to be applied. Agricultural researchers developed criteria for identifying and quantifying damaging pests, as well as thresholds to help commercial growers determine at what point economic, as compared to cosmetic, losses would occur. Concomitantly, chemicals that were more friendly to the environment were being developed. The fungicides used today are, as a group, the least toxic to mammals (including people) and the most effectively targeted at fungi of any fungicides ever used. In the past the philosophy behind pest control was to use general biocides in low enough doses so as not to be lethal to humans. The philosophy now is to develop chemicals that more accurately target the pest. For example, pesticides may target chitin, a compound that is found only in insects and fungi.

ICM continues to be developed, and one can suspect that, like the biological systems in which we work, it will continue to evolve to accommodate our food-production needs. In the meantime the terms "sustainability" or "sustainable cropping systems" have also come into common use. Sustainable agriculture, as the name suggests, refers to cropping systems that can be maintained over a long period of time. The system must both be profitable and have a minimal or neutral environmental impact. It does not suggest the elimination of pesticides any more than ICM does, but rather the knowledgeable, sensible, and restrained use of them.

newer pesticides are formulated to reduce the ability of pests to build up resistance, rotating pesticides for a given pest is still good practice.

4. Never apply insecticides during bloom time, since it will kill the bees that pollinate the flowers. Applying pesticides in the evening will also limit exposure to bees.

ESTABLISHING A PEST AND PEST-MANAGEMENT PHILOSOPHY

Just as each of us arrives at a personal or spiritual philosophy in our own way and in our own time, the same is true for developing our gardening or pest-management philosophy. One strong piece of advice I offer to all gardeners, however, is that approaching your garden or your pests blindly and without careful thought will be neither satisfying nor successful. Whenever you use a pesticide spray, be sure that you know what you are doing and why you are doing it. Read the directions carefully and consult with experts in your area for suggestions or potential caveats.

I do not spray my backyard garden with chemical pesticides unless it is essential. I feel that I can share some of my bounty with my insect neighbors, and I also simply do not like the process of spraying. I'd rather mow the lawn—and that's quite a statement from a person whose main goal over the years has been to minimize the size of her lawn. I would certainly rather pull weeds. Every person will have his or her own peculiar likes and dislikes. My advice: Obtain information, make informed decisions, and don't hesitate to listen to your gut feelings.

The question of "organic" gardening is gaining increasing attention in our society, and I have my own biases on the matter. If you want to follow that philosophy, make sure you understand exactly what it means. "Organic food" has come to be defined as food that is grown without the use of any synthetic chemicals, whether fertilizers, growth hormones, or pesticides, but the insinuation that, by definition, organically grown food is safer is simply not true. Lead arsenate, nicotine, and copper are all organic compounds that have been used as pesticides at one time or another, yet all are toxic to animals and humans as well as insects. Rotenone and pyrrolnitrin, both organic products, are more toxic to humans than many synthetic pesticides. In addition, organically produced food is more prone to rot (many rots can be carcinogenic or even toxic) and often has residues of sulfur or copper, both of which are biocides. You may be attracted to the idea of organic food, but as with most things, be aware of what you're buying into.

Pesticides in Perspective

If people who lived just 100 years ago could see us today, they would be astounded at both the abundance of our food supply and our collective ignorance about its production. On one hand, this ignorance is a wonderful thing. Because we don't have to know everything about our food and how it is produced, we can expend our energies in other directions. Much of the technological progress and the artistic expression that we all enjoy today would not be possible if each of us had to worry about producing our own food. But this lack of knowledge is also a very dangerous thing. Particularly in the Western world, people who have never experienced hunger assume that food will forever be there in quantity, diversity, and amazing abundance, regardless of what they do or believe. One result of this is that many people have joined the crusade against pesticide use, believing it to be detrimental to the safety of our food and the quality of our health. The reality is that we could not produce enough food to feed ourselves without the help of synthetic pesticides.

Poisons are very scary. We live with extremely toxic substances in our homes all the time, but the thought of pesticide residues that we can't see being in our food is particularly unnerving. After all, we can live without Chlorox, but we can't live without food. Take heart. There is little reason to suspect that our food supply is unsafe, given that we are all living longer, healthier lives. In fact, one of the greatest plagues in the United States is that we eat too much and suffer from the diseases of abundance. *My* greatest fear is that well-intentioned but uninformed policy makers will set agricultural policy, particularly as it relates to pesticides, that serves to drive domestic producers out of business, making us increasingly dependent on other countries for our food.

This is not to say that we have not made mistakes regarding pesticides, or that we won't make more mistakes in the future, nor that our systems for producing food are ideal. Far from it. We need to shoulder responsibility for past mistakes, learn from those mistakes, and look to the future rationally and constructively.

Surely each of us cannot know everything about the entirety of agricultural production, but there are some things each of us can do. Try to know as much as possible about your food. Make decisions based on informed fact, not vague fears. Buy locally whenever possible. Buying locally not only contributes to the economics and diversity of your community, but the folks that you are buying from are eating the same thing that they're selling to you. They are bound to grow responsibly. And while you're at it, grow some of your own food. The education is like no other, and you benefit in every possible way.

DIGRESSION

On Nature and Food Production

The growing of a lot of a single plant species in a small area is not a situation found in nature, yet this is how humans produce food. The act of producing food takes us out of the realm of nature and into the realm of technology, and the production of a dependable, sustainable food supply enabled human civilizations to develop. The technophobes might argue that it was a mistake, that we'd be better off if we were more closely tied to the land. Personally, I wouldn't wish that tenuous and tedious existence on anyone, though vast numbers of people throughout the world still endure such uncertainty of survival. Surely there is some middle ground, and growing some of your own food is a great place to begin.

I particularly enjoy seeing people engaged in fruit production of any sort in their backyard because it offers so many lessons about the natural order. Remember, plants that produce edible fruit do so to attract creatures to eat it. It is a remarkable dispersal strategy, almost as good as sprouting legs. "Come eat me!" shouts the plant. "I taste great, and you can take the seeds with you. Just drop them off wherever it's convenient." Even when these edible and ornamental products are being grown for your personal consumption, they continue to call everyone else's name as well. The sugars and aromatics are just as attractive to hungry fungi, insects, birds, and squirrels as they are to you. Even the foliage is an attractant, enticing everything from insects to deer for a snack of leaves. The berry planting thus provides an amazing laboratory for observing the remarkable complexity of nature. The backyard grower has the opportunity to watch the changes brought about by the simple act of planting a berry plant in their garden, their very own ecosystem.

White Straw-berries.

CHAPTER 2

Berries in the Landscape

It is hard to imagine an entity with more aesthetic appeal than a berry fruit. The beauty resides in its vibrant color, its sensual shape, its inviting smoothness, its fruity smell. The fact that the fruit is borne on plants with such variety of shape, form, and color only adds to its allure. At first glance, it appears to be the perfect package of utility and form. Why, then, aren't berry plants used more frequently in the landscape? There are two answers. One is that many gardeners are simply not familiar with berry-producing plants. The second answer is that, in addition to the fabulous possibilities, many of these plants have certain pitfalls. Rather than seeing these as immutable shortcomings, we can develop more realistic expectations about how the plants will perform by better understanding their limitations.

Each of the chapters in this book includes a section called "Niches in the Landscape," which offers specific suggestions for using each crop in the landscape. Before jumping into the discussion of your preferred crop, however, take the time to look over the general concepts presented here regarding selecting berry plants for the landscape.

USING BERRY PLANTS IN THE LANDSCAPE: POSSIBILITIES

Small-fruit plants can take a variety of forms and uses in the landscape, from low groundcovers to rounded shrubs to long-trailing vines (Figure 2.1). Familiarizing yourself with a plant's expected form is an important first step in planning your edible-yet-attractive garden. Some specific suggestions for using berry plants follow, but remember that your imagination is just as fertile as mine. Your garden space is unique, as are your tastes, needs, and environment, and the best way to use the plants in the landscape is however they best suit your situation.

Berry plants as groundcovers and low edgings. The low-growing berry plants make terrific groundcovers. For neutral soils (pH 5.5–7.0), strawberries are wonderful low-growing plants. Only a few have to be planted, and they quickly fill in the space with runners and daughter plants. I have also used the non-runnering alpine strawberry *(Fragaria vesca)* as an edging around beds. In this case I had a grapevine growing against a wall trellis, and I wanted to keep the area around the base of it weed free. I installed a semicircle of bricks around the vine against the house, planted the little strawberries along the inside edge of the bricks, and heavily mulched the space between the plants. And voila—grapes and little strawberries growing together in an area of about 10 square feet (about one square meter).

The lowbush blueberry *(Vaccinium angustifolium)* is a terrific choice for more acidic soils (pH 4.0–5.0). Cranberries *(Vaccinium macrocarpon)* can also be used, but they are a little more demanding in their requirements. Lingonberry *(Vaccinium vitis-idaea)* plants, which at 12 to 18 inches (30–45 cm) high are slightly taller than most groundcovers, also do well in acidic soils. Great care should be taken prior to planting these acid-loving plants, even if the soil's pH level is acceptable. If the pH is on the high side, amending the soil with sulfur first will help lower the pH level. (Chapter 5 includes a table for acidifying the soil with sulfur for blueberry plants.) If the soil contains a low level of organic matter (2 percent or lower), copious amounts of peat moss need to be added as well.

Berry plants as hedges or fences. I love the use of berry plants as hedges or fences. What better way to seclude yourself from a hostile world than with a fruitful plant? The possibilities for using berry plants for this purpose are seemingly endless. Elderberry *(Sambucus*

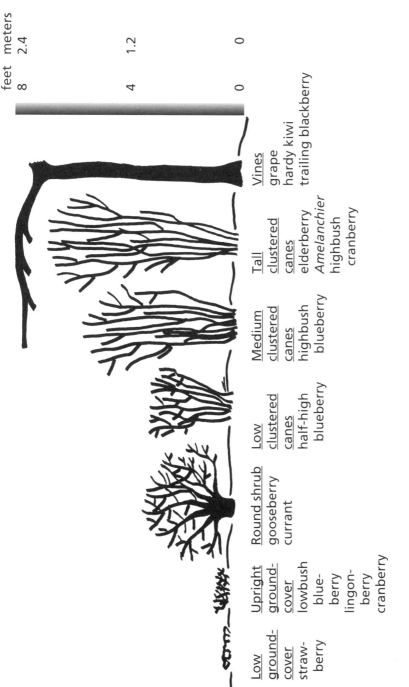

						feet	meters
						8	2.4
						4	1.2
						0	0

| Low ground-cover strawberry | Upright ground-cover lowbush blueberry lingon-berry cranberry | Round shrub gooseberry currant | Low clustered canes half-high blueberry | Medium clustered canes highbush blueberry | Tall clustered canes elderberry *Amelanchier* highbush cranberry | Vines grape hardy kiwi trailing blackberry |

Figure 2.1. Berry plant forms for the landscape. (Forms may vary considerably depending on the cultivar.)

canadensis) can be used to construct a tall, 12-foot (4-m), non-thorny hedge. A slightly shorter one can be grown from highbush cranberry *(Viburnum trilobum)* or some species of *Amelanchier*. In more acidic soils, try a blueberry hedge. These are all plants that lack thorns and do not produce suckers to irritate (or enthrall) your neighbors. Sometimes, though, thorns can be a good thing, if, for example, you want to present a formidable barrier to someone or something. In this case the gooseberry *(Ribes grossularia)* is the plant of choice. Note that although thorny blackberries are a bit more persuasive, they sucker copiously. (See the comments about invasive plants and neighbors under "Pitfalls.")

The berry plants themselves can be the fence, or they can be trained to grow on existing fences. I have grapes *(Vitis)* growing on a low, 3-foot (1-m), split-rail fence. Thornless blackberries or tayberries work just as well, though they need to be tied to the support structure since they lack tendrils. Maypop *(Passiflora incarnata)* vines also offer potential, but since they are herbaceous perennials, they are not present through the whole season. Hardy kiwi *(Actinidia arguta)* can fill a fence, indeed a very tall fence, quickly as well.

Berry plants as arbor dwellers. Several berry plants are vigorous enough to fill an arbor as easily as ornamental vines such as wisteria and trumpet vine. First on the list is hardy kiwi, although it needs a fairly big arbor to accommodate its vigor. Grapevines are the other obvious selection for arbor training. They provide wonderful thick shade, and the fruit hanging down provide visual appeal from flowering in early spring through harvest in late summer and fall. Take care to consider the cold tenderness of the grape cultivar you select; specific information can be found in Chapter 6.

Berry plants for aesthetic appeal. Berry plants have a lot to offer in terms of color and aesthetic appeal. Specific information for each crop is found in subsequent chapters, but to whet your palate, here are some of my favorite ornamental characteristics among berry plants.

Strawberries for early spring flowering and fruiting. Nothing is lovelier than a healthy strawberry canopy in bloom (Plate 2). The flowers are large and white with bright yellow anthers, and in most years they are prolific. The yielding of the flowers to fruit is a wonderful process to observe, particularly to those of us starved for plants after a long dreary winter.

Blueberries for flowering, fall color, and winter color. The blueberry bears exquisite little bell-shaped flowers in clusters (Plate 18). In autumn, leaves of most cultivars turn a vibrant red (Plate 19), and as the leaves fall off, they reveal red stems to rival the red-twigged dogwoods *(Cornus)* in intensity and hue (Plate 20). Did I mention that the fruit is wonderful, too?

Elderberry for green hedges and unusual flowers and fruit. I love the leaves and form of the elderberry. It is not exotic but rather solid and utilitarian. The form of the flower cluster is reminiscent of an umbrella, and the ensuing clusters of dark purple fruit have great visual appeal (Plates 37 and 38). And this plant has so many uses in the landscape, the home, and the kitchen.

Gooseberries and currants for hedges and color of fruit and flowers. Gooseberry plants make a terrific 3- to 6-foot (1–1.8 m) thorny hedge that tolerates more shade than the average fruit plant. The leaves of many gooseberry and currant cultivars turn a striking red in the fall (Plate 29), and the shapes and colors of the fruit also provide interest for the landscape (Plates 30 and 31).

Highbush cranberry for color, color, and color. The highbush cranberry is a vigorous, beautifully formed bush that turns bright red in fall and has the most beautiful jewel-like red fruit (Plate 39)—never mind that the flavor is marginal. As a landscape plant, highbush cranberry is hard to beat. It does well in climates that are quite cold, and it can form useful hedges. So add sugar to the fruit and make jelly or sauce, or leave the berries for the wildlife.

USING BERRY PLANTS IN THE LANDSCAPE:
PITFALLS

"Uh-oh," you say. "Pitfalls!?" I'm afraid it's true. Though I love to wax poetic about the berry plant's wonderful combination of usefulness and beauty, we are all best served by being fully informed about the possible difficulties before we sail forth into our yards. Despite the precautions and additional work that is required for growing edible ornamentals, however, my love of these plants and their potential in the landscape is undiminished. We may initially resent the necessary extra effort, but berry plants eventually become all the more endearing for it. Perhaps this section is more appropriately called "considerations" rather than pitfalls. Consider the following points before you plant, and not only will you have realistic expectations, but you will be able to plant these berries in appropriate locations around your home.

Crop maintenance is not optional. While ripe and healthy fruit is lovely to look at, rotting fruit on ill-cared-for plants is truly unattractive. This unattractiveness goes beyond the visual, as the rotting fruit can take on unpleasant smells and attract unwelcome visitors such as insects and bees. The latter consideration can be a particular nuisance, even a hazard, if you are planting grapes on an arbor, for example, and intend to sit under it during the summer months. In such cases, you have several choices. One option is to remove the flower clusters as they appear, thus eliminating most of the maintenance required during the summer. The second and better option— as far as I'm concerned—is to keep the grape plants consistently and regularly well maintained. Prune the plants every winter to discourage fungal diseases, control excess suckers, and control diseases on the crop as needed. If you are growing the crop in a dry environment, maintenance does not take much effort, and the most that you may need to do is apply a spray for Japanese beetles, if they are a problem. In wet areas or years, though, you may need to pay more attention and more actively control diseases and insect pests.

Many berry plants require pruning during their dormant period, and failing to carry out this essential task is inviting disaster. Pruning not only ensures a crop of good-sized sweet fruit, it keeps rows of plants neat and narrow so that the canopy does not get so thick that light and air cannot penetrate.

Fruit plants may go through "unattractive" stages. Most perennial landscape plants have periods when they are absent or not at their most ornamental, and strawberries are a good example. They make a lovely lush groundcover in the fall and spring, but after fruiting in early summer they go through a quasi-dormancy, during which time they look, for lack of a better word, ratty. At this point you need to renovate the strawberry plants, removing leaves and thinning out the plants. (This is described further in Chapter 3.) So, first they fruit, then they look a little bedraggled, then you cut them back. They regrow by about midsummer, so the plants are at less than their best for only a short time. Still, you need to consider this aspect as you plan your planting.

Before deciding what to do about your plants in their "off" seasons, you should carefully read the sections in this book dealing with the specific berries. Fall-fruiting raspberries, for example, are often cut down to the base during the dormant season. As a result, the plants will seem to be gone entirely, but you can use this to your advantage. This apparent disappearance is a common trait in other garden perennials, including peonies and bleeding hearts, so being aware of it can help you with placement of the plants in your garden. One effective solution is to plant your fall-bearing raspberries against a foundation, with spring-flowering bulbs and perennials in front. With this arrangement, first the bulbs flower, then the low-growing perennials, and as this is happening, the green stems of the raspberries provide a lovely backdrop for the flowering perennials.

Some berry species are invasive. Thorny blackberries and raspberries come to mind first when thinking about invasive berry plants, but even the humble strawberry can be invasive in the right environment. One way to control the growth of the plants is to "containerize" them in the soil. You can place barriers, such as thick pieces of plastic made for this purpose, along the edge of where you want the plants to grow. For raspberries, the barriers need to be at least 12 inches (30 cm) deep, and if your soil is deep, this may not be enough. I take a very hard line with the raspberries that edge my house, around which I regrettably did not install a barrier prior to planting. The plants are separated from the lawn only by an edging of bricks. Once summer comes, they throw up suckers in the adjacent lawn, and I relentlessly run over those little shoots with the lawn mower.

If you do this soon enough, it discourages the plant from growing there. However, you eventually may have to go in and dig up the root of the plant and prune it back from the lawn area. I adore raspberries, so the little bit of extra effort doesn't upset me. Hopefully, with this prior knowledge, it will upset you even less.

The issue of invasiveness brings up another potentially sensitive issue: neighborly relations. Though red raspberries make a wonderful hedge (and the summer-bearing types are present all year round), if you plant your wonderful hedge on or near a property line, those suckers will come up in your neighbor's yard as well as your own. One option is to install barriers to minimize these unwanted suckers, and hope all goes well. You can also just plant the raspberries somewhere else. My preferred solution is discussing the issue directly with said neighbor—though this is highly dependent on the individuals and your relationship with them. Some neighbors will embrace the idea of a raspberry hedge if you offer to let them harvest the fruit from their side. Others may not care one way or the other, and still others will be horrified at the concept of the unknown. If the latter is the case, at least you tried, but once your neighbor has responded in the negative, you have little choice but to plant your lovely raspberries elsewhere.

CHAPTER 3

Strawberries

FAMILY: ROSACEAE, THE ROSE FAMILY

PRIMARY SPECIES:

Fragaria ×ananassa Duch.—common garden strawberry
Fragaria chiloensis Duch.—beach strawberry, Chilean strawberry
Fragaria vesca L.—alpine strawberry, wood strawberry
Fragaria virginiana Duch.—meadow strawberry, scarlet
   strawberry

Strawberries—such small plants, such beautiful fruit, such wonderful flavor. At a time when these luscious fruits are being produced for export in regions far from where they are being consumed, the quality of the strawberries one finds at the grocery store may not be as good as it once was. Strawberries grown in places like California and Florida, which have longer growing seasons than other regions, are bred for firmness, size, and color, rather than flavor. The good news is that you can easily grow strawberries in your own private paradise, however small, and the flavor will be wonderful. The strawberry can be thought of as the tomato of the berry world: you can certainly buy them in the grocery store, but the difference between that variety and the ones you grow in your own backyard is like night and day. In addition, the plants make a wonderful groundcover in the garden, and they are highly productive. Many cultivars are also quite disease resistant.

HISTORICAL BACKGROUND AND
OTHER INTERESTING FACTS

Strawberries are an ancient crop. The first written reference to the strawberry is from ancient Rome, but the berries were likely collected from the wild for medicinal purposes and as a source of food long before recorded history.

The question of why these fruits are called "strawberries" is widely debated. The name may be based on the fact that the seeds are the color of straw, or that in medieval England the berries were often strung on pieces of straw and sold. An alternative explanation is that the natural growth habit of the plant results in fruits "strawn" (strewn) on the ground. The name most certainly does not stem from the current practice of applying straw as a mulch for winter protection.

The history of the modern cultivated strawberry is an interesting one. The cultivated plant, *Fragaria* ×*ananassa*, is a hybrid between *F. virginiana*, the meadow strawberry, and *F. chiloensis*, the Chilean strawberry. The Chilean strawberry first made its way to European gardens in the early eighteenth century. In 1712 a French spy named Amédée François Frézier was sent by King Louis XIV to survey and map the coasts of Chile and Peru to obtain information about the Spanish fortifications there in anticipation of war. Monsieur Frézier was not just a spy, however—he was also an amateur horticulturist. As such, he was extremely impressed with the large, tasty strawberry fruit that grew wild on the Chilean coast, and he dug up several of the most vigorous plants he found and transported them back to France. (Quarantine restrictions had not been invented at this point in history.) Only five plants survived the rigorous journey across the ocean, and one plant was given to the Jardin des Plantes in Paris. The plants were eventually distributed around Europe, and the Chilean strawberry, *F. chiloensis*, became commonly cultivated throughout the continent. Because *F. chiloensis* is dioecious (fruiting plants have only female flowers), other species that bear male or perfect (bisexual) flowers were interplanted to ensure pollination and fruiting. The pollinator used was often the North American native *F. virginiana*. The hybridization of these

DIGRESSION

Life, Death, and Fresh Strawberries

My great-aunt was a very unusual woman, but like most children, I took her presence, her activities, her self, completely for granted. To me, she was just another relative who, for no good reason, loved me. (Oh that all children should have such security!) She would drive her 1950 Oldsmobile to our house in suburban Washington, D.C., on hot June days, open the trunk, and voila! Fresh strawberries, whole flats of them, would be placed in my arms to bring to my mother in the house. During the week, my great-aunt was the head librarian for the National Bureau of Standards Library (a prestigious position, particularly for a woman in the 1940s and '50s), but on the weekends, she drove out to her country place in Centreville, Virginia, and grew things. My mother told me later that when my great-aunt was in her early forties she experienced a brush with death, and she bought the country place and renewed her relationship with the land after that. Whatever her motivation, she provided my brother and me with fresh strawberries—and an unpretentious but lasting role model.

two species, probably in several locations, led to the development of today's commercial strawberry, *F. ×ananassa*. The hybrid was clearly superior to all the other strawberry species available in Europe at the time. Since then, breeding efforts have improved fruit quality, productivity, pest resistance, winter hardiness, and various ornamental qualities. This work is ongoing, and many strawberries produced today are superior in productivity and pest resistance to any previously produced in history.

Beyond its relatively short western European history, the strawberry has been cultivated extensively in Chile for many centuries. Long before the European discovery of the New World, probably as far back as 2000 years ago or more, the Chilean strawberry was most likely domesticated by the indigenous Mapuches. The Mapuches were hunter-gatherers, but they learned about agriculture from the Picunches, who in turn had been influenced by Incan invaders. These native peoples consumed both wild and domesticated strawberries, which were eaten fresh or dried or made into a fermented juice known as *lahuene*. The domesticated fruits were probably the larger, white form of strawberry, which has been found at three locations in southern Chile. The red-fruited forms were certainly consumed as well, but since they were abundant in the wild, it was not necessary to cultivate them. One legend has it that red strawberries were planted by the indigenous peoples as traps for the Spanish soldiers. The Indians would place the plants in small, open spots in the forest, and when the soldiers dropped their weapons to pick the tempting morsels, they were sprung upon and attacked by the natives.

The Chilean strawberry was transported to other South American locales as well. The largest land area of cultivated strawberries was at Huachi-Grande, near Ambato, Ecuador, where an estimated 1200 to 1700 acres (500–700 hectares) were used to grow strawberries from at least the late 1700s until 1970. In the early 1900s it was written that the fruit was three times the size of the European strawberry and was produced throughout the year. The fruit was not only large but tough. In 1921 a North American pomologist, Wilson Popenoe, wrote:

> It is the custom in Ecuador to throw the fruits into boxes: they are then carried six or seven miles on mule-back to the city of Ambato, where they are sorted by hand, for shipment by train to Quito or Guayaquil. There is probably no other strawberry in the world which could tolerate this sort of handling.

The traditional plantings of the Chilean strawberry began to disappear in the 1950s, when they were mixed with Northern

Hemisphere cultivars of *Fragaria* ×*ananassa*. They were eventually completely replaced by California cultivars, including 'Chandler' and 'Pajaro'. Several expeditions to Chile by North American researchers have sought to collect and preserve some of these remarkable Chilean strawberries. (Among the researchers are J. F. Hancock from Michigan State University, J. S. Cameron from Washington State University, and C. Finn from the U.S. Department of Agriculture in Corvallis, Oregon.) These collections have been conducted in collaboration with the governments of both countries, and it is hoped that the plants will yield valuable traits to breeding programs throughout the world.

Today, strawberries are produced in every state in the United States and in nearly every country in the world, most notably Italy, Poland, Russia, and Japan. This wide distribution suggests that the strawberry plant is widely adapted, and as a genus, this is true. However, many individual genotypes or cultivars of strawberries are narrowly adapted to local conditions, and so selecting cultivars that are proven to perform well in your specific region is particularly important.

BIOLOGY OF THE PLANT: KNOWING IT AND USING IT TO YOUR ADVANTAGE

The strawberry plant is in many ways unique among fruit plants. It is a herbaceous perennial composed of leaves, a crown (a compressed, modified stem), and a root system (Figure 3.1). The root system is composed of two types of roots: those that are semipermanent, lasting for more than a season, and those that are transient in nature, lasting only days or weeks. In light sandy soils the roots may extend as deep as 12 inches (30 cm), with half of the root mass in the lower 6 inches (15 cm). In heavier soils, such as clay loams, 90 percent of the roots may be located in the top 6 inches (15 cm) of soil. This shallow root system is, in part, responsible for the plant's sensitivity to deficient or excessive water in the soil. Another aspect of the strawberry root system that has practical importance to the grower is that new roots arise from the base of the developing leaves. Since leaves (and along with them, roots) are formed successively higher on the crown as the plant ages, the strawberry tends to grow "out of the ground." For this reason, mounding soil around the bases of the plants at renovation time, particularly as the bed ages, is good practice. It supports the base of the plant and gives the newly forming roots a place to call home.

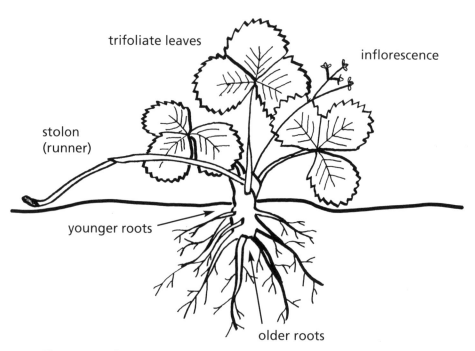

Figure 3.1. The strawberry plant.

Each leaf of the strawberry plant is composed of three leaflets, each oval in shape and with serrated edges. Leaves can exhibit considerable differences in size, from alpine strawberries, the leaflets of which are often less than 1 inch (2.5 cm) long, to some common short-day cultivars, which may have leaflets up to 2 inches (5 cm) long. The runners, or stolons, arise from buds in the leaf axils and are the strawberry plant's device for asexual propagation. Runners form during the long days of summer, and they generally require a day length of more than 12 hours for formation. The matted-row system of culture, which is the method of strawberry cultivation recommended in this book, takes advantage of the plant's runnering capacity as a means of establishing many plants from a few.

The flower cluster (inflorescence) of the strawberry plant arises from the terminal buds. Bud formation occurs deep in the plant tissue and is invisible to even the most observant onlooker. The inflorescence formed from this single bud contains a number of flowers, which will result in a number of fruit, with about 30 days between flower opening and fruit ripening. The terminal flower opens first and is referred to as the king flower. The king flower also has the highest number of cells in it. Why is this important? Because it will yield the largest fruit, appropriately called the king fruit. Unfortunately, since it opens first, the king flower is also more likely to be damaged by late frosts. The remaining flowers on the inflorescence open sequentially down the stem, from the terminus to the base of the inflorescence. In other words, the second flowers to open are those located just below the terminal flower, and they will open slightly later (usually a day or two) and have slightly smaller fruit. This arrangement means that the fruit is smaller as the season progresses. It is also a good reason to avoid frost, if you can.

More than one inflorescence may be borne on a single plant if branch crowns (small compressed branches on the thicker main crown) have developed, since each branch crown can also terminate in a flower cluster. After several years, however, if too many branch crowns develop on an individual plant, intraplant competition for resources can result in reduced berry size as berry number increases. For this reason, 3- to 4-year-old plants are not as desirable in a planting bed as younger plants, which have fewer crowns.

The strawberry fruit is an aggregate fruit, composed of achenes (a type of seed) that are fused together on a tissue (the receptacle) at the end of the flowering axis. The majority of the consumable portion of the fruit, therefore, is receptacle tissue. Fruit size, which ranges from ¼ inch (0.5 cm) to 2 inches (5 cm), is dependent on a number of factors, including the fruit's location on the inflorescence, the density of the crowns on the individual plant, and the particular cultivar (certain cultivars are simply larger or have less variation in size within a given cluster), as well as environmental factors such as water availability and plant density.

The fruit will also vary somewhat in shape, primarily as a result of genetics. Some cultivars produce fruit with a more spherical shape, whereas others bear long and thin fruit. Certain cultivars tend to form a long "neck"—a disappointing trait. In such plants, the area of the fruit just under the cap (calyx) becomes distended and develops a thin skin, making that area weak and prone to skin rupture or insect attack. Color can vary among strawberry cultivars from fairly light oranges to very dark reds or near purples.

Strawberry Types

The different strawberry types are defined primarily by their time of flower bud initiation, and hence fruiting. The two main types of strawberries are short-day (also referred to as June-bearing) strawberries, which initiate flower buds when the days are short, and day-neutral strawberries, which will form flower buds regardless of day length. This difference in time of flower bud initiation translates to differences in time of fruiting.

Strawberry types can also be distinguished by the different species from which they were bred. Most cultivated strawberries are hybrids of two or more species, although the alpine strawberry is a separate species *(Fragaria vesca)*. It is little grown but is included here because of its potential as a garden plant and as a delightful addition to the plate.

Short-day or June-bearing strawberries. The short-day strawberry is by far the most widely grown type of strawberry. Also known as the June-bearing strawberry, it bears its fruit during that month in most regions of the Northern Hemisphere. This type forms flower buds during the short days of autumn (late September through early November), becomes dormant in the winter, and then flowers and fruits when the weather turns warm again in the spring. Some bud formation may continue through the short, warm days in spring as well. The plant must have a full, well-established leaf canopy because the leaves provide the energy for flower bud initiation. Note that the day-length response relates only to when flower buds are formed and has nothing to do with when the plant actually blooms.

Temperature also plays a role in flower bud formation. Temperatures below 60°F (16°C) are ideal for bud formation; generally, if night temperatures exceed 70°F (21°C), bud initiation is inhibited. The ability of the plant to substitute cool temperatures for short days accounts for the plant's production in areas of higher elevations. In this case, short-day strawberry plants may form flower buds whenever stimulated by cool temperatures, so they may behave more like day-neutral plants than short-day plants.

Day-neutral strawberries. Day-neutral strawberry plants, which yield fruit almost continuously from spring through fall, are becoming increasingly important commercially and are useful for home producers too. They initiate flower buds regardless of day length, thus producing some fruit throughout the summer and a sizable fall crop that is a great bonus for backyard growers. The plants will flower and produce fruit and runners simultaneously, with runner plants often flowering prior to rooting.

Day-neutral cultivars begin fruiting at roughly the same time as the short-day strawberries, usually between mid-May and mid-June. At this time, plants produce a medium-sized crop of medium-sized fruit. The crop borne by day-neutrals in the spring is not as large, and individual berries are not as large, as the crop that a short-day cultivar would give. Another small crop is offered in the middle of the summer, with a few scattered fruit in between. This crop is often the smallest in size, particularly in warmer climates, and may suffer from the heat, drought, or insects prevalent in midsummer. Although the spring and summer crop is small compared to that of the short-day strawberry, the real bonus of these plants is the crop that issues forth in the fall. Starting in late summer (August in most cases), day-neutral strawberries begin producing fruit again, and they will do so until the first hard frost.

These strawberries have relatively low root-to-shoot ratios, and consequently they are especially sensitive to high soil temperatures. The negative effects of high temperatures can be ameliorated by a heavy straw mulch or a white-on-black plastic mulch to keep soil temperatures low. The plants perform best in cooler climates, specifically USDA zones 5 and north.

Day-neutral strawberries should not be confused with ever-bearing strawberries, which bear some fruit in summer and some in fall. They initiate most of their flower buds under long days, and generally lack the productivity and berry quality of the day-neutrals. Ever-bearing cultivars are occasionally offered in nursery catalogs.

Alpine strawberries. Though less well known than the short-day strawberry in North America, the alpine or wood strawberry *(Fragaria vesca)* is the most widely distributed strawberry plant, occurring throughout Europe, northern Asia, northern Africa, and North America. These small herbaceous perennial plants can be used as ornamentals or for fruit production. The fruit is often soft and small, but it can also be very aromatic and tasty. Most commercially available alpine strawberries are non-running and day-neutral, so they will bear fruit continuously from spring through fall. Available cultivars include 'Alexandria', 'Ruegen', and 'Mignonette'. A few white or yellow cultivars are also offered, such as 'Alpine Yellow' and 'Pineapple Crush'.

CULTIVAR SELECTION

Appropriate cultivar selection is vital to the success of any strawberry planting. Strawberries are extremely sensitive to local conditions, and a cultivar that performs well in one location may do poorly in another. In addition, cultivars are often bred specifically to be grown in certain production systems. Cultivars from eastern, midwestern, and northwestern North America have been bred primarily for perennial (matted-row) culture, whereas those bred for the industries of California and the Southeast perform best in annual culture systems. Cultivars for the Pacific Northwest have been bred primarily for processing. A list of recommended cultivars by region is given at the end of the chapter. All cultivars listed are selections of the garden strawberry *Fragaria ×ananassa*.

Because of the variations in cultivar performance, I strongly advise that you consult with local experts, such as other producers or county extension agents, before planting a large area of an untried cultivar. The best means of selecting cultivars is to conduct a small test plot on the planting site, using the preferred training system.

Cultivars are listed as early, midseason, or late, based on the harvest seasons shown in Table 3.1. The typical short-day strawberry bears ripe fruit for only about 2 weeks, but backyard growers can extend the season in their gardens by planting several cultivars to span the harvest period. By including early, midseason, and late cultivars in a planting, the gardener can enjoy ripe berries from the backyard for as long as 5 or 6 weeks during late spring and summer. Note that the harvest season for the southeastern United States is much longer than that in other regions, spanning December through March.

Table 3.1. Typical Strawberry Harvest Times by Region

Region	Short-day Cultivars	Day-neutral Cultivars
New England	mid-June–mid-July	mid-August–frost
Mid-Atlantic	June	June–October
Midwest	June	June–October
South Central	May	June
Southeast	December–March	December–March
Pacific Northwest	June	May–October

SHORT-DAY CULTIVARS

'Allstar'. Midseason. Produces elongated, flavorful berries that are lighter in color than those of most cultivars. Good fruit size. Productive. Has become the standard midseason berry in the eastern and midwestern United States.

'Annapolis'. Early. Fruit medium-large, firm, and glossy, with good flavor. Plants runner freely. Fairly susceptible to *Botrytis*.

'Arking'. Late. Productive plants with large fruit. Late-season ripening helps extend season. South-central United States only.

'Benton'. Midseason. Fruit is firm, large, and dark red. The color is
    too dark for preserves for the commercial market, but that is
    merely a cosmetic, not a taste, issue. Pacific Northwest only.
'Camarosa'. Midseason. Firm fruit that ripens evenly over several
    months. Susceptible to powdery mildew. Southeast only.
'Cardinal'. Midseason. Widely planted in Arkansas and surrounding
    states for its high production. Has deep red color and good
    disease resistance. Good for fresh eating or freezing. South-
    central United States only.
'Cavendish'. Midseason. Very large, firm fruit with good flavor.
    Very productive and moderately vigorous. Tends to ripen un-
    evenly in hot years.
'Delite'. Late. Large berries, average to poor flavor. Very resistant to
    disease.
'DelMarvel'. Midseason. Very vigorous plants, with high produc-
    tion of large, firm, aromatic fruit.
'Earliglow'. Early. Medium-sized berry with excellent flavor. Plant
    is only moderately productive. 'Earliglow' is the standard for
    early cultivars.
'Guardian'. Midseason. Very productive. Firm, large fruit, some-
    times rough or uneven looking. *Botrytis* can be prevalent. The
    area on the fruit just below the cap tends to become elongated
    and thin-skinned. The long "neck" breaks easily and provides
    easy entry for slugs and sap beetles.
'Honeoye'. Midseason. Large fruit, productive. Lack of resistance to
    red stele root rot is a concern. Fruit tends to become soft in hot
    weather. Flavor is distinctive, perfumey.
'Hood'. Early-midseason. Fruit large, bright red, and quite firm.
    Plants susceptible to viruses. Pacific Northwest only.
'Jewel'. Midseason. Large, soft fruit; can be very dark. Tends to
    soften in hot weather. Very productive, though dense foliage
    can encourage *Botrytis*. Lack of root-rot resistance is a concern.
'Kent'. Midseason. Extremely productive plant with large, firm
    fruit. Yields fruit in middle of the plants, resulting in high rot, so
    planting rows should be kept narrow. Average flavor.
'Lateglow'. Midseason. Productive. Good size and flavor. First
    berries are extremely large, though size decreases over the sea-

son. An extremely vigorous plant that needs to be renovated judiciously.

'Latestar'. Late. Mild fruit flavor, but variable yields and fruit size. Vigorous plants that runner well. Flowers and ripens a few days later than 'Allstar'.

'Lester'. Midseason. Productive plant with good-sized berries. Flavor is good, though size tends to run down quickly. Fruit is fairly susceptible to *Botrytis*.

'MicMac'. Midseason. Fairly productive with large, firm, light red fruit. Plants are quite vigorous, but no known resistance to red stele rot. New England only.

'Mohawk'. Early. Medium-sized fruit, larger than that of 'Earliglow' but not as flavorful. Tolerant of *Botrytis*. Particularly variable from site to site.

'Northeaster'. Early. Very large and firm fruit with aromatic flavor and aroma. King berries are slightly rough. Not a strong plant-maker, but well adapted to heavy soils.

'Oso Grande'. Midseason. Once the most common cultivar in Florida, it is being replaced by 'Sweet Charlie' and 'Camarosa'. Low yields early in the season, and fruit sometimes ripens unevenly. Produces fewer misshapen fruit than other Florida cultivars. Southeast only.

'Primetime'. Midseason. Medium-firm berry with mild, lightly aromatic flavor. It is a relatively new, untested cultivar, but in trials it has yielded as well as and was as large-fruited as 'Allstar'. Produces well on either light or heavy soils. Good *Botrytis* resistance.

'Rainier'. Late. Large, bright red fruit is excellent for all processing purposes. Pacific Northwest only.

'Raritan'. Midseason. A widely planted cultivar in spite of disease susceptibility. First fruits are large, but size decreases more rapidly than on most cultivars. Very flavorful.

'Redchief'. Midseason. Productive, with good color and size. Flavor average. Excellent disease resistance.

'Rosa Linda'. Early. Extremely productive cultivar. Early fruit often has green tips. Appears to have some resistance to powdery mildew, mites, angular leaf spot, and gray mold. Southeast only.

'Seneca'. Midseason. Round, large, medium-red, exceptionally firm fruit with firm skin. Plant is vigorous. Mediocre flavor, but firmness of fruit may be useful for shipping or playing softball.

'Shuksan'. Midseason. Large, glossy, bright red fruit with a tough skin. Fruit is firm. Good for freezing and for preserves. Pacific Northwest only.

'Sparkle'. Late. Flavorful, high-quality, attractive but soft fruit. Plant tends to grow very thickly, increasing likelihood of *Botrytis* and limiting air penetration. Size decreases rapidly during harvest season.

'Sumas'. Early. Large fruit with medium-glossy red interior and exterior. Moderately firm. Pacific Northwest only.

'Sweet Charlie'. Early. The standard against which all other Florida cultivars are compared. Early fruiting, high productivity, and good fruit quality. Susceptible to gray mold. Southeast only.

'Totem'. Midseason. Dark red, large fruit with red interior color. Pacific Northwest only.

'Veestar'. Early. Productive, with medium bright berries. Performs well in Mid-Atlantic region. Shows some *Botrytis* resistance.

DAY-NEUTRAL CULTIVARS

'Fern'. Begins fruiting earlier than 'Hecker', with larger and better quality fruit. Pacific Northwest only.

'Hecker'. Medium-sized, dark reddish orange fruit. Productive. Flavor not great. Pacific Northwest only.

'Seascape'. Large fruit with good flavor. Relatively new and untested outside of California, so grow only on a trial basis at first. Pacific Northwest only.

'Selva'. Fruit large and dark. Very firm with good flavor when ripe. Reports from Florida indicate high susceptibility to spider mites and powdery mildew. This cultivar is grown primarily for its early yield, but inferior flavor and low productivity make it a poor choice for the backyard in the Southeast. Southeast and Pacific Northwest only.

'Tribute'. Fruits slightly later than 'Tristar' and has larger berries. Flavor not as strong, and plants are more vigorous.

'Tristar'. Bears an early crop. Fruit is smaller than that of 'Tribute'.

Flavor is excellent. Firm flesh and skin. Moderate vigor. Size is reduced in hot weather.

A word on taste. Taste is obviously an important consideration when choosing cultivars. Any locally grown strawberry is likely to taste better than the imported types (primarily because the imported ones have to be picked on the green side of ripe for successful shipping), but the proper selection of cultivars also makes a huge difference in flavor.

Tastes vary with the individual, of course, but few dispute that the flavor of 'Earliglow' is the most aromatic, sweet, and strawberry-like. It is the standard against which all others are compared. 'Raritan' also has excellent flavor, but unfortunately it lacks resistance to red stele root rot disease. A few other cultivars are noteworthy for their flavor. The perfumey quality of 'Honeoye' is a distinctive taste that people either love or hate. 'Allstar' has a pleasant flavor, but its light orange color may influence those who taste with their eyes as well as their noses and mouths.

HOW TO GROW STRAWBERRIES: PLANTING THROUGH HARVEST

Site Selection and Preparation

You should select the site of your strawberry bed the year before planting. Early site selection allows proper soil preparation, an essential first step toward successful production (see Chapter 1, "General Principles"). Strawberries should not be planted where potatoes, tomatoes, eggplants, peppers, or raspberries have been planted for the past 5 years. These crops may harbor the *Verticillium* organism, which is a serious pathogen of strawberry. Many cultivars are resistant to this pathogen, but none is immune. Plantings also should not follow sod, because the grubs that infest sod roots consume strawberry roots as well, and the grass can become a persistent weed problem in the planting. Realistically, many backyard growers have no choice but to plant their strawberries in an area that was sod prior to planting. To minimize potential problems, you should break up the sod and dig the soil as deeply as possible, keeping an eye out for grubs. If you see them, expose them to the air and/or remove them by hand. Repeat this process until you no longer see any of the pests. If you have a heavy grub infestation, you may wish to treat the site with a labeled insecticide. Be sure to take care of this problem prior to planting. Chemicals that are labeled for removing grubs from established strawberry plantings can only be applied by licensed users, and it often requires sacrificing the crop for a full year afterward. Sites that are heavily infested with sedge *(Carex)*, nutgrass *(Cyperus esculentus)*, quackgrass *(Agropyron repens)*, Johnson grass *(Sorghum halapense)*, or Canada thistle *(Cirsium arvense)* should be avoided or treated with systemic herbicides prior to planting. Cover cropping with competitive species such as rye *(Secale cereale)* or Sudan grass *(Sorghum sudanense)* in the years prior to planting will also suppress weeds.

Strawberries require full sun and adequate air drainage. A gentle slope (5 to 7 percent) lessens the danger of spring frost damage to flower buds by improving air drainage, although steep slopes (over 12 percent) should be avoided because of the difficulties of cultivation and soil erosion.

Strawberry plants grow and produce fruit satisfactorily in a wide range of soil types, from sands to heavy loams. They are not notably sensitive to soil pH, but they grow best on soils with a pH of 6.0–6.5. Soil should be tested for lime and mineral requirements the spring or summer prior to planting. Testing in the previous year allows you to apply lime and phosphorus, which are relatively immobile and thus require time to move through the soil, in the fall prior to planting.

Best yields are obtained in deep, fertile soils that have good internal drainage and high organic matter. The organic matter content of the soil can be improved prior to planting by incorporating manure in the soil or by planting cover and/or green manure crops. Because of their shallow root system, strawberry plants are particularly sensitive to water in the root zone, either too much water or too little. Soils that have poor drainage induce smaller root systems due to reduced oxygen for root respiration. Poor drainage also

---

DIGRESSION

Full Sun

"Full sun"—many plants require it, and you certainly need it for optimal fruit production, but what exactly does it mean? Full sun means that the site is not shaded by any obstructions (houses, trees, other plants) at any time during the day. Obviously, for a home site, this can be rather difficult, since the house and landscaping dramatically reduce the availability of unobstructed sites. My experience with strawberries is that they need at least 8 to 10 hours of direct sunlight to produce a reasonable amount of fruit. If you have a choice, plant strawberries where they will get their sun in the morning (an eastern or southern exposure) so that the dew will dry quickly, minimizing the chance of fruit rots. Providing morning sun is not essential, however, and again, it is not always practical, since the morning sun is usually low and there may be obstructions from adjacent properties.

---

encourages the proliferation of fungal diseases that may infect the roots.

Irrigation is required for growing strawberries because the shallow-rooted nature of the plant makes it particularly susceptible to drought. Trickle irrigation (discussed in Chapter 1) has been used successfully to provide adequate soil moisture for strawberries; however, because overhead irrigation is necessary in many regions to protect the blossoms against frost, few commercial producers in these areas install trickle systems. Home gardeners have more options for frost protection since their plots are relatively small, and trickle irrigation is a viable alternative for small-scale growing.

Strawberry size can be dramatically increased by timely irrigation as the berry enlarges. Avoid overwatering, as too much water will dilute the flavor of the berry and give it a bland, unappealing taste.

Planting and Establishment

The method of strawberry production recommended in this book is called the matted-row system. The strawberry's perennial nature is used to best advantage in the matted rows by allowing the plants to be replenished with new growth each year. If properly maintained, the matted-row system will yield strawberries for 5 to 8 years or even longer. This perennial production system is inexpensive to establish, particularly compared to annual systems, in which the strawberry plants are planted, fruited, and removed in the course of a single year.

Strawberry plants should be kept in a shady area or a refrigerator up until planting. Place the roots in water about a half hour prior to planting. Do not allow the roots to dry out during the planting process. Strawberries are best planted in April as soon as the soil is in good condition—that is, well-worked soil without excess moisture. Planting after the first of June is not recommended.

Short-day strawberries should be planted 18 to 24 inches (45–60 cm) apart in rows at least 36 inches (90 cm) apart, with the soil line above the roots but not covering the growing point of the crown. The wide spacing of the plants makes for a relatively inexpensive initial investment, and the plant's ability to form runners freely allows it to create the bed in the first season.

The site should be irrigated immediately after planting. Optimal soil-moisture levels must be maintained throughout the first season to allow the plants to become well established. After planting, apply 2 pounds (1 kg) of a balanced 10-10-10 fertilizer per 100 feet (30 m) in each row, with an additional 2 pounds applied in late August. Young plants will look very small and insignificant when you first plant them (Plate 5)—but take heart. They will grow and flourish, given time and tending.

To avoid flowering and fruiting stress on the young plant, flower buds should be removed in the first year by cutting off the inflores-

cence at the base. Flower buds and runners on day-neutral strawberries need to be removed only through early July of the first year
and may be allowed to fruit from then on. Removal of flowers
allows the plants to direct their energy toward establishing a root
system and developing a healthy, large leaf canopy to fuel next
year's crop. The importance of establishing a healthy stand of plants
cannot be overemphasized. Remember, the main objective of the
first year is to establish a healthy canopy that will provide you with
delicious fruit for many years to come.

Overwintering

Strawberry plants require mulching for protection from the cold
and from soil heaving that can result from sudden drops in temperature. Approximately 4 inches (10 cm) of clean (weed-free) wheat,
oat, or rye straw or salt marsh hay applied in December serves as an
effective mulch. Do not apply mulch in clumps, which can smother
plants. Mulch should be removed from the tops of the plants and
moved to the center of the row in spring, usually mid-March to
early April, after the danger of freezing has past but before much
leaf yellowing occurs. The straw mulch left in the rows provides a
bed on which the berries can ripen.

Harvest and Postharvest

At last—a year and a few months after planting—you're ready to
harvest! Berries generally will be ripe 28 to 30 days after full bloom
and should be harvested every 2 to 3 days. (See Table 3.1 for typical harvest times in the United States.) Strawberries should be
picked when they are fully colored. Pick them in the morning, after
the plants have dried, to maximize the shelf-life of the berries, and
be sure to retain the caps. The picked berries should be kept out of
direct sun and refrigerated as soon as possible. Do not wash the
berries until just prior to use.

My first agricultural job was as a college student harvesting
strawberries for ten hours each day, and I came to detest these
plants that I have since grown to love and respect. One thinks that

one will acclimate to bending over all day long, but in fact, even though I was only 19, I felt more debilitated every day. There was a good lesson in this: Don't plant more than you can comfortably pick, and only pick in the morning. Lesson learned.

Renovation

Thinning, narrowing, and mowing your strawberry beds, known as renovation, invigorates the plants and produces larger fruit. Beds that retain too many plants will yield small berries that are difficult to find under the dense foliage. The renovation process should begin immediately after harvest is completed. This gives the plants time to develop a sufficient canopy, which will, come fall, determine the amount and quality of the flower buds that will in turn produce fruit the following spring.

Renovation entails removing weeds, narrowing rows to 6 to 12 inches (15–30 cm), and thinning the plants to one plant about every 4 to 5 inches (10–12.5 cm) in the row. Row narrowing is best done with a rototiller, though a shovel can be used on small plantings. Try to select for the strongest runner (daughter) plants, and remove mother plants when they are 3 to 4 years old. Clip or mow leaves off and fertilize plants with about 5 pounds (2.3 kg) of 10-10-10 per 100 feet (30 m) of row. Irrigate if the weather is exceptionally dry.

If renovation is done properly, your first response should be, "Oh, my gosh! What have I done?" The planting will look completely devastated, and you will wonder how it will ever recover. Again, take heart. Continue to water and tend to the needs of the planting, and you will be amazed at the vigor with which it returns. In research plantings, I often have to narrow our rows even more drastically, down to a width of 3 to 6 inches (7.5–15 cm), or else the rows will grow together again by fall. If you see this happening, you can narrow the rows further later in the season.

With proper renovation and pest control each year, a strawberry planting should produce abundant large berries for at least 5 years.

Other Production Systems

Though I prefer the matted row because it takes advantage of the plants' natural tendencies and maximizes output per cost, other systems can be used to grow strawberries. If space is limited or the soil is unsuited to strawberry cultivation, strawberry plants can be grown in pots or pyramids. Pyramids are structures that hold soil in rings or squares, with successively smaller rings or squares stacked on top of the base. They are available from many garden supply stores or mail-order sources. In addition, strawberries are often grown on a commercial scale as annuals, planted on raised beds on plastic. Runners are removed rather than used to make the bed in the first year. The advantage of this system is that it produces strawberries in the first year (though only in the first year), and the plastic minimizes weed problems and keeps the strawberries relatively clean. Disadvantages include high expense, only annual production, and the use of non-renewable, rarely recycled plastics.

Frost Protection

Strawberry flower buds and fruit are susceptible to frost injury any time after bud break. In areas with late frosts, a crop can be substantially damaged even after the berries are developing. Early-blooming cultivars are more likely to be injured by frost than late cultivars. The simple spreading of several layers of newspaper or wool blankets on top of the planting overnight when a frost is expected can be enough to prevent any blossom kill. Frost blankets are also available. These are usually opaque, polypropylene, nonwoven fabrics that are reusable. Frost damage results in flowers with black centers, rather than yellow ones. Frost-damaged flowers will not develop into fruit.

In larger scale commercial production, strawberry blossoms and berries are protected against frost by overhead irrigation. The principle behind this method is that as water freezes, heat (called the heat of fusion) is released by the state change of water from liquid to ice. As long as an adequate layer of freezing water covers the bud or berry, the temperature will remain at or near the freezing point

(32°F, 0°C). The critical temperatures at which the various stages of strawberry blossoms are injured by frost are as follows: tight bud, 22°F (–6°C); half-opened blossom, 27°F (–3°C); open blossom, 30°F (–1°C); and fruit, 28°F (–2°C). Though small producers can use irrigation for frost protection, it is usually more practical to employ frost blankets.

Day-Neutral Strawberries: A Different Critter

Day-neutral strawberry plants require slightly different management strategies, since they have a slightly different physiology than their short-day counterparts. The following are some key principles for successfully growing the day-neutral types.

1. Day-neutral strawberries should be planted closer together, about 5 to 9 inches (12.5–22.5 cm) apart. They can be planted in staggered double rows, if desired. Additionally, day-neutral plants should be mulched immediately after planting since they are sensitive to warm soil temperatures. Mulch with about 4 inches (10 cm) of clean straw.
2. Day-neutral cultivars require a more constant nitrogen rate throughout the planting year. Apply 1 pound (0.5 kg) of ammonium nitrate per 100 feet (30 m) of row once a month from June through the first of September.
3. Renovation is not recommended for day-neutral strawberries. Plants will need to be replaced every third year.

NICHES IN THE LANDSCAPE

From the purely ornamental viewpoint, strawberry plants make lovely low-growing groundcovers. They have glossy, medium dark green leaves that turn red in the fall. The plants will fill in a sunny spot in a matter of a season or two. Fruiting is not as prolific on plants grown in large beds as compared to rows, since rows allow for more sunlight penetration and air movement. It is also more difficult to locate the fruit in dense beds, so be sure to look carefully under leaves when harvesting—and watch where you step. Nurseries are releasing some purely ornamental strawberries, such as 'Pink Panda' (a sterile pink-flowered cultivar), that flower over most of the growing season and never produce fruit. In the right spot, these can be quite aggressive in the landscape and need to be contained.

The alpine strawberry *(Fragaria vesca)*, also referred to as *fraise des bois* or wood strawberry, is a fine plant for edgings. A smaller plant than the hybrid strawberry of commerce, it produces tiny, cone-shaped fruit. Some cultivars available through nurseries bear fruit that is quite tasty, but they do not offer high yields. A few on your cereal can be just the thing in the morning, though. As described in Chapter 1, I have used alpine strawberries to edge a bed that had a grape plant growing in it.

PESTS IN THE PLANTING

There's no avoiding it. You are going to have to deal with some pests if you want to grow lovely strawberries. Most of the disease and insect pests that are documented as plaguing strawberries are outlined in Tables 3.2 and 3.4. For recommended chemical and cultural controls, contact your local extension office or consultants. Also be sure to read Chapter 1 of this book for extensive recommendations on controlling pests using cultural management.

Weeds

Weeds will, without a doubt, plague your strawberry plantings. The strawberry plant is particularly sensitive to competition from weeds because it is short, so taller plants can easily block the sun, and it is shallow rooted, so it does not complete well for water and nutrients in the soil. The only cure is to be vigilant about weeding. The most problematic time for new growers is at planting, before the plants have filled in their area, because nature loves to fill in bare soil, especially in late summer. Pull the weeds, and keep on top of the problem. Going through the planting and pulling weeds once a week is optimal, and at least once every two weeks is required. Herbicides?

Some herbicides are labeled for use with strawberries, and commercial production guides will list them and the directions for their use, but for the small-scale grower, they are unnecessary. Opaque plastic works too, at least for a while, but because strawberries are grown in matted rows, and the runners need to root, it is not a practical solution. If you are very patient, you could poke holes in the plastic and carefully set the new runner plants to align with the holes, but if you're going to do that, you might as well spend your time pulling the weeds. A final reminder: Be sure to deal with the really noxious perennial weeds *before* you plant.

The one exception to the preceding philosophy of weed control is if your planting is overrun with grasses. There are certain extremely useful herbicides that will remove grasses specifically, while leaving broadleaf plants (in this case, our strawberries) unaffected. A herbicide called Poast (active chemical ingredient, sethoxydim) is available and can be used on strawberry plants—as always, be sure to follow the directions on the label.

Diseases

Strawberries have a whole host of fungal diseases that will either molest or kill them (Table 3.2). Fortunately, the plant breeders have helped us out considerably by developing many resistant cultivars, and you can help yourself, too. First, purchase and grow disease-resistant plants wherever possible. Today's strawberry cultivars offer great resistance to *Verticillium* wilt and red stele, though certainly not all cultivars have this resistance; refer to Table 3.3, or a reputable nursery's catalog, for information on disease-resistant cultivars. You can further help your situation by being very picky about where you plant strawberries. If puddles of water remain on the site after a light rain, you are almost guaranteed to have root-rot problems. The site you select must be well drained. If you do not have any suitable sites, remember that strawberries grow quite nicely in pots or pyramids. You can also modify the soil and engineer the drainage in container systems to allow you to grow the plants in spite of poor soil.

Gray mold. Gray mold, caused by the fungus *Botrytis cinerea*, is by far the most troublesome and most common disease problem (Plate 6). This fuzzy mold forms on ripe berries, and in extreme conditions, on green fruit as well. The fungal spores infect the plant in blossom, and they lie dormant in the developing fruit until the sugars in the fruit are high enough to encourage the spores to grow and eventually produce more spores on the ripe fruit. The spores formed on the ripe fruit can then go on to infect other ripening fruit from the outside (called a secondary infection), and so on and so on.

The time when the plants are blooming is critical. Chances are, if you have dry weather during this period, you will not have much trouble with gray mold. If you see a fruit with mold on it in your planting, get it out of there! As you harvest, you will inevitably miss a few ripe fruit, and these may become infected and threaten other fruit. Picking up that rotten fruit and disposing of it in the compost pile is a nasty job, but force yourself to do it, and you can control the disease without resorting to pesticides.

Another good cultural management technique for controlling gray mold is to make sure that the plants are not too dense in the planting. A density of about one plant every 4 to 5 inches (10–12.5 cm) is optimal. If the plants are closer than that, they take longer to dry after rain or irrigation, making a great environment for the fungus. Gray mold develops when free water is about, so anything you can do to reduce drying time and increase air circulation will help control this disease. Evidence also suggests that excessive nitrogen applied during the growing season will predispose the fruit to gray mold.

Let's say that we have had a very rainy spring, bloom is upon us, and more rain is likely to come. We have done everything right culturally (good plant density, well-drained site), and we would really like to harvest some strawberries. Under these conditions, a fungicide spray is warranted. (For a detailed discussion of pesticides, see Chapter 1.) A mixture of Captan and Benomyl (benomyl) or Ronilan (vinclosolin) at bloom time will vastly improve the chances of harvesting a crop. These pesticides do not accumulate in the plant tissue, and since bloom is 30 days from harvest, they are quite safe for application to your berries.

Table 3.2. Common Strawberry Diseases and Causal Organisms in the
United States

Name of Disease	Plant Parts Affected	Causal Organism
angular leaf spot	leaves, systemic	*Xanthomonas fragariae* (bacterium)
anthracnose rot	fruit, crowns, leaves	*Colletotrichum* (fungus)
anthracnose fruit rot (black spot)	fruit	*Colletotrichum* and *Gloeosporium* (fungi)
black root rot	roots	*Pythium, Rhizoctonia,* and other fungi
gray mold	fruit, crowns, roots	*Botrytis cinerea* (fungus)
leaf scorch	leaves, systemic	*Diplocarpon earliana* (fungus)
leaf spot	leaves	*Mycosphaerella fragariae* (fungus)
leather rot (vascular collapse)	fruit, crowns	*Phytophthora cactorum* (fungus)
Phomopsis leaf blight	leaves, fruit	*Phomopsis (Dendrophoma) obscurans* (fungus)
powdery mildew	leaves, fruit	*Sphaerotheca macularis* (fungus)
red stele root rot	roots	*Phytophthora fragariae* (fungus)
Rhizoctonia fruit rot (hard rot)	fruit, crowns, leaves, roots	*Rhizoctonia solani* and *R. fragariae* (fungi)
Rhizopus rot (leak)	fruit	*Rhizopus* (fungus)

Other diseases. Although red stele, *Verticillium,* and powdery mildew are all common diseases of the strawberry, they are rarely a serious problem for the home gardener—provided that the right site and cultivars are selected. Red stele (caused by the fungus *Phytophthora fragariae*) will only be a problem in wet sites with heavy soils. Even so, resistant cultivars can sometimes overcome these negatives. *Verticillium* can be completely avoided by not planting your strawberries in a site that has contained other *Verticillium*-susceptible plants, such as raspberry, tomato, potato, and eggplant. Though some resistant cultivars are available, *Verticillium* resistance

Name of Disease	Plant Parts Affected	Causal Organism
stunt	roots	*Pythium* (fungus)
Verticillium wilt	roots	*Verticillium albo-atrum* (fungus)
dagger	roots	*Xiphenema* (virus)
leaf and stem nematode	leaves	*Ditylenchus dipsaci* (virus)
necrotic shock	systemic	likely a necrotic shock virus
root knot	roots	*Meloidogyne* (virus)
root lesion	roots	*Pratylenchus* (virus)
spring dwarf	crowns	*Aphelenchoides fragariae* (virus)
strawberry crinkle	systemic	aphid-vectored strain crinkle virus
strawberry feather leaf	systemic	likely a virus-like particle
strawberry latent crowns	systemic	aphid-vectored strain latent crowns virus
strawberry leaf roll	systemic	likely a strain of leaf-roll virus
strawberry mild yellow edge	systemic	aphid-vectored strain mild yellow edge virus
strawberry mottle	systemic	aphid-vectored strain mottle virus
strawberry pallidosis	systemic	likely a pallidosis virus
strawberry veinbanding	systemic	aphid-vectored strain veinbanding virus

is not nearly as reliable as red stele resistance, due to the nature of the causal organism. Symptoms of both diseases include weak growth and often the complete collapse of the plant.

Powdery mildew is never a problem on strawberry fruit, but it may infest leaves in very damp years or in foggy sites. This fungal disease can be a problem if it occurs in the fall and limits plant photosynthesis. Since flower bud initiation takes place in the fall, if the plant is unable to photosynthesize due to the disease, its ability to form next year's flower buds will be limited. This is rarely a problem, however, and can be taken care of by appropriate site selection.

Table 3.3. Disease Resistance of Common Strawberry Cultivars

Cultivar	Verticillium Wilt	Red Stele	Leaf Diseases*	Powdery Mildew
'Allstar'	resistant–tolerant	resistant	tolerant	tolerant
'Annapolis'	intermediate	resistant	susceptible	unknown
'Cavendish'	intermediate	resistant	unknown	susceptible
'Delite'	resistant	resistant	resistant	unknown
'DelMarvel'	resistant	resistant	resistant	unknown
'Earliglow'	resistant	resistant	resistant	partially resistant
'Guardian'	resistant	resistant	resistant	susceptible
'Honeoye'	susceptible	susceptible	partially resistant	unknown
'Jewel'	susceptible	susceptible	resistant	resistant
'Kent'	unknown	unknown	unknown	unknown
'Lateglow'	resistant	resistant	tolerant	tolerant
'Latestar'	resistant	resistant	resistant	unknown
'Lester'	susceptible	resistant	resistant	unknown
'Mohawk'	resistant	resistant	unknown	tolerant
'Northeaster'	resistant	resistant	intermediate	susceptible
'Primetime'	resistant	resistant	resistant	unknown
'Raritan'	susceptible	susceptible	susceptible	unknown
'Redchief'	partially resistant	resistant	resistant	resistant
'Seneca'	susceptible	susceptible	unknown	unknown
'Sparkle'	susceptible	resistant	susceptible	susceptible
'Tribute'	partially resistant	resistant	tolerant	resistant
'Tristar'	resistant	resistant	tolerant	resistant
'Veestar'	tolerant	susceptible	tolerant	unknown

*Includes leafscorch and leafspot.

Low-lying areas should be avoided because of poor air circulation and propensity to frost.

Insects

The insect pests that seriously injure strawberry plants on a regular basis are few, fortunately. The primary threats are discussed here and in Table 3.4.

Tarnished plant bug. A relative of the stinkbug, only smaller, the tarnished plant bug *(Lygus)* can lurk in strawberries and cause damage from bloom time through fruiting. It has a long needlelike protuberance for a mouth, which it injects into the blossom or the developing fruit and slurps out the contents of the seed (achene). We don't really want the seeds anyway, so why is this a problem? The living seed sends messages to the developing fruit, and if some of the achenes are dead, the message will not be sent, and the fruit tissue in that area will not develop. The result: deformed fruit. This deformation usually occurs on the tip of the berry, giving it a buttonlike appearance (Plate 7). It does not hurt the fruit in any other way—the fruit is still edible and tasty—and so some folks opt to ignore the deformed fruit. If it gets bad enough, though, the damage from tarnished plant bug can take a bite out of your production. Pre- and post-bloom sprays of an appropriate insecticide are recommended. As mentioned earlier, never apply an insecticide during bloom since it will also kill the bees that are pollinating the flowers. Applying pesticides in the evening will limit exposure to the bees.

Sap beetles. Sap beetles *(Stelidota geminata)* simply love ripe strawberry fruit. These little black beetles are especially attracted to fruit that has been damaged by birds or slugs, adding insult to injury by contributing further grossness to an already disgusting fruit. The best remedy is to keep the fruit well harvested, something you probably intended to do anyway. As with gray mold disease, removing moldy and overripe fruit from the planting will improve control efforts. The delicious smells from the rotting fruit is what attracts

Table 3.4. Major Strawberry Insect and Mite Pests in the United States

Common Name of Pest	Scientific Name of Pest	Actions
cutworm	*Agrotis*	attacks fruit, flowers, and buds
field cricket	*Gryllidae*	attacks fruit, flowers, and buds
flower thrip	*Thysanoptera*	attacks fruit, flowers, and buds
lygus or tarnished plant bug	*Lygus*	attacks fruit, flowers, and buds
sap beetle	*Stelidota geminata*	attacks fruit, flowers, and buds
strawberry clipper or bud weevil	*Anthonomus signatus*	attacks fruit, flowers, and buds
flea beetle	*Altica ignita*	attacks leaves
grape colaspis	*Colaspis flavida*	attacks leaves
potato leafhopper	*Empoasca fabae*	attacks leaves
strawberry aphid	*Chaetosiphon fragaefolii, C. jacobi, C. minor, C. thomasi*	attacks leaves
strawberry leafroller	*Ancylis comptana-fragariae*	attacks leaves

the sap beetles in the first place. It has been suggested that by placing an old container of rotting fruit far from the strawberry planting you can lure the beetles away from the planting. It's worth a try if you have a lot of these pests in your area, but keeping the plot well-picked should be sufficient.

Strawberry clipper or strawberry bud weevil. A debate is raging in the small-fruit community about whether or not we really need to control the strawberry clipper *(Anthonomus signatus)*. This insect damages the plant by laying eggs in a stem in the flowering cluster, causing the stem to break and killing the flower. If you see several broken stems in your planting before bloom, you probably have been hit by the strawberry clipper, although you will rarely see the

Common Name of Pest	Scientific Name of Pest	Actions
two-spotted spider mite	*Tetranychus urtricae, T. telarius*	attacks leaves
arion slug	*Arion subfuscus*	attacks leaves, fruit
cyclamen mite	*Stenerotarsonemus pallidus*	feeds on stems and crowns
meadow spittlebug	*Philaenus spumarius*	feeds on stems and crowns
strawberry crown borer	*Tyloderma fragariae*	feeds on stems and crowns
strawberry crown miner	*Aristotelia fragariae*	feeds on stems and crowns
strawberry crown moth	*Synanthedon bibionipennis*	feeds on stems and crowns
black vine weevil	*Otiorhynchus sulcatus*	attacks roots
garden symphylan	*Scutigerella immaculata*	attacks roots
obscure root weevil	*Sciopithis obscurus*	attacks roots
strawbeery root weevil	*Otiorhynchus ovatus*	attacks roots
strawberry root aphid	*Aphis forbesi*	attacks roots
strawberry root worm	*Paria fragariae*	attacks roots
white grub	*Phyllophaga*	attacks roots

offending insect. All the older literature recommends insecticide sprays for control, but more recent research has found that, though individual fruits are lost, the plant compensates by developing new flowers or by increasing the size of the remaining fruit. The jury is still out on this, but if you see the tell-tale broken stems, you have several options. Probably the best approach is to simply wait and see how the crop develops. If you sustain too many losses at the end of the season, you should plan on spraying the following year. Or better yet, you can conduct your own experiment. Apply the insecticide recommended by your local extension office on half of your strawberry patch and not the other, and see if you can tell the difference in yield between the treated and untreated sections.

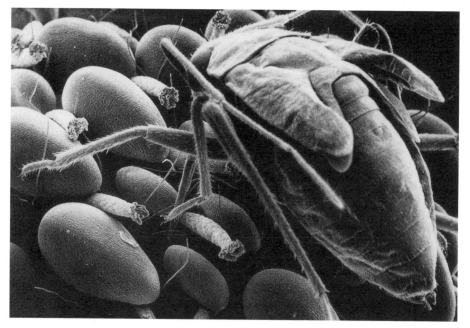

Figure 3.2. A scanning electron photograph of tarnished plant bug. (Photo by David Handley, University of Maine)

Slugs. Slugs are not a problem every year, but when they are a problem, they are *really* a problem. They eat holes in ripe or nearly ripe fruit, usually at the cap (calyx) end of the fruit and often on the underside as well if the fruit was laying in the soil. Slugs can provide entry holes for other pests such as sap beetles as well. I have to say that the worst thing I have experienced while harvesting strawberries (aside from a sore back) was picking up a large, fully ripe fruit from the patch and seeing not only a large hole on the bottom but also the slimy culprit that caused it slithering along the fruit—it was especially harrowing since the fruit was inches from my mouth! I suppose it could have been worse; I could have eaten it. So, what to do about slugs. First of all, slugs are a problem only in rainy years, unless you are lucky enough to live in slug-infested territory like the Pacific Northwest. In most climates, the weather eliminates slugs as a threat for about a third of the growing season. Secondly, slugs are, in fact, attracted to beer, so setting out small tin cans filled halfway with beer will trap a lot of these slimy pests. Some imaginative work by Marvin Pritts at Cornell University found that slugs were more attracted to expensive, imported beers than to the run-of-the-mill sorts. Unfortunately, the research also showed that, though an enormous number of slugs were trapped, damage to the fruit was not significantly reduced using the beer-trap method. Bear in mind, however, that this study was done at a commercial-sized planting. It is my suspicion (call it intuition) that beer traps would be an effective means of control in smaller, garden-sized plantings. But go with the expensive beer.

Diatomaceous earth is also purported to be a slug killer—it is supposed to slice their bodies as they crawl over it—but I have not seen any evidence of its effectiveness. As a last resort, you can scatter slug baits around the backyard site. I call this a last resort because slug baits can also be consumed by dogs, cats, and other wildlife, but these baits are ephemeral and will wash away with the first rain.

Birds

Birds are rarely a serious problem for strawberries, though they can decimate a blueberry planting. Netting is the best approach if birds are taking more than their share. Robins and starlings are usually the worst offenders.

FREQUENTLY ASKED QUESTIONS

What's the best tasting strawberry? People have different tastes and preferences when it comes to strawberry flavor. A few cultivars that are popular for the taste of their berries include 'Earliglow' (by far the best), 'Raritan', 'Honeoye', and 'Allstar'. 'Raritan' and 'Honeoye' both lack disease resistance, however, so you need to balance that potential shortcoming with flavor considerations. If you have a very well-drained soil that has not had strawberries planted in it before, you may want to try growing some 'Raritan' plants, just for the flavor of the berries.

As mentioned earlier, the fruit of any cultivar will taste better when it is grown to full ripeness locally, as compared to those picked early and shipped "green." It is hard to go wrong when you grow your own.

Why are my berries deformed? Deformed berries are usually a result of tarnished plant bug injury (as discussed earlier in the chapter). Fruit can also be deformed from frost. Frost most often kills the flower, resulting in no fruit, although occasionally it will only damage a portion of the flower. This portion will not develop properly, so the berry will look lopsided. You can still eat and enjoy them, and relish the idea that you are either sharing your bounty with some bugs, or that you barely escaped a fruit-killing frost.

What's the white foamy stuff on my berry plants that looks like spit? The foam is caused by spittle bugs *(Philaenus spumarius)*. It does not harm the fruit, and rarely is it a major problem. The nymphs of this insect cover themselves with the peculiar spittle-like substance for protection until they develop into the adult stage. Spittle bugs are usually present at bloom time through harvest. Plunging your hand into a substance that looks like spit can be unpleasant, but it is harmless. If it gets to be too bad, a spray of malathion will get rid of the critters.

Do I really have to renovate my planting every year? Yes! Renovation rejuvenates the planting and makes for larger, better quality fruit. The consequence of not renovating is many small plants with small berries, which are a nuisance to harvest. High plant density results in higher disease incidence as well.

RECOMMENDED STRAWBERRY CULTIVARS BY REGION

The following lists suggest the cultivars most suitable for various regions of the United States; more descriptive information is given earlier in the chapter. Refer to Table 3.1 for details on harvest season.

MID-ATLANTIC AND MIDWEST

Early Season
'Annapolis'
'Earliglow'
'Mohawk'
'Northeaster'
'Veestar'

Midseason
'Allstar'
'DelMarvel'
'Guardian'
'Honeoye'
'Jewel'
'Kent'
'Lester'
'Primetime'
'Raritan'
'Redchief'
'Seneca'

Late Season
'Delite'
'Latestar'
'Sparkle'

Day-Neutral
'Tribute'
'Tristar'

NEW ENGLAND

Early Season
'Annapolis'
'Earliglow'
'Northeaster'

Midseason
'Allstar'
'Cavendish'
'Honeoye'
'Jewel'
'MicMac'

Day-Neutral
'Tribute'

SOUTH CENTRAL

Early Season
'Earliglow'

Midseason
'Cardinal'
'DelMarvel'

Late Season
'Arking'

SOUTHEAST

Early Season
'Rosa Linda'

Midseason
'Camarosa'
'Oso Grande'

PACIFIC NORTHWEST

Early Season
'Hood'
'Sumas'

Midseason
'Benton'
'Shuksan'
'Totem'

Late Season
'Rainier'

Day-Neutral
'Fern'
'Hecker'
'Seascape'
'Selva'
'Tribute'
'Tristar'

CHAPTER 4

Brambles

FAMILY: ROSACEAE, THE ROSE FAMILY

PRIMARY SPECIES:
Subgenus *Ideobatus*—raspberry
    Rubus idaeus L.—red raspberry
    Rubus occidentalis L.—black raspberry
Subgenus *Eubatus*—blackberry
    Rubus bartoni Newton
    Rubus laciniatus Willd.
    Rubus nitidioides Wats.
    Rubus procerus Muell.
    Rubus ruticanus var. *inermis* E. Merc.
    Rubus thysiger Banning & Focke
    Rubus ulmifolius Schott.
    Rubus ursinus Cham. & Schlecht.

I have always thought that if there truly is a food of the gods, it must be raspberries. Sweet but not too sweet, stimulating but not brash, so full of heavenly aroma. It is also the crop that I most often recommend for people who have only a small bit of land. A 10-foot (3-m) row of raspberry plants in your backyard gives you enough berries to eat in season and enough to freeze or use to make jam. What a great Christmas present: bright red raspberry jam that tastes like it just came out of the garden, just as winter's darkness is starting to descend. If planted in an appropriate site, these plants also require little in the way of pest control or maintenance.

HISTORICAL BACKGROUND AND
OTHER INTERESTING FACTS

A bramble is defined as any plant belonging to the genus *Rubus*. The best-known brambles are raspberries and blackberries. Several types of raspberries and blackberries are extensively cultivated, and hybrids between the two, such as tayberries, boysenberries, and loganberries, are produced on a limited scale, though most are narrowly adapted only to the Pacific Northwest of North America.

The red raspberry *(Rubus idaeus)* has been cultivated in Europe since at least the sixteenth century. The species name was most likely selected by the botanist Carolus Linnaeus after a reference from the Roman scholar Pliny, who wrote about wild raspberries having come from Mount Ida in Greece. Palladius, a Roman writer from the fourth century B.C., named the raspberry in a treatise on garden plants.

The earliest written evidence of red raspberry cultivation in North America is in a 1771 list of plants. Commercial raspberry production, and the selection and breeding efforts that typically accompany commercial production, likely did not begin on a large scale until as late as the 1800s, even though the crop was known and planted in a limited manner before then. In 1876 Andrew S. Fuller wrote the *Small Fruit Culturist*, the first source of practical information for small-fruit producers. At this time in history, numerous publications had long been available on the culture of tree fruits and grapes, but Fuller's book was a milestone for bramble growing. In 1880, slightly less than 12,225 acres (4950 hectares) of red raspberries were in production in the United States; by 1948, the plants were being cultivated on 370,500 acres (150,000 hectares), with New York, Michigan, Oregon, Ohio, and Pennsylvania leading in production. The middle of the twentieth century was the heyday of red raspberry cultivation in the eastern and midwestern United States. After World War II, however, production plummeted, primarily the result of plant diseases and labor shortages. The introduction of aphid-resistant cultivars and micropropagation techniques have led to a new, though modest, rebirth, with production acreage in the United States at about 133,380 acres (54,000 hectares) today.

The black raspberry *(Rubus occidentalis)* has been domesticated only since the mid-1800s. The cultivated plants remain close to their wild, North American–native relatives in productivity and growth habit. When I first came to Pennsylvania, I noticed an interesting trend. Producers told me that they did not grow red raspberries because they could not sell them. In fact, one grower told me that, for lack of customers, he had to feed his red raspberries to his pigs. Horrifying! As I explored market preferences across the state, I found that in rural areas producers had little success selling red raspberries but great success with black raspberries. This may be due to the fact that black raspberries grow wild in Pennsylvania and are a traditional food source for rural dwellers. The urban folks, however, often disdained the stronger flavored, seedier black raspberry in favor of the red raspberry, its tamer and, some might argue, more refined cousin.

Purple raspberries were recognized as hybrids between red and black raspberries as early as 1870. They are currently bred in several raspberry programs across the United States. The plants are particularly vigorous, though the purple berries usually lack the sweetness of the black or red berries. They make a beautiful jam, however, and tend to fruit a little later (late June in central Pennsylvania), extending the season a bit.

The history of the blackberry proves more contentious than that of the raspberry. Early European settlers in North America saw blackberry plants more as a weed than as a potential crop, and great effort was put into killing them, though the berries were likely gathered from wild stands and put to good use. Although blackberries were domesticated in Europe by the seventeenth century, they were not cultivated by North Americans until the nineteenth century. A sort of natural breeding program ensued as settlers moved west across the continent, clearing ground as they went and providing the open areas that blackberries often pioneer. Various species of blackberries hybridized freely, and two selections from those populations, 'Lawton' and 'Dochester', were marketed in 1850. The superior nature of these selections (as compared to those gathered in the wild) sparked a great deal of interest in blackberries as a cultivated crop, and private and, later, public breeding programs took up the cause.

Current bramble production is centered in Russia, Poland, Yugoslavia, the United Kingdom, North America, and Chile. The largest production area in North America is in the Pacific Northwest, where the climate is relatively mild. This industry produces high-quality fruit that is used primarily for processing. Production in the Midwest, the Mid-Atlantic, and New England is stable or rising, with red raspberries most prevalent, followed by black and purple raspberries. The bramble-producing industries in these regions are small, and fruit is grown primarily for fresh consumption. Red raspberry production in California is also increasing and may become more significant in the near future. Chile is the latest up-and-coming contender. Because the growing season there is opposite that of the Northern Hemisphere, and because the raspberry is so perishable, Chilean bramble production should complement, rather than compete with, production in North America and Europe.

BIOLOGY OF THE PLANT: KNOWING IT AND USING IT TO YOUR ADVANTAGE

Rubus species typically have perennial roots and biennial shoots (Figures 4.1 and 4.2). The shoots (called canes) grow vegetatively in the first growing season. These vegetative canes are called primocanes. The primocanes go dormant for the winter and then leaf out, flower, fruit, and die during the second growing season. The canes that flower, fruit, and die after the dormant period are referred to as floricanes. From early spring through the end of harvest, both primocanes and floricanes are present in a bramble planting. In certain training and trellis systems, these two growth phases are grown separately (by training them to opposite sides of the trellis) to minimize competition and to maximize air circulation among the canes, which in turn reduces infection by fungal diseases.

Bramble fruits range from just over pea-sized (about 1 gram) to about the size of a quarter (3.5–4 grams). Shape is also variable, ranging from almost spherical to oval, oblong, or conical. In general, raspberries are more spherical or conical in shape, whereas blackberries are more ovoid. Size and shape are determined prima-

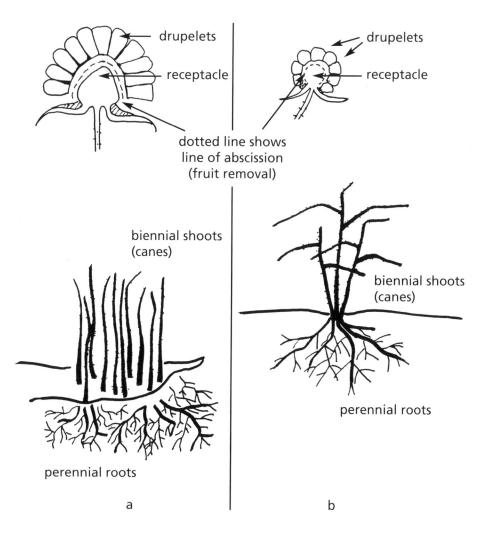

Figure 4.1. The raspberry plant: a) red raspberry, b) black raspberry.

rily by the genetic makeup of the cultivar, though certainly if water or nutrients are restricted, size will suffer.

Each fruit is composed of many individual sections called drupelets. The drupelets are loosely held together by intertwining hairs at the base of the fruit, as well as by a waxy deposition on the surface. Raspberry fruits detach from the receptacle when harvested

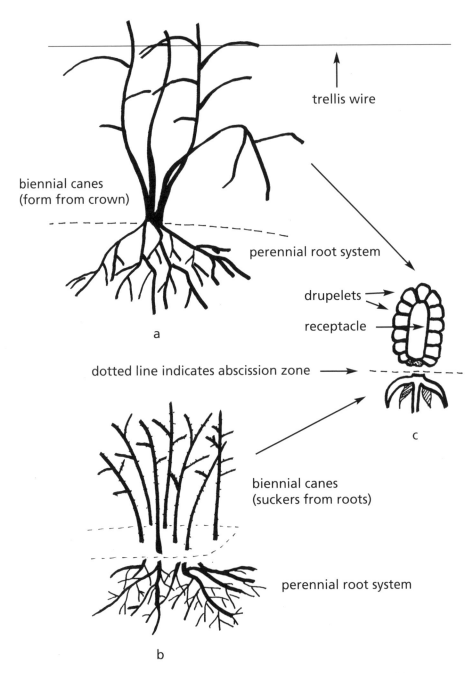

trellis wire

biennial canes
(form from crown)

perennial root system

drupelets

receptacle

a

dotted line indicates abscission zone

biennial canes
(suckers from roots)

c

perennial root system

b

Figure 4.2. The blackberry plant: a) trailing thornless blackberry,
b) upright thorny blackberry, c) fruit detail.

ripe, resulting in a fruit with a cup-shaped cavity where it was previously attached to the plant. Blackberry fruits, by contrast, detach from above the receptacle when ripe, so the receptacle is consumed as part of the fruit, appearing as a center of white tissue inside the fruit. The "plug" of tissue in the center of the fruit helps prevent crushing, which is one reason why blackberry fruits have a slightly longer shelf-life than raspberry fruits.

Types of Raspberries

Red, black, and purple raspberries are the three most commonly grown raspberry types, although yellow or gold raspberries are also produced. The word *type* is used intentionally, because the difference among them is not only the color of the fruit, but also the growth habit (and hence the cultural practices), pest susceptibility, and other characteristics.

Raspberry plants range in height from about thigh-high, such as some of the more cold hardy types grown in New England, to 6 or 7 feet (about 2 m) tall. Leaves are usually composed of three (sometimes five) leaflets, are light to medium green in color, and have serrated edges.

Red raspberries *(Rubus idaeus)* are further divided into two types: summer-fruiting and primocane-fruiting. Summer-fruiting red raspberries bear their fruit in summer (June and July in the Northern Hemisphere). They have the typical biennial life cycle of a bramble, so fruit is borne only on the second-year canes, and the canes die after fruiting.

Primocane-fruiting red raspberries are an exception to the typical bramble life cycle. They fruit during the first year on the new canes, usually in late summer through fall (fruiting ceases at the first hard frost). Also known as ever-bearing or fall-fruiting raspberries, they will fruit again in the spring on the buds basipetal to (closer to the base of the plant than) the last buds that fruited the previous fall. About 10 percent of the total yield is usually borne in the summer, with about 90 percent in the fall.

Because both types of red raspberries produce new canes (colloquially called suckers) primarily from the root system, they are usually grown in hedgerows (see Figure 4.3). In the Pacific Northwest, however, they are often grown in concentrated groups of canes, called "hills" or "stools," on 6-foot (2-m) high trellises to facilitate machine harvesting. Red raspberries are typically the most winter-hardy of the raspberries, although those bred for the Pacific Northwest are relatively cold tender.

As the name suggests, black raspberries bear dark purple to black fruit (Plate 13), usually slightly earlier in the season than red raspberries. These plants belong to the species *Rubus occidentalis*, and the cultivar 'Jewel' is the standard for the northeastern and midwestern United States. Black raspberries initiate new canes from the crown of the plant rather than from root suckers, and therefore they are grown in a hill system in which each plant is grown independently, with pruning and maintenance done on a per plant basis (see Figure 4.4). They require summer tipping, unlike red raspberries, because individual canes can grow to unmanageable lengths, and if grown unchecked, they will tip-root. Black raspberries are more cold tender than red raspberries.

Purple raspberries are hybrids between red and black raspberries. They initiate new canes predominately from the crown but may form suckers between plants as well. They are grown in the same manner as black raspberries and are intermediate between the parent species in cold hardiness.

Gold or yellow raspberries are mutant forms of red or black raspberries. Though not widely grown, they are increasingly being released by nurseries because of their novelty appeal. Most are not an improvement over the red raspberries in flavor, growth habit, or productivity, although the cultivar 'Anne', from the University of Maryland's breeding program, is an exception (Plate 14). 'Anne' is not particularly productive, but its berry has a remarkable flavor, worth growing for the wonderful jam it makes. The flavor is mildly raspberry-like but also has traces of banana and strawberry-like aromas. To date, all the yellows and golds bear their fruit in fall, but plant breeders are working toward developing a worthy summer bearer.

Types of Blackberries

Four types of blackberries are currently grown: thorny erect types, which dominate wild populations; thorny trailing types; thornless trailing types; and thornless upright types. Thorny blackberries have excellent fruit quality, but they are grown less extensively in cultivation because the thorns present an obstacle in harvesting. OK, the thorns are nothing short of brutal. Like rose thorns, blackberry thorns recurve backward, so if they don't get you going in, they'll get you coming out. Still, the flavor of the thorny blackberry fruit far surpasses that of the other types. Though less cold tolerant than raspberries, thorny blackberries are hardier than the thornless types.

The trailing thornless blackberries were developed by the United States Department of Agriculture beginning in the early 1960s. They are the most cold tender of the blackberries—suitable only in zone 6 and warmer areas—but they are extremely vigorous when grown on a suitable site (Plate 16). They produce large, $3/4$- to $1 1/2$-inch (1.8–3.75 cm) diameter, prostrate canes that require trellising. Fruit flavor is somewhat tart, but the fruit is excellent for processing into pies, jams, syrups, and other goodies.

A breeding effort initiated in the 1980s at the University of Arkansas has yielded several worthy upright forms of thornless blackberry. Cold hardiness is still not as good as in the thorny types, but it is better than that of many trailing thornless types. When trialed in central Pennsylvania, the upright thornless cultivars were not hardy, although production from southern Pennsylvania to Arkansas is feasible. Production in the Southeast will be limited by inadequate chilling.

A fourth, less common blackberry type is grown only in the Pacific Northwest. Trailing thorny blackberries, also referred to as western trailing blackberries, are quite cold tender and require more chilling than is provided in areas of the southern United States. Cultural management techniques are the same as those for trailing thornless types.

Tayberries and Other Lesser Known Brambles

Raspberries and blackberries are the brambles most commonly produced and consumed in the United States, but several other brambles have also been developed, both as novelties and for their often superior flavor. These include tayberries, tummelberries, loganberries, and boysenberries, all of which are hybrids between red raspberries and blackberries. They are produced on a relatively small scale, and only tayberries should be considered for production outside of the Pacific Northwest and California, since the others are quite cold tender. More similar to the trailing blackberry than to the raspberry, these hybrid types have a trailing rather than upright growth habit, and the fruit adheres to the receptacle.

Tayberry plants produce red, elongated bramble fruits that retain their receptacle when harvested. The fruit makes a beautiful ruby-red jam, but it is extremely soft when fully ripe and recommended only for pick-your-own commercial operations, backyards, or for processing. Tayberries should be grown according to the recommendations for trailing blackberries.

CULTIVAR SELECTION

Selecting appropriate cultivars is perhaps the most important decision involved in growing brambles, and it is certainly a difficult one to change once the plants are established. Prospective growers should consult with neighbors, local county extension personnel, and local nurseries for the most up-to-date information on cultivars for their location. Several cultivars are resistant to the raspberry aphid, which is a useful trait since this aphid transmits a virus.

When purchasing bramble plants, be sure to obtain them from a reputable nursery. Tissue-cultured plants are preferred because they are easier to establish and are more likely to be free from disease than dormant canes. See the Appendix for sources of plant materials.

Many noteworthy bramble cultivars are described here; a list of recommended cultivars by region is given at the end of this chapter.

Typical harvest dates for the various regions of the United States are shown in Table 4.1. Season, hardiness, and productivity data for the individual bramble cultivars discussed here is included in Table 4.2.

Table 4.1. Typical Bramble Harvest Times by Region

Region	Summer-bearing Raspberries	Ever-bearing Raspberries	Blackberries
New England	mid-July	late August	n/a*
Mid-Atlantic	July	late August	late July–early August
Midwest	July	late August	late July–early August
South Central	late May	late August	late May–mid-July
Southeast	March–June	March–September	April–early June
Pacific Northwest	mid-June	late August	late June–frost

*Blackberries are not recommended for New England because the low winter temperatures are too cold.

SUMMER-BEARING RED RASPBERRY CULTIVARS

'Amos'. A recent release that was a sister seedling to 'Sentry'. Fruit quality is comparable to 'Sentry', but plants are not as vigorous and do not require as much sucker removal on fertile sites.

'Boyne'. Very winter hardy and productive. Berries are dark red, small to medium in size. Plants are short.

'Canby'. Moderately winter hardy and nearly thornless. Productive, with attractive medium to large fruit. Has performed well in western Pennsylvania, but many growers complain of a lack of hardiness.

'Chilliwack'. Bright red, firm fruit with excellent flavor. Canes are quite vigorous and nearly spine-free. Medium productivity. Some root-rot resistance. Very early. Pacific Northwest only.

'Hilton'. Large, cone-shaped berries. Plants are vigorous, but cold hardiness is lacking. Fruit flavor and firmness are only good. May be difficult to pull off the bush if not fully ripe.

'Killarney'. A sibling of 'Boyne'. Very early fruit is medium-sized and bright red. Hardy, and well armed with spines. Produces many suckers. Like 'Boyne', the plant is short.

'Latham'. Excellent cold hardiness. Plant is susceptible to mildew but resists viruses fairly well. Fruit size is small to medium, flavor is acceptable, firmness is good. Relatively long bearing season. Old standard eastern cultivar.

'Meeker'. Medium to large fruit with good flavor. Ripens later than 'Willamette'. Very productive, but susceptible to winter injury. Pacific Northwest only.

'Newburgh'. Medium-sized berries with good flavor and good cold hardiness. Relatively productive, but fruit may be crumbly and may ripen unevenly. Particularly attractive to Japanese beetles and two-spotted spider mites.

'Nova'. Midseason cultivar with medium-sized, firm fruit. Flavor is somewhat acidic. Plants have good vigor and few thorns. Very hardy. New England only.

'Reveille'. Very early berry. Good cold hardiness and vigor. Fruit is too soft for shipping, but excellent flavor and good size make it useful in the home garden.

'Sentry'. A vigorous cultivar with large, firm fruit. Fruit is exceptionally attractive and flavorful, though more susceptible than most to gray mold. It is moderate in winter hardiness and productivity.

'Taylor'. Late season for a summer bearer. Medium fruit size, good flavor, and moderate winter hardiness. Very susceptible to mosaic virus, fungal diseases, and two-spotted spider mites.

'Titan'. A productive cultivar with mild-flavored (some would say bland), very large cone-shaped berries. Plants have excellent vigor but poor winter hardiness. The fruit is soft, and some growers feel the appearance is too rough (drupelets are uneven). 'Titan' is particularly susceptible to *Phytophthora* root rot, so make sure soils are especially well drained. Resistant to the raspberry aphid.

'Tulameen'. Produces very large fruit that is firm, bright red, and has excellent flavor. Extremely susceptible to root rot. Pacific Northwest only.

'Willamette'. Medium to large fruit, dark red with mild flavor. Ripens early. Susceptible to root rot, and not productive in heavy (clay) soils. Long considered the standard summer-bearer for the Pacific Northwest. Pacific Northwest only.

FALL-BEARING RED RASPBERRIES

'August Red'. Ripens early compared to other fall-bearing cultivars. Produces short, spiny canes of only moderate vigor. Fruit is somewhat rough and flavor is mild. New England only.

'Autumn Bliss' (Plate 11). Extremely high yielding and vigorous. Canes are of large diameter and medium height; they tend to sucker in clumps around the original plants. Considerably earlier than 'Heritage', though fruit quality is not as consistent.

'Autumn Britten'. Medium height and good productivity. Later season than 'Autumn Bliss'. In Pennsylvania trials, fruit size and quality were good at the beginning of the season but diminished as the season progressed.

'Caroline'. High-yielding, excellent-flavored fruit, though the fruit can be rough in appearance. Strong raspberry taste. This plant has a lot of variation in cane height, with the shorter canes bearing earlier in the season than the taller ones.

'Dinkum' (Plate 12). A tall plant with moderate cane density. Productivity is medium to low, and the season is fairly late, but the berries are exceptionally beautiful. They are slightly conical but rounded and have very even drupelets. Flavor and firmness are also excellent. Grow this one for quality, not quantity.

'Dormanred'. Somewhat trailing in habit. Well-adapted to hot envionments. Fruit quality is very marginal, but this cultivar is one of the few that survives the heat of the South. Southeast and south-central United States only.

'Fall Red'. Canes are short to medium in height, and the plant produces many suckers. Spiny. Fruit is medium-sized and the flavor is good, but fruit is quite soft. Ripens early for a fall-bearer. New England only.

'Heritage'. Medium-sized, firm fruit of excellent quality. Season begins in mid- to late August in Pennsylvania and continues through severe frost or freeze. Fruit tolerates light frosts well.

Plants are very vigorous and sucker well. The standard among fall-bearing types, with the only limitation that it begins bearing too late for northern climes.

'Polana'. A short plant with attractive and shiny fruit (similar to that of 'Dinkum'), but this cultivar is susceptible to having a split receptacle, which results in difficulty with fruit removal. Flavor is good, not excellent.

'Redwing'. Very productive. Ripens earlier than 'Heritage' in some years or some sites. Fruit is large and has good flavor but tends to be soft. Tall canes fill rows evenly. At its best, fruit quality is as good as 'Heritage', but is not consistently so.

'Ruby'. Very large and extremely attractive fruit, but flavor is bland. In some years, the fruit may be rough looking. Hard to remove in some years. Yields were much lower compared to 'Heritage' in two Pennsylvania trials. Particularly susceptible to root rots and crown gall.

'Summit'. Matures about 10 days earlier than 'Heritage'. Fruit is medium-sized and dark red. This cultivar was tested in Pennsylvania and performed miserably. Pacific Northwest only.

BLACK RASPBERRY CULTIVARS

'Allen'. Large and attractive fruit on vigorous, productive plants. Fruit size is comparable to 'Jewel'. Flavor is mild, hardiness intermediate.

'Blackhawk'. An older cultivar that is enjoying a revival. Moderately productive with large firm fruit. Season is slightly later than most.

'Bristol'. High-yielding and early, with medium-sized fruit of excellent flavor. Susceptible to anthracnose, but tolerant of powdery mildew. It is the most widely grown black raspberry in Pennsylvania.

'Cumberland'. Difficult to distinguish from 'Bristol'.

'Haut'. Firm, medium-sized fruit with good flavor. Comparable in most traits to 'Bristol'.

'Jewel'. A particularly vigorous and productive plant with excellent cold hardiness. Fruit is larger than 'Bristol'. It is more susceptible to gray mold after harvest. Some resistance to powdery mildew. The standard for the northeastern and midwestern United States.

'Munger'. The primary black raspberry cultivar in Oregon. Fruit is small to medium in size and blue-black in color. Has good flavor and firmness. Needs well-drained soils. Pacific Northwest only.

'Mysore'. Tropical or subtropical. Quite vigorous in warm sites with good quality fruit. Southeast only.

PURPLE RASPBERRIES

'Brandywine'. Produces firm, round, tart, reddish fruit. Very vigorous, with good winter hardiness. Suckers grow only from the crown, so plants will not spread.

'Royalty'. Cone-shaped fruit that is sweeter than 'Brandywine'. Fruit is too soft for shipping, although it can be picked slightly before ripeness for this purpose. Suckers freely from roots, growing more like a red raspberry in hedgerows. It is resistant to raspberry aphids, which spread some viruses, but is especially susceptible to crown gall.

YELLOW RASPBERRIES

'Anne' (Plate 14). A medium to tall plant that produces very few primocanes, limiting its yield. Fruit is a true yellow color, large, slightly rough in appearance. The wonderful flavor has overtones of banana; the flavor improves as the season progresses. Worth growing for the unusual and delicious jam it makes.

'Autumn Harvest'. A vigorous plant with an unusually high degree of branching. Produces abundant but very small fruit that is mediocre in flavor.

'Goldie' (Plate 15). Similar to the fall-bearing red 'Heritage' in time of fruiting and productivity. Fruit is actually more of a pink or orange color by the time it is easily removed from the receptacle. Fruit is prone to sun bleaching. This cultivar was a mutation of 'Heritage' and sometimes reverts back to the red form.

UPRIGHT THORNY BLACKBERRIES

'Brazos'. Later fruiting than other southeastern blackberries. Good-sized fruit with large druplets. Self-pollinates, so another cultivar is not needed for fruit set. Southeast only.

'Choctaw'. Very productive, bearing large fruit with small seeds. Hardiness is questionable.

'Darrow'. Plants are very erect, vigorous, and winter hardy. An old standard but often difficult to find these days.

'Illini'. Very hardy and very thorny. Good fruit quality. New England and northern Midwest only.

'Kiowa'. Large (10–12 grams), flavorful fruit. Plant has a long ripening season and is quite productive. Very thorny and erect. South-central U.S. only.

'Oklawaha'. Productive, but with small drupelets. Cross-pollination with another cultivar improves fruit size and set. Southeast only.

'Shawnee'. Very productive plant that bears extremely large, sweet fruit late in the season. Hardiness is purported to reach 10°F (–12°C), but this cultivar has not been widely planted in the Midwest or Northeast due to poor winter survival.

TRAILING THORNY BLACKBERRIES

'Black Butte'. Berries are extremely large but only fair in flavor. Plants not terribly productive. Pacific Northwest only.

'Kotata'. Large, glassy black berries with good flavor and firmness. Canes are quite thorny and vigorous. Productive. Pacific Northwest only.

'Marion'. A midseason berry known for its excellent flavor. Large, bright black, medium-firm fruit. Very thorny and productive. Pacific Northwest only.

'Olallie'. Medium to large berries that are bright black and firm. Plants are vigorous and productive but fairly cold tender. Pacific Northwest only.

UPRIGHT THORNLESS BLACKBERRIES

'Arapaho'. The earliest of the upright thornless blackberries. Fruit is medium-sized, short, and conical with small seeds.

'Navaho'. Fruits relatively late, with medium-sized fruit and good flavor. Resistant to anthracnose and root rot.

TRAILING THORNLESS BLACKBERRIES

'Chester'. Ripens later than 'Hull' or 'Dirksen' but has better flavor and slightly better cold hardiness.

'Dirksen'. One of the hardiest and most consistent of the trailing types. Excellent fruit quality and improved flavor compared to some of the early cultivars.

'Hull'. Flavor is sweeter and less tart than other trailing cultivars. Berry does not lose its color in high temperatures.

'Thornless Evergreen'. Medium-sized, firm berries are dark black and mildly flavored. Fruits late (mid-August to mid-September), and plant is very productive. Suckers arising from roots are often thorny. Pacific Northwest only.

'Triple Crown'. Produces very large berries with good flavor. Relatively new and untested.

HYBRID BRAMBLES

'Boysenberry'. Very large, soft, deep maroon berries. The flavor is distinctive and excellent, sought after by gourmets. Canes are quite thorny, though some thornless clones are available. Pacific Northwest only.

'Loganberry'. Early season. Berries are medium in size, elongated, and dark red. Though soft, they have good flavor. A thornless clone is available, but most clones are thorny. Pacific Northwest only.

'Tayberry'. Long canes need to be trellised. Produces early in the season. Berries are deep red, soft, and have a distinctive flavor. Canes are extremely thorny.

Table 4.2. Bramble Cultivars by Season, Hardiness, and Productivity

In this table, season refers to the earliness or lateness of a cultivar relative to its bramble type. For example, 'August Red' is early relative to other fall-bearing red raspberries. Refer to the lists at the end of the chapter to ascertain which cultivars perform best in your region.

Cultivar	Season	Hardiness	Relative Productivity

RASPBERRIES

Summer-Bearing Red (bear fruit from late June to late July in most regions)

Cultivar	Season	Hardiness	Relative Productivity
'Amos'	early	moderately hardy	medium
'Boyne'	early	hardy	medium
'Canby'	early	moderately hardy	medium
'Chilliwack'	midseason	tender	medium
'Hilton'	late	tender	medium
'Killarney'	early	hardy	high
'Latham'	late	very hardy	medium
'Meeker'	midseason	tender	high
'Newburgh'	late	moderately hardy	high
'Nova'	midseason	very hardy	medium
'Reveille'	early	hardy	high
'Sentry'	midseason	moderately hardy	medium
'Taylor'	late	moderately hardy	medium
'Titan'	midseason	moderately hardy	high
'Tulameen'	early	tender	medium
'Willamette'	early	tender	high

Fall-Bearing Red (bear fruit from August to November in most regions)

Cultivar	Season	Hardiness	Relative Productivity
'August Red'	early	hardy	medium
'Autumn Bliss'	early	hardy	high
'Autumn Britten'	early-mid	hardy	high
'Caroline'	midseason	hardy	high
'Dinkum'	late	hardy	medium
'Dormanred'	midseason	hardy	high
'Fall Red'	early	hardy	medium
'Heritage'	late	hardy	high
'Polana'	late	hardy	medium
'Redwing'	mid-late	hardy	high
'Ruby'	midseason	hardy	high
'Summit'	early	hardy	high

Cultivar	Season	Hardiness	Relative Productivity
Black (bear fruit from mid-June to mid-July in most regions)			
'Allen'	early	moderately hardy	medium
'Blackhawk'	midseason	tender	medium
'Bristol'	early	tender	high
'Cumberland'	early	tender	high
'Haut'	early	moderately hardy	medium
'Jewel'	early	hardy	high
'Munger'	early	tender	high
'Mysore'	early	tender	medium
Purple (bear fruit from late June to late July in most regions)			
'Brandywine'	midseason	hardy	medium
'Royalty'	midseason	moderately hardy	high
Fall-Bearing Yellow (bear fruit from August to November in most regions)			
'Anne'	late	hardy	low
'Autumn Harvest'	late	hardy	high
'Goldie'	midseason	hardy	high

BLACKBERRIES

Cultivar	Season	Hardiness	Relative Productivity
Upright Thorny (bear fruit from early July to late August in most regions)			
'Brazos'	late	tender	medium
'Choctaw'	midseason	tender	high
'Darrow'	late	hardy	medium
'Illini'	late	very hardy	medium
'Kiowa'	midseason	tender	high
'Oklawaha'	early	tender	medium
'Shawnee'	late	tender	high
Trailing Thorny (bear fruit from late June to late August in the Pacific Northwest)			
'Black Butte'	midseason	tender	medium
'Kotata'	midseason	tender	high
'Marion'	midseason	tender	high
'Olallie'	midseason	tender	high
Upright Thornless (bear fruit from late May to late July in most regions)			
'Arapaho'	early	tender	high
'Navaho'	mid-late	tender	high

Table 4.2. Continued

Cultivar	Season	Hardiness	Relative Productivity
Trailing Thornless (bear fruit from late July to late August in most regions)			
'Chester'	late	tender	high
'Dirksen'	late	tender	high
'Hull'	midseason	tender	high
'Thornless Evergreen'	late	tender	high
'Triple Crown'	late	tender	high

A word on taste. How the berries taste is probably the most important question for the home gardener. With some cultivars, it seems that size and taste have an inverse relationship—if it's big, it tastes lousy. The red raspberry cultivar 'Titan' is a good example of this. 'Titan' has a large berry that tends to be watery in flavor, particularly in wet seasons, though all raspberries suffer from this tendency to varying degrees. 'Caroline' and 'Anne', two recent releases from the University of Maryland, are good sized *and* have good to great flavor, though they are not the most productive of plants. 'Sentry' and 'Amos' are my favorite raspberries for flavor among the summer fruiters, and good old 'Heritage' is hard to beat among the fall-bearing types for flavor and production, though fruit size is often small.

Black raspberries are more flavorful than the reds, and there is little variation in flavor from cultivar to cultivar. They are generally less far-removed from the native form, whereas the red raspberries are often fairly complex hybrids.

The cultivar 'Shawnee' (which has thorns from Hades) is the best flavored blackberry, but the thornless 'Arapaho' and 'Navaho' have good flavor too. Many folks find these three blackberry cultivars to be on the seedy side, however, so if this is a concern for you, beware. As mentioned earlier, the trailing thornless blackberries are generally tarter than the other types; 'Chester' and 'Triple Crown' have the best flavor among them.

Flavor is variable from person to person, but I am generally comfortable recommending those just mentioned; these are not only my opinions but an amalgam of opinions of knowledgeable and experienced berry experts. Be aware, however, that raspberry flavor varies a great deal from location to location. For example, 'Heritage' is always a favorite in southern Pennsylvania, where the soils are fairly heavy, but my colleagues on the eastern shore of Maryland say the flavor of that cultivar is lacking when grown in the lighter, sandier soils of the area. If you are unsure, plant a few plants, fruit them for a couple of years, and replant if you don't like them. Testing is part of the journey—and getting there is half the fun.

HOW TO GROW BRAMBLES: PLANTING THROUGH HARVEST

Site Selection and Preparation

Brambles require full sun and well-drained soil. They do not tolerate wet soils. I realize that I say this for all the small-fruit crops—and it is always true—but it is the most true for red raspberries. Prior to planting, the organic matter content of the soil can be increased by adding manure (at about 3 pounds per 100 square feet) or by planting cover crops or green manure crops. Control perennial weeds before planting your brambles by incorporating a competitive cover crop or by applying nonselective herbicides to the site. Do not plant brambles in soils in which *Verticillium*-susceptible crops (tomatoes, potatoes, peppers, eggplants, or strawberries) have been grown, since brambles are also susceptible to this disease.

The soil should be tested at least one year before planting. As with other small-fruit crops, lime and phosphorus should be applied the fall prior to planting. Potassium can be applied in the fall or spring, and nitrogen in the spring just prior to planting. After this initial soil adjustment, only nitrogen should be added annually, unless tissue (leaf) analysis indicates a nutrient deficiency in the plant.

Brambles benefit from irrigation, especially during fruit swell, which occurs the week prior to ripening. I have conducted irrigation experiments and found that the response of the raspberry plant is very linear—that is, the more water you give it, the taller it gets. Up to a point, this is a good thing, but raspberries can get too much of a good thing. Certainly you should never let your raspberry planting become dry at a soil depth of 6 inches (15 cm) or so, but you also do not want your plants to get so tall that they cannot support the fruit they are bearing. This is usually only a problem with the primocane-fruiting types of red raspberries. Trickle irrigation is preferable to overhead sprinkling for brambles, because wetting the fruit increases the incidence of disease. Plants generally require about 2 inches (5 cm) of water per week during the growing season and up to 4 inches (10 cm) per week during harvest.

Planting and Establishment

If you are planting dormant canes, do so in early spring, as soon as the soil can be worked. Dormant plant roots should be soaked in water thoroughly prior to planting and planted in a deep hole. If the soil lacks fertility, or is particularly heavy (full of clay) or light (sandy), incorporate some peat moss by replacing about half the soil with peat in the planting hole. First-generation tissue-cultured plants, which are preferred, can be planted as soon as the danger of frost has passed.

Plants should be spaced within rows as follows: red raspberries (all types), 24 inches (60 cm); black raspberries, 30 inches (75 cm); purple raspberries, 40 inches (100 cm); thorny and thornless upright blackberries, 40 inches (100 cm); and thornless trailing blackberries, 6½ feet (2 m) apart. Spacing between rows should be about 6 to 8 feet (1.8–2.4 m), although the row spacing depends on the size of the equipment that will be used to maintain (mow, cultivate, spray, or mechanically harvest) the planting. At least 4 feet (1.2 m) more than the widest implement should be left between rows if more than one row is planted.

Weed control in the first year is essential. Research has shown that applying a clean straw mulch 4 inches (10 cm) deep to newly planted tissue-cultured raspberries provides good weed control. For red raspberries, which send suckers up from the roots, be sure to mulch between plants within the rows, too. Establishing a permanent sod cover between the rows is recommended for brambles. *Brambles are one of the few crops for which I do not recommend mulching after the first year, unless the soils are very sandy.* Mulch on heavy or clayey soils can encourage the development of *Phytophthora* root rot, a soil-borne fungal disease that weakens and eventually kills red raspberry plants.

Plants should establish and begin to grow quickly in the first season. Red raspberries begin to fill in the spaces between plants, and black raspberries produce new canes from the crown area. The black raspberry canes tend to grow prostrate (along the ground) in the first year. Stake them up if you can. The next year they will be more upright, and eventually they will be very upright indeed. First fruit on the primocane-fruiting red raspberries will appear in the first year, but the other bramble types will not produce fruit until the following year—remember that all other brambles produce fruit only on two-year-old canes. Even so, you will not have a full crop for 3 to 4 years after planting—but be patient. With luck, you'll have enough fruit in that first or second year to give you courage to wait.

Plant Nutrition and Fertilization

If the soil was properly adjusted prior to planting to meet the nutrient requirements of your brambles, only nitrogen will need to be added after planting. Apply 0.5 pounds of actual nitrogen per 100 linear feet (0.25 kg per 30 m) of row once the soil has settled around the roots well. (See Chapter 1 for an explanation of "actual nitrogen.") In subsequent years, you can increase the nitrogen levels to as high as 1 pound of actual nitrogen per 100 linear feet (0.5 kg per 30 m) of row, applied in the late spring (April or May). Primocane-fruiting cultivars should have an additional 0.2 to 0.3 pounds of nitrogen added in late June or early July. If you have not tested your soil prior to planting, use balanced 10-10-10 fertilizer to be safe. To obtain the desired nitrogen content, use 5 pounds (2.3 kg) of 10-10-10 after the soil has settled, since 10-10-10 is only 10 percent nitrogen.

Pruning Brambles

Fruiting canes of all cultivated brambles, except for fall-bearing raspberries, die after fruiting is completed. These dead floricanes should be removed immediately after fruiting to improve air circulation through the canopy.

Pruning red raspberries. Summer-bearing red raspberries will grow naturally in a hedgerow system, as illustrated in Figure 4.3. The new shoots, originating from the root system, will fill in the entire length of the row. No summer pruning (except for removing spent floricanes) is necessary, although suckers growing outside the desired area may be removed at any time. In fact, if your raspberries are growing in a good location, they'll probably attempt a mutiny and try to take over your yard and the rest of the universe. Mowing the canes back when they are small is usually sufficient to keep them in check.

Dormant pruning for red raspberries can be accomplished any time the canes are fully dormant (November through March in the northern United States). All dead, damaged, or weak canes should be removed, and the beds narrowed to 12 to 18 inches (30–45 cm). This is a very important step. If the beds get too wide, sunlight (which fuels fruit bud development) cannot penetrate well, and the canopy gets so dense that it does not dry quickly, which leads to the development of fungal diseases. Further, the rows become difficult to work in, and fruit within the canopy is often not seen, left to rot, and disseminates disease-causing spores—a bad thing. After narrowing the rows, thin the canes so that there is about one cane every 4 to 6 inches (10–15 cm) within the row. Try to leave the healthiest canes with the largest cane diameter. Once thinned, the remaining canes should be tipped to 4 to 5 feet (1.2–1.5 m) in height, removing about the top one-fourth of each cane (Figure 4.3). The canes you leave standing should look sturdy. Imagine hanging a crop of fruit on them: Will they stay upright, or topple over?

Primocane-fruiting red raspberries, as the name suggests, bear fruit on canes produced in the first season. In late summer, the canes terminate growth and develop flower buds. Flowering and fruit development begins at the tip of the cane and continues succes-

Figure 4.3. Pruning summer-bearing red raspberries in a hedgerow: a) before pruning, b) after pruning. The diagonal lines indicate where the tops of the canes are cut (tipped) after thinning.

sively down the cane toward the base. When the weather becomes cold enough, flowering and fruiting ceases. To dormant prune primocane-fruiting raspberries, most commercial producers simply remove all the canes at the base, and begin the cycle again the next spring. These large-scale growers cut the canes using a large, tractor-mounted mower, but you can emulate this by cutting all the canes at ground level, leaving about a 1 inch (2.5 cm) stub. Alternatively, canes that fruited in the fall can be left in place and allowed to fruit the following summer. Unpruned canes on this type of raspberry begin flowering at the node below the last fruit of the previous year, and they will bear fruit in early to midsummer. As a home gardener, you can opt to leave the canes over the winter and get a few fruit from them the following season—remember that primocane-fruiting raspberries offer about 10 percent of their total yield in the summer. Or you can mow the canes off and just gather the fall crop. Many small-scale producers plant both primocane fruiters and summer bearers and then mow the primocane fruiters, getting summer fruit from their summer bearers. The choice is yours.

Pruning black and purple raspberries. In addition to removal of spent floricanes, black and purple raspberries require summer tipping (Figure 4.4). They should have their tips removed ("tipped") at 40 to 48 inches (1–1.2 m) if they are not grown on a trellis. Tipping encourages the development of lateral fruiting branches and increases the strength of the cane. This pruning should be done fairly early in the season, at which point only 3 to 6 inches (7.5–15 cm) of new growth needs to be removed. Tipping the plants later than this—when removal of more than 6 inches (15 cm) of new growth is required to bring the height back to 4 feet (1.2 m)—can increase the incidence of cane blight, since the wound resulting from removing larger diameter wood takes longer to heal.

All dead, damaged, and weak canes should be removed from dormant black raspberry plants. Thin the remaining canes to five to ten per plant. Lateral branches should be headed back to 4 to 6 inches (10–15 cm) for black raspberries, or 6 to 10 inches (15–25 cm) for the purple ones. More vigorous plants can support longer lateral branches. If a trellis system is used, even a nominal one such as the passive support trellis shown in Figure 4.5c, canes can be tipped higher (up to 5 feet or 1.5 m) as long as they are supported by the trellis.

Pruning blackberries. Erect blackberries have strong upright canes. They should be pruned similarly to black and purple raspberries:

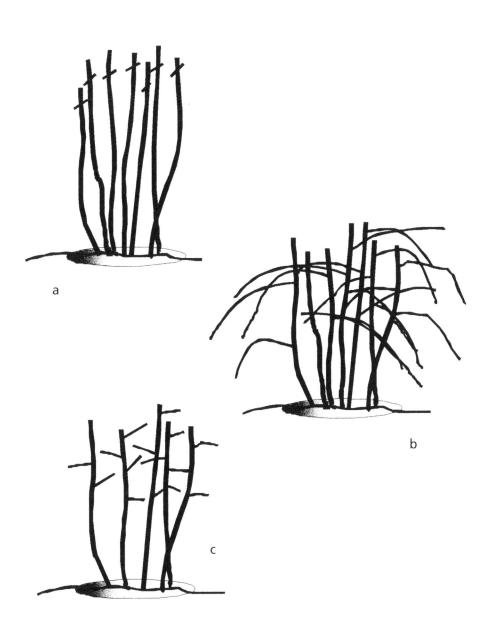

Figure 4.4. Pruning black and purple raspberries: a) summer pruning, with diagonal lines indicating where the new canes are cut (tipped); b) after tipping the canes will grow and develop lateral branches by the end of summer; c) after dormant pruning, with the canes thinned and headed back.

tipped back to 40 to 48 inches (1–1.2 m) in the summer, with laterals cut back to 12 to 18 inches (30–45 cm). Because they produce new shoots from the root system, erect blackberries are grown in hedgerows, like red raspberries, and should be thinned to about 10 inches (25 cm) apart during dormant pruning.

Trailing blackberries are not erect in habit and thus require trellising. A simple trellis with wires at heights of 3 and 6 feet (about 1 and 2 m) is the most common approach (see Figure 4.5d), although the plants also can be trained to fences or other structures up to 8 feet (2.4 m) in height. Plant height will depend on soil fertility and water availability. They should be tipped to about 6 inches (15 cm) above the highest trellis wire and tied to it during the summer months. For dormant pruning, retain about five to eight of the strongest canes and remove laterals that originate on the lower 36 inches (90 cm) of the main canes. The remaining laterals should be shortened to 12 to 18 inches (30–45 cm).

Trellis Systems for Raspberries

The need for standard trellises (as shown in Figure 4.5d) is well established for trailing blackberries and tayberries, but they are not absolutely necessary for most raspberries. If the grower tips the plants low enough during dormant pruning, the plants *will* stand on their own. However, the value of providing support for raspberry plants has long been recognized. In 1919 Andrew Fuller, author of the great work *Small Fruit Culturist*, commented that "it is questionable whether anything is saved by not staking raspberries. . . . The cost is but a trifle in comparison to the value of the fruit lost when [staking is] not used, especially when it commands so large a price as it does in our Eastern markets." Trellis systems generally do not affect the type of pruning a plant receives—black raspberries still need to be tipped in summer, whereas red raspberries do not. Rather, the trellis allows the plant to support more surface area for fruit production.

The 2-meter "I" trellis system (Figure 4.5d) is routinely used in the large processing-production areas of the Pacific Northwest. The trellis allows for increased productivity by supporting a larger plant

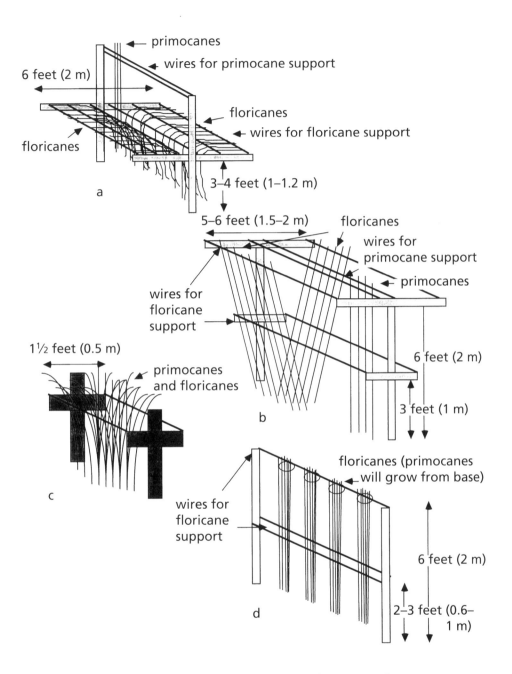

Figure 4.5. Trellis systems for bramble plants: a) horizontal or "T" system; b) "V" system; c) hedgerows (passive support); d) "I" system

canopy and aids in mechanical harvesting. In these systems, canes are bundled or woven onto the trellis and secured. Several other trellis systems useful for bramble production are shown in Figure 4.5.

Harvest and Postharvest

Brambles, like all small-fruit crops, should be harvested in the morning, after the dew has dried. Morning harvesting minimizes the amount of heat that builds up while the berries are in the field and will result in longer shelf-life. Ripe berries detach easily and should be stacked no more than three or four high in shallow containers; stacking them higher than this will crush the berries on the bottom. When in the thick of the harvest season, I often put "extra" berries directly into a container in the freezer as I go, for quick and easy accruing of berries for my coveted jam.

Raspberries are notorious for their short shelf-life. This is due, in part, to the morphology of the fruit, which is composed of many loosely attached drupelets. It is also a result of the fruit's high rate of respiration (an indication of metabolic activity) after harvest, which is the highest of any temperate-zone fruit. Raspberry fruit is also very susceptible to postharvest infections of gray mold, caused by the fungus *Botrytis cinerea*.

To maximize shelf-life, you can employ a preharvest fungal control (using local fungicide recommendations), particularly in wet seasons. Harvesting berries during the coolest part of the morning is also beneficial. Harvested berries should be kept out of direct sunlight and refrigerated or frozen as soon as possible. Blackberries can be handled similarly, although their shelf-life is several days longer than that of raspberries.

NICHES IN THE LANDSCAPE

As the saying goes, "Good fences make good neighbors." If this is true, then raspberry and blackberry hedges surely make for good relationships with those living in close proximity to you. Thornless blackberries can be trained to any structure, including a fence, that does not exceed 8 feet (2.4 m) in height, though 6 feet (1.8 m) is probably a more typical height. The blackberry canes must be tied to the structure, however, since they do not have tendrils (as grapes do) to hold them on. Fortunately, this is not a big task. Relatively few canes are produced per plant, and a little careful training of the canes as they grow takes a small amount of time, though a great amount of *timing*. Be sure to train the canes while they are still green. They have a tendency to break off at the base if bent too far, so tie them vertically first, and then train the tips of the shoots horizontally, if desired.

Red raspberry plants make a wonderful hedge as well, although as discussed in Chapter 2, their suckering nature has the potential to cause tension with your neighbors. The summer-bearing types will have a constant presence once established, whereas the fall-bearers can either be kept year-round (fruiting in both fall and summer) or mowed so that the hedge "disappears" during the dormant season, only to grow up again in the summer. I have fall-bearing red raspberries planted along the foundation of my house, under a window, where they face a warm southern exposure. They thrive here—the soil is well drained—and I often wander out on late-August mornings to pick a few for my cereal. This is wealth.

The thorny blackberries make for a great hedge if you are looking for intimidation. Even my overly enthusiastic Border-collie mix does not venture near these rascals. Bear in mind that if you use thorny blackberry plants to separate your property, you may need to work with your neighbors. They can chose to mow the suckers that come up on their property from the root system—this is probably the easiest control—and the offer of the berries from their side of the hedge should more than make up for the inconvenience.

Fall-bearing red raspberries fit well in ornamental plantings with spring-flowering plants that tend to die off or look ratty as the summer progresses. I am thinking of plants like bleeding heart *(Dicentra)* or peony *(Paeonia)*—two of my favorite old-fashioned friends. These perennials will just be flowering and finishing up as the raspberries are getting to be 1 to 2 feet (30–60 cm) tall. Be sure to isolate the root systems, using a plastic underground barrier. Otherwise the raspberry plants will overtake the ornamentals, though peonies are worthy opponents.

PESTS IN THE PLANTING

Raspberries and blackberries, if planted in a good site, are relatively devoid of pest problems, with a few notable exceptions that I will discuss here. Weeds need to be controlled vigilantly until the plants are established, but once established, brambles are excellent competitors, and few weeds will succeed in their presence. If grasses are a severe problem in early establishment, refer to the recommendations for strawberries in Chapter 3.

The major disease and insect pests that plague brambles are outlined in Tables 4.3 and 4.4. For recommended chemical and cultural controls, contact your local extension office or consultants. Also be sure to read Chapter 1 of this book for extensive recommendations on controlling pests using cultural management.

Diseases

Viral diseases. Just as viruses cannot be controlled but only outlived by humans, they also cannot be controlled in plants. Unfortunately, in plants, viruses are rarely outlived either. For whatever evolutionary reason, once a plant is infected with one of the vigor-debilitating viruses, it will not recover (it lacks our immune system) and must be removed so as not to infect its neighbors. The bottom line is that, at all costs, we want to avoid viruses. There are three primary ways to do this.

1. Purchase your plants from a reputable nursery that advertises its plants as "virus tested." Despite the convenience, digging up plants from your neighbor's garden has many risks, which are discussed in Chapter 1. You need to balance the risks with the convenience.
2. If wild bramble plants are growing in the immediate vicinity (within 500 feet or 150 m of your planting), remove them. They are reservoirs not only for viruses but also for a systemic fungal disease called orange rust.
3. Control the vectors (carriers) of the viruses. The primary vectors for raspberry viruses are aphids and microscopic soil worms

Table 4.3. Common Bramble Diseases and Causal Organisms in the United States

Name of Disease	Plant Parts Affected	Causal Organism
crown gall, cane gall	cane, crown	*Agrobacterium tumafaciens* (bacterium)
anthracnose	cane, leaves, fruit	*Elsinoe venetum* (fungus)
cane blight	cane	*Leptosphaeria coniothyruim* (fungus)
gray mold	fruit, cane	*Botrytis cinerea* (fungus)
late leaf rust	leaves, fruit	*Pucciniastrum americanum* (fungus)
orange rust	leaves, systemic	*Gymnoconia peckiana* or *Kunkelia nitens* (fungi)
Phytophthora root rot	root	*Phytophthora* (fungus)
powdery mildew	leaves	*Sphaerotheca humuli* (fungus)
spur blight	cane	*Didymella applanata* (fungus)
Verticillium wilt	systemic	*Verticillium albo-atrum* (fungus)
mosaic	systemic	aphid-vectored complex of viruses
leaf curl	systemic	aphid-vectored virus
crumbly berry	systemic	nematode-vectored tomato ringspot virus
black raspberry streak	systemic	unknown vector and virus
blackberry sterility	systemic	unknown vector and virus

called nematodes. You can have your soil tested for nematodes, but unless the soil is very sandy or your area has a history of nematodes, it probably is not necessary to do so. If native bramble populations are in the area *and* aphids are feeding on your raspberry plants, spray the planting with an anti-aphid insecticide. Malathion works well, but you should also check out other locally recommended controls. Remember that brambles are closely related to roses and tend to attract the same complex of pests.

How do you know if you have a virus? Diagnosis is not easy. Often plants will simply be stunted and not grow well. A virus found in red raspberries makes the fruit "crumbly," causing the drupelets to fall apart when you pick them. Mosaic virus, a problem in black raspberries, can cause a mosaic-like pattern to develop on the lower leaves in the spring, but it is an easy symptom to miss. You can send samples to a virus-testing laboratory to confirm whether the leaves are infected. However, viruses are not often a problem when the preceding precautions are followed and the site is sunny and well drained.

Gray mold. The gray mold (caused by the fungus *Botrytis cinerea*) that affects brambles is the same gray mold that can afflict strawberry plants. Unfortunately, much less is known about its infection process in brambles, so we tend to assume that it is similar to that in strawberries. There is an important practical difference, though. Gray mold almost never develops on fruit that is still attached to the plant, unless the fruit is over-ripe. If you keep your fruit well harvested, refrigerate or freeze it as soon as you pick it, and consume it promptly, you can pretty much avoid gray mold on bramble fruit. Gray mold can form on fruit in the refrigerator, however, particularly if you did not spray for the fungus when the berries were on the plant. It develops in the refrigerator much more rapidly than it does with strawberries, so be aware of the possibility—and eat the berries quickly.

In exceptionally wet years, gray mold can develop on fruit on the bush. In my second year in Pennsylvania, we had a terrifically wet spring and early summer. It was so wet that I actually saw slugs feeding on raspberries that were 4 feet (1.2 m) off the ground. I also saw gray mold develop on raspberry fruit that was just ripening on the plant. In all honesty, it is not clear that any amount of spraying would help in that situation anyway, since the spray is washed off as soon as it is applied.

Anthracnose. The anthracnose-causing fungus *Elsinoe venetum* is occasionally a problem on brambles. Anthracnose results in lesions on canes, particularly of black raspberries, but it can also cause individual drupelets to look "scabby" in wet years. A dormant liquid lime-sulfur spray—which stinks, is caustic, and is a pain to use, but sometimes necessary—can be applied just as the plants are starting to grow, when leaves are ¼ to ½ inch (0.5–1.25 cm) expanded. For those folks who are opposed to using synthetic pesticides, lime sulfur occurs naturally and is approved for use for organic growers. If the plants are planted in a good site and pruned properly, however, spraying will rarely be necessary. Sprays of Captan and Benlate (benomyl) can be applied if anthracnose becomes a problem on the berries during harvest.

Phytophthora root rot. A fungal disease that you may encounter, especially on marginal, poorly drained sites and in particularly wet years, is the root rot caused by *Phytophthora rubi*. Generally only a problem on red raspberries, *Phytophthora* root rot is characterized by short, spindly canes. In summer-fruiting types it can also result in high plant mortality after the winter. If the site is marginally wet, planting on raised beds will help enormously to reduce the incidence of this disease. Plant the brambles on top of 12- to 18-inch (30–45 cm) tall mounds or berms. Be aware that these beds may require more maintenance. Specifically, when you pull weeds, you need to make sure that you do not pull any more soil off the berm than is necessary. You also may need to go back and routinely mound up more soil if the raspberry roots become exposed.

Two fungicides—Ridomil (metalaxyl), a soil drench, and Alliette (fosetyl-A), a foliar material—are labeled and somewhat effective for controlling *Phytophthora* root rot. Both require a pesticide license, however, and there is some evidence of pathogen resistance to the materials. They are not nearly as effective as the cultural controls, so I do not recommend these pesticides for backyard growers.

Insects

Japanese beetles. You can expect to see Japanese beetles annually on your brambles. If numbers are low, as they tend to be in cooler years, I usually ignore them or simply knock them off my plants as I pass by. In most years, however, the pest starts doing enough damage to the

Table 4.4. Major Bramble Insect and Mite Pests in the United States

Common Name of Pest	Scientific Name of Pest	Actions
aphids	*Amphorophora agathonica, Aphis rubicola*	attacks fruit and leaves
blackberry leafminer	*Metallus rubi*	attacks fruit and leaves
eastern raspberry fruitworm	*Byturus rubi*	attacks fruit and leaves
Japanese beetle	*Popillia japonica*	attacks fruit and leaves
raspberry sawfly	*Monophadnoides geniculatus*	attacks fruit and leaves
rose chafer	*Macrodactylus subspinosus*	attacks fruit and leaves
sap beetle	*Glischrochilus quadrisignatus, G. fasciatus*	attacks fruit and leaves
strawberry bud weevil	*Anthonomus signatus*	attacks fruit and leaves
tarnished plant bug	*Lygus lineolaris*	attacks fruit and leaves
two-spotted spider mite	*Tetranychus urticae*	attacks fruit and leaves
yellow jackets	family Vespidae	attacks fruit and leaves
flat-headed cane borers	*Agrilus ruficollis, A. rubicola*	attacks canes, crown, and roots
raspberry cane borer	*Oberea bimaculata*	attacks canes, crown, and roots
raspberry cane maggot	*Pegomya rubivora*	attacks canes, crown, and roots
raspberry crown borer	*Pennisetia marginata*	attacks canes, crown, and roots
root weevils	*Otiorhynchus*	attacks canes, crown, and roots
tree crickets	*Oecanthus*	attacks canes, crown, and roots

leaves that I get nervous. (Remember that leaves are providing fuel for the entire plant system.) In fact, I have seen the numbers get so high that these beetles were actually procreating on my raspberry fruit. This is a pretty bad situation. Both malathion and Sevin (carbaryl) work well on Japanese beetles, so I use these pesticides as needed. After spraying, you need to wait at least one day before harvesting the fruit, and even then, a slight pesticide odor can be detected. It is best to get the pests under control well prior to harvest, if possible. And of course, rinse the fruit very thoroughly before consuming. Neither of these materials is absorbed by the fruit, so you only need to clean the surface well. Fortunately, Japanese beetles usually create the biggest problem after summer-bearing fruit is harvested and well before fall-bearing types begin fruiting.

Chemicals do work well in controlling Japanese beetles, but several non-pesticide alternatives are available. One option is to simply knock the beetles off the plant and into a bucket of soapy water. The soap coats them, and they eventually die. This should be done in the cooler part of the day, if possible, since the beetles will be less likely to fly off before you get them. Pheromone traps are another much-advertised means of controlling Japanese beetles. These traps are plastic bags that contain the mating scent of the beetle. In a good Japanese beetle year (which is, by definition, a tough raspberry year), these bags will quickly fill with beetles, requiring emptying at least once a day. The problem is that these bags are probably bringing in all the neighborhood beetles, and you may not be making much of a dent in the overall population. The bottom line: You may still have injury from these little beasts, particularly in abundant years. Another older remedy is the use of milky spore, which is a bacteria that infects the Japanese beetle grubs when they are still in the ground. It is usually sold as a powder that you can spread on any turf area, where the grubs overwinter, during the dormant season (fall through spring). A couple of caveats, however. Milky spore only works in warmer climates, specifically USDA hardiness zones 6–10. Another shortcoming is that all the turf in the vicinity needs to be treated in order for the control to be effective. In other words, there's no point in treating your own yard when the guy behind you doesn't treat his, because the

Japanese beetles can easily get to your yard from your neighbor's. When I was a child, our entire suburban neighborhood decided to treat all the lawns with milky spore. As I recall, we had a great abundance of Japanese beetles for a number of years, inspiring the grown-ups to bond together and deal with the problem. It seemed to work, but the presence of these critters does seems to ebb and flow over the years by some unknown natural force.

Sap beetles and tarnished plant bug. These two pests can plague raspberries and blackberries as they can strawberries, but they usually are not as big a problem on brambles. Refer to Chapter 3 for more information.

Birds

I almost chose not to include birds in this chapter because in my experience birds rarely bother raspberries. This is amazing to me, because I think that raspberries are so delicious and I cannot understand why birds don't love them as much as I do. Birds are a big problem in early grapes, a big problem in blueberries, an occasional small problem in strawberries, but almost never a problem in raspberries. The one time that birds were a problem for my raspberries was in an extremely dry year—the driest on record in many eastern and midwestern locales.

FREQUENTLY ASKED QUESTIONS

What raspberry produces the biggest fruit? Some may think that size doesn't matter, but when it comes to filling a container with pea-sized raspberries, this becomes a contentious issue. 'Titan' is by far the largest summer-fruiting red raspberry, and 'Ruby' is the largest fall fruiter. Among black raspberries, 'Jewel' and 'Allen' offer superior size.

What's the best flavored raspberry? The two biggest ones, 'Titan' and 'Ruby', have a bland (the nursery catalogs will call it "mild") flavor. I personally like a red raspberry that grabs me by the lapels and throws me up against the wall, or at least gets my attention. 'Heritage' tastes great when grown in loam or clay loam; its flavor seems to dwindle in sandier soils. 'Sentry' and 'Amos' are also nicely flavored. The recent introductions 'Anne' and 'Caroline' (a yellow and fall-bearing red raspberry, respectively) both have good to excellent flavor. I especially like 'Anne' because it has banana and strawberry overtones.

Flavor is less variable in black raspberries than it is in red raspberries, and they have more flavor as a general rule. So go for size with black raspberries. They all taste great, though they also tend to be seedier than the reds.

Why are my bramble canes dying after they fruit? This is usually the new grower's first question. The normal bramble life cycle is to produce a vegetative cane, called a primocane, in the first year. That cane overwinters, and then it is referred to as a floricane. After the winter, the floricane leafs out, flowers, fruits, and dies. At the same time that the floricane is going through flowering, fruiting, and dying, the plant's root system is putting out new primocanes that will provide the fruit for next year. Only the root system of brambles is perennial—the shoots are biennial. The one exception to this life cycle is the ever-bearing or primocane-fruiting red raspberry, which produces canes, flowers, and fruit in a single season and does not die after first fruiting.

Why does my red raspberry fruit crumble when I pick it? Crumbly fruit can be caused by a number of things. It often occurs in situations where the weather was not ideal for pollination. If you had rainy or overcast weather during bloom, your plants may not have been adequately pollinated, and this will cause the fruit to fall apart. Sometimes cool conditions can cause crumbly fruit, because the division between the receptacle and the fruit does not form completely. This problem is called plugging, and it just means that the fruit will not let go of the receptacle tissue.

The most serious cause of crumbly fruit in red raspberries is a viral disease that is transmitted by soil-borne microscopic worms called nematodes. If you observe this condition over several consecutive years, the virus is probably the culprit. Unfortunately, there is no cure. Raspberries should be pulled out and not replanted until the nematodes are eradicated.

Why do some of the little sections of my raspberry fruit look scabby or bleached? Raspberries that are exposed to bright, direct sunlight often become bleached looking. This is called sunscald and is only a cosmetic problem. The fruit is still perfectly edible, though it tends to rot more quickly, so consume it or freeze it before that happens.

Fruit that has a scablike spot on it most likely has been infected by the fungal disease anthracnose. It is usually only present if the plants have not been pruned properly, if they are planted in a bad site, or if it is a particularly wet season. This disease can be controlled with commercially available fungicides, but this should be your last solution, with site selection and good management your first.

How can I keep my raspberries from taking over the universe, or even my yard? During dormant pruning, make sure to narrow your raspberry or blackberry rows to 12 to 18 inches (30–45 cm). Then, during the growing season, be vigilant about thinning the plantings. When new canes sprout along the sides of rows, or in the middle of adjacent lawn, mow them down with vigor and purpose. Continue to do this throughout the season, and you should be able to achieve some modest level of control. Any canes that slip by can be taken out during the next dormant pruning.

RECOMMENDED BRAMBLE CULTIVARS BY REGION

The following lists suggest the cultivars most suitable for various regions of the United States; more descriptive information is given earlier in the chapter.

MID-ATLANTIC AND
MIDWEST

Summer-Bearing Red Raspberries
'Amos'
'Canby'
'Hilton'
'Latham'
'Reveille'
'Sentry'
'Taylor'
'Titan'

Fall-Bearing Red Raspberries
'Autumn Bliss'
'Caroline'
'Dinkum'
'Heritage'

Black Raspberries
'Allen'
'Bristol'
'Cumberland'
'Haut'
'Jewel'

Purple Raspberries
'Brandywine'
'Royalty'

Yellow Raspberry
'Anne'

Thorny Upright Blackberries
'Choctaw'
'Darrow'
'Shawnee'

Thornless Upright Blackberries
'Arapaho'
'Navaho'

Thornless Trailing Blackberries
'Chester'
'Dirksen'
'Hull'

NEW ENGLAND

Summer-Bearing Red Raspberries
'Boyne'
'Killarney'
'Latham'
'Newburgh'
'Nova'
'Taylor'

Fall-Bearing Red Raspberries
'August Red'
'Autumn Bliss'
'Fall Red'
'Heritage'

Black Raspberry
'Jewel'

Thorny Upright Blackberries
'Darrow'
'Illini'

SOUTH CENTRAL

Fall-Bearing Red Raspberries
'Dormanred'
'Heritage'

Thorny Upright Blackberries
'Kiowa'
'Shawnee'

Thornless Upright Blackberries
'Arapaho'
'Navaho'

SOUTHEAST

Fall-Bearing Red Raspberry
'Dormanred'

Black Raspberry
'Mysore'

Thorny Upright Blackberry
'Brazos'
'Oklawaha'

PACIFIC NORTHWEST

Summer-Bearing Red Raspberries
'Chilliwack'
'Meeker'
'Newburgh'
'Tulameen'
'Willamette'

Fall-Bearing Red Raspberries
'Amity'
'Heritage'
'Summit'

Black Raspberries
'Bristol'
'Cumberland'
'Munger'

Yellow Raspberry
'Goldie'

Thorny Upright Blackberries
'Cherokee'
'Shawnee'

Thorny Trailing Blackberries
'Black Butte'
'Kotata'
'Marion'
'Olallie'

Thornless Upright Blackberry
'Navaho'

Thornless Trailing Blackberry
'Chester'
'Hull'
'Thornless Evergreen'
'Triple Crown'

CHAPTER 5

Blueberries

FAMILY: ERICACEAE, THE CALCIFUGES

PRIMARY SPECIES:

Vaccinium angustifolium Ait.—lowbush blueberry
Vaccinium ashei Reade—rabbiteye blueberry
Vaccinium corymbosum L.—highbush blueberry

Blueberries: one of the very few edible (delicious!) blue foods. Eat them out of hand, in pie, in jam—how can you go wrong? Without a bit of pucker in their flavor, these gentle North American natives are truly wonders of the New World, and a homegrown success story. Blueberries have been grown in cultivation only since the middle of the twentieth century, so their growth and flavor are much like that of their wild ancestors. In fact, the lowbush blueberry *(Vaccinium angustifolium)* industry in Maine and the maritime provinces of Canada consists of managed populations of wild plants, truly a glowing example of sustainable agriculture.

Blueberries are a relatively recent passion for me. When I worked in New Jersey (the second largest area for blueberry production in the United States), blueberries were not in my job description. They were such an important crop that they required a full-time person all to themselves. Once transplanted to Pennsylvania some 12 years ago, I began working on blueberries with a passion and have loved them ever since. I am particularly fascinated by their ability to survive, even thrive, in conditions where other plants can't.

Most of the information that follows pertains to the northern highbush blueberry *(Vaccinium corymbosum)*, although I will digress a bit to talk about the other types. The culture of southern highbush and rabbiteye blueberries is similar to that of the highbush blueberry.

HISTORICAL BACKGROUND AND
OTHER INTERESTING FACTS

Several species of blueberry are indigenous to the United States. These include the lowbush blueberry *(Vaccinium angustifolium)*, of commercial importance in Maine and eastern Canada, and the rabbiteye blueberry *(V. ashei)*, which is commonly cultivated in the southern United States. The most economically important of the species is the highbush blueberry *(V. corymbosum)*, which is widely grown in the Mid-Atlantic, Midwest, and Pacific Northwest of the United States as well as the Pacific Northwest of Canada. Substantial industries are also developing in New Zealand, Australia, Germany, and most recently, Chile.

The highbush blueberry plant is indigenous to North America, and native peoples long used it both as a fresh product and dried. Interest in growing the crop on a commercial scale first emerged in the mid-1800s, but the blueberry's value as a fruit crop was not exploited until the 1920s, perhaps because the European settlers were not familiar with the plant and therefore did not seek it out, or perhaps it was so easy to harvest in the wild that it was unnecessary to cultivate it. Selection and breeding research was initiated shortly after the turn of the century by Elizabeth White, a cranberry producer in Whitesbog, New Jersey, and Frederick Coville, a plant breeder working for the United States Department of Agriculture. White used "monetary incentives" to obtain the largest fruited blueberry plants flourishing in the Pine Barrens of New Jersey. The story goes that she asked natives of the barrens to bring her large fruit, and if the fruit failed to pass through her wedding band, she acquired the bush from which the berries came. White then transplanted these bushes to a site for observation. Coville, at the USDA in

Beltsville, Maryland, became interested in the crop and, in 1906, began the first blueberry breeding program with the material that White had selected from the wild. One of those original wild selections, 'Rubel', continues to be cultivated commercially, albeit on limited acreage.

Following on the heels of this early work in the Mid-Atlantic region, the development of the blueberry industry in Michigan began in the 1930s, largely through the testing, research, and advocacy of professor Stanley Johnston at the Michigan Agricultural College (now Michigan State University). At the time, the land along Lake Michigan was considered useless and thus was inordinately cheap. Blueberry plants were extremely well adapted to these soils and thrived under the conditions along the lake, and thus a blueberry industry developed along the lake's eastern shore. The problem that was both anticipated and realized was that the farms were so remote that moving the berries to market was a considerable hardship. In response, the Michigan Blueberry Growers Cooperative was started as a marketing organization, and it exists today as an international firm known as MBG Marketing. Today Michigan is the leading area for blueberry production in the world.

The third significant blueberry-producing region in the United States got its start in the 1930s and '40s as well. Though their soils were not typical for native blueberries, producers in the Pacific Northwest found that amending the soils was worth the large investment since production was so high in the area. Of all the regions in the United States, the Pacific Northwest is experiencing the greatest growth in highbush blueberry production today. Unlike the bramble and strawberry fruits grown in the Pacific Northwest, most blueberries are produced for selling fresh at market rather than for processing.

Lowbush blueberries are grown primarily in the northeastern corner of North America. The industry is founded on naturally occurring populations of wild *Vaccinium angustifolium*. Producers manage these populations by controlling weeds and applying fertilizers, and the fruit, removed by hand-held rakes, is used primarily in processing. Breeding efforts have done little to improve the existing populations, which are genetically diverse. The rabbiteye blueberry *(V. ashei)*, produced in the southeastern United States, is a larger, more heat-tolerant species that exhibits broader soil adaptation than the highbush species. It is relatively susceptible to cold injury, however, and the fruit quality is, in most people's opinions, not as good as that of the highbush blueberry. In the wild, this species produces an enormous bush, often reaching 20 feet (6 m) in height. The rabbiteye was one of the first blueberry species to be examined and developed as a commercial crop. In the late 1800s M. A. Sapp of Florida transplanted and observed several rabbiteye seedlings. His experiment was enormously successful and resulted in the beginning of a small industry based on transplanting wild selections to cultivated settings. However, this rabbiteye industry was unable to compete with the northern highbush industry that developed rapidly in the 1930s, and it languished until a breeding effort was initiated by several horticultural researchers the following decade. Those programs continue today.

The southern highbush—which emerged from complex hybrids involving *Vaccinium corymbosum, V. darrowii, V. ashei,* and *V. tenellum*—was developed for warmer regions where fruit production is limited by the shortage of chilling hours typically required in blueberry cultivation. Breeding efforts toward a low-chilling highbush blueberry began in 1948 with R. H. Sharpe in Florida. Sharpe saw an opportunity in marrying the fruit quality of the northern highbush *(V. corymbosum)* with the soil adaptation and low chilling requirement of *V. darrowii.* 'Sharpblue', 'Flordablue', and 'Avonblue' were the first cultivars released from that program, in 1976 and 1977—which highlights the long-term nature of such breeding programs. As with rabbiteye blueberries, the fruit quality of the southern highbush is generally not as good as that of the highbush, but breeding efforts are ongoing in both rabbiteye and southern highbush, and we can expect to see improved fruit quality as time goes on.

The fact that blueberries are native to North America is significant to backyard growers in the United States and Canada. For one thing, because the plant evolved here, it co-evolved with numerous pests. Bad news, right? No, good news, because the plants also evolved mechanisms for pest resistance. When planted on a suitable site, blueberry bushes are often pest free.

The blueberry is a somewhat troublesome and anomalous plant, quite different from most of our other berry plants in that it requires soil in which most plants would not thrive or even grow—in other words, it thrives in lousy soil. Well, "lousy" may be too judgmental, but by the horticultural standards of pH and available nutrients, it is true. Blueberry plants grow in soils that are acidic (pH 4.5–5.0), uniformly moist (not wet), and nutrient-poor. The soils are often high in organic matter, and although organic matter is usually associated with high nutrition, this is true only in a long-term sense. Organic matter is important because it provides a slow-release reservoir of nutrients, but when a plant is trying to bust out and grow and reproduce, the nitrogen in the organic matter is not readily available to the plant, and the plant can go hungry, in spite of that storehouse of reserves in the soil. So, plants that grow in these soils need to develop a strategy for getting more nutrients than are readily available. Pitcher plants *(Sarracenia)*, which often grow in acidic, nutrient-poor soils alongside wild blueberries, adopted a strategy of insectivory; that is, they capture insects and absorb nutrients (primarily nitrogen) from the decaying bodies in addition to what they get from the soil via their root systems.

Blueberries also developed an elegant strategy for acquiring nutrients from tough soils, and that is what initially sparked my research interest in them. (My palate was sparked considerably earlier.) Blueberry plants have a fungus living in their root systems that helps them acquire nutrients. The fungus and the blueberry plant have a symbiotic relationship, meaning that the two organisms cooperate with and benefit from each other—the fungus provides nutrients for the plant, and the plant provides the fungus with food (carbohydrates from photosynthesis). The cooperation, the root and the fungus together, is called mycorrhiza (*myco* is Latin for "fungus" and *rhiza* means "root"; the plural is mycorrhizae). There has been some question as to the importance of mycorrhizae in commercial plants, but recent surveys have found that commercially produced blueberries in the eastern and midwestern United States, as well as some in Chile, are heavily infected with mycorrhizal fungi.

DIGRESSION

Mycorrhizae

Most terrestrial plant species have some sort of mycorrhizal relationship, the most common being vesicular arbuscular mycorrhizae (VAM), which is found in strawberry and raspberry plants, among others. This relationship allows the infected plants (which are "hosts" or "co-symbionts" with the fungi) to take up more phosphorus and several other nutrients. The VAM relationship is also usually an obligate one, meaning that the plant cannot live without the fungus, and the fungus cannot complete its life cycle without the plant. The blueberry mycorrhizae (ericoid mycorrhizae) are unique because they are formed with fungi from a different fungal class, called Ascomycetes (Plate 22). These fungi can exist either as symbionts with the plants or as free-living organisms in the soil. While vesicular arbuscular mycorrhizae are primarily responsible for the uptake of phosphorus (a relatively immobile nutrient), the ericoid mycorrhizae are most important for their role in acquiring nitrogen from tightly bound sources, such as the proteins in organic matter. The fungus exudes a protein-cleaving substance called protease that breaks down the organic matter and makes the nitrogen available to the plant. What does the fungus get out of it? Sugars, the economic unit of life. The plant produces sugars through the process of photosynthesis and then passes some of the wealth on to the fungal symbiont. "I'll give you nutrients, you give me sugars" is sort of a biological variation on "I'll scratch your back, you scratch mine."

BIOLOGY OF THE PLANT: KNOWING IT AND USING IT TO YOUR ADVANTAGE

The highbush blueberry *(Vaccinium corymbosum)* is a perennial dicotyledon with a relatively shallow root system and woody canes that originate from the crown of the plant (Figure 5.1). The root system is fibrous but is devoid of root hairs. In most plants root hairs serve to increase surface area for the uptake of water and nutrients, so the lack of root hairs makes the blueberry plant more sensitive to fluctuating soil-water conditions. The distribution of the root system in the soil is dependent on plant age and soil conditions, and it can vary widely. Plants grown in heavier, clay soils have a more compact root system, whereas those growing in sandier soils have root systems that are widely distributed. In mature highbush blueberries, the root system is usually found primarily within the drip line of the plant, though some roots may extend as far as 6 feet (1.8 m) beyond the crown of the plant. Root depth can extend as much as 30 inches (75 cm) into the soil, though most roots are in the top 18 inches (45 cm) of soil.

A mature cultivated highbush blueberry commonly has 15 to 18 shoots, or canes. Growth habit varies among cultivars, with some forming very upright bushes and others more spreading in habit. Fruit is borne on buds formed during the previous growing season. With close observation, you will notice that the flower buds are plumper than the leaf buds and develop on the tips of the branches, as opposed to laying flat against the stem, as is the case with the leaf buds. The leaves generally start to grow in the spring a week or two before the flowers develop. Blueberry plants grow in flushes. The number of flushes in a season is somewhat dependent on the cultivar, but in most cultivars and in most areas, two distinct flushes are evident: one in June and one in August. After the August flush, the next season's flower buds are initiated, beginning at the tip of the shoot and progressing toward the base. Typically five to seven flower buds are initiated per shoot, though as many as fifteen and as few as one have been reported. By mid-autumn, the observant grower should be able to distinguish the plump flower buds on the tips of the shoots, which hold the secrets to next year's harvest.

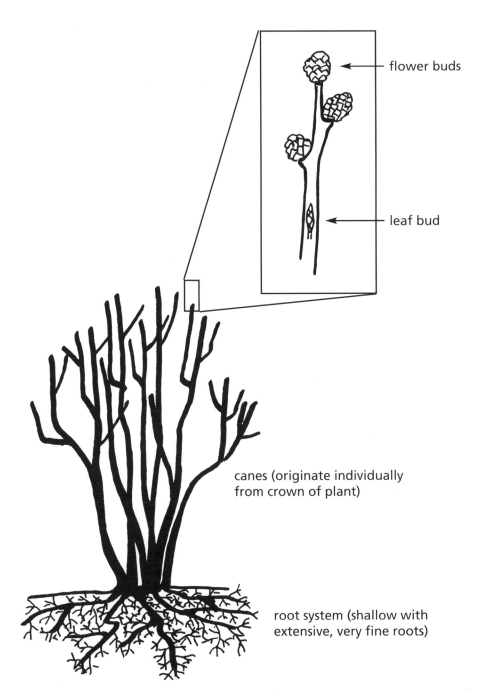

flower buds

leaf bud

canes (originate individually from crown of plant)

root system (shallow with extensive, very fine roots)

Figure 5.1. The blueberry plant.

Plate 1. Commercially grown strawberries demonstrate the dense rows formed by the plants.

Plate 2. A strawberry canopy in bloom in May.

Plate 3. A strawberry blossom being pollinated by a honeybee.

Plate 4. An abundance of beautiful strawberry fruit. (Photo by David Handley, University of Maine)

Plate 5. This newly planted strawberry plant will eventually form a dense planting, as shown in Plate 1. (Photo by David Handley, University of Maine)

Plate 6. Gray mold, caused by *Botrytis cinerea,* on strawberry fruit. (Photo by Jim Dill, University of Maine)

Plate 7. Strawberry fruit showing fruit-tip distortion (also called "catfacing") from tarnished plant bug injury.

Plate 8. Red raspberries make excellent hedges when properly trained.

Plate 9. High-vigor boysenberries used to form a hedge in New Zealand. Thornless blackberries and tayberries also have the vigor to fill a 6-foot (1.8 m) trellis like this one. (Photo by David Handley, University of Maine)

Plate 10. A blackberry flower.

Plate 11. 'Autumn Bliss' is a hardy and productive fall-bearing red raspberry.

Plate 12. The fall-bearing raspberry 'Dinkum' produces beautiful, flavorful fruit.

Plate 13. Black raspberry fruit on the bush.

Plate 14. 'Anne' is a relatively new yellow raspberry with a wonderful aromatic flavor.

Plate 15. 'Goldie' produces berries that are pinkish or orange when ripe for harvesting.

Plate 16. Thornless blackberries are extremely prolific.

Plate 17. A native stand of lowbush blueberry plants in Maine.

Plate 18. The white snowball bloom on blueberries offers great ornamental interest.

Plate 19. Blueberry plants offer spectacular red, purple, and orange colors in fall.

Plate 20. Some blueberry cultivars have red stems and pink blooms, particularly early in the blooming period.

Plate 21. Luscious ripe blueberry fruit. (Photo by Kathy Demchak, Penn State University)

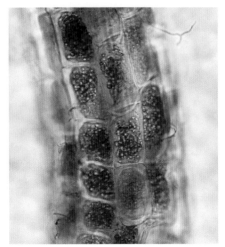

Plate 22. A mycorrhizal infection in cleared and stained root cells of a blueberry plant. The blue coils are fungi inside the cells. (Photo by Kathy Demchak, Penn State University)

Plate 23. Grape vines trained to a high-wire cordon.

Plate 24. Grape flowers in bloom.

Plate 25. The seedless table grape 'Canadice' is a hardy cultivar for colder climates.

Plate 26. 'Niagara' is a common juice grape grown in the eastern and northern United States. (Photo by David Handley, University of Maine)

Plate 27. 'Cayuga White' produces a dry white wine and is well adapted to American soils.

Plate 28. The dark red wine made from the cultivar 'Chambourcin' has spicy or pepper tones.

Plate 29. American black currant *(Ribes americanum)* displaying its attractive fall color. (Photo by Kim Hummer)

Plate 30. Gooseberry fruit on the bush.

Plate 31. The fruit of red currant, shown here ready for harvest, is red, slightly transparent, and simply lovely to look at.

Plate 32. Currants grafted on the trunk of a tree species of *Ribes*. Though not sold this way in the United States, these shrubs have ornamental value and offer an easier picking height.

Plate 33. Hardy kiwi shows its vigorous twining growth habit by summer.

Plate 34. The dense, glossy foliage of hardy kiwi.

Plate 35. A green-fruited hardy kiwi cultivar ready for harvest. (Photo by David Handley, University of Maine)

Plate 36. Hardy kiwi also produces red-fruited cultivars. (Photo by David Handley, University of Maine)

Plate 37. A full-sized elderberry bush makes an attractive addition to the landscape.

Plate 38. A cluster of elderberry fruit.

Plate 39. Though the fruit is tart, the fruit and foliage of highbush cranberry offer great ornamental potential. (Photo by David Handley, University of Maine)

Plate 40. Green fruit on a serviceberry bush. When ripe, the fruit is blue and looks much like a blueberry, though it usually lacks sweetness. (Photo by Clarence C. Peters)

Fruit size in blueberries is determined both by the plant's genetic makeup and by climatic conditions. Native blueberry plants in the wild produce fruit that is generally much smaller than the cultivated blueberry fruit that we see in our grocery stores and fruit stands. (Certainly, anyone who has ever picked wild blueberries that were smaller than peas has marveled, nay despaired, at how long it takes to fill a bucket, or even a pint, with these small packets of aromatic flavor.) Because the lowbush blueberries cultivated in the northeast consist of managed wild populations, their fruit is always smaller than the highbush blueberry's. In addition to these genetic variations, berry size is affected by the amount of available nutrients and water when flower buds are initiated in late summer and when the fruit develops the following summer. Insufficient water during fruit sizing, in particular, will lead to smaller berries. Keep in mind, though, that too much water can lead to bland, if large, fruit.

Pollination can also influence fruit size. Blueberries can be either self-pollinated or cross-pollinated, but the fruit will be noticeably larger if the flowers are pollinated with pollen from a different cultivar. Cool temperatures (below 50°F or 10°C) can further restrict pollination in two ways. The first is that bees, which are the primary blueberry pollinators, do not fly as much when the weather is cool or rainy. The second problem is that even if the pollen has landed on the stigma (in other words, the flower is pollinated), it still needs to germinate, grow a tube down the stigma, and fertilize the waiting egg. If the weather is cool, this process is slowed down considerably. Native bumble bees are the best pollinators for blueberries since they pollinate over a wide range of weather conditions and are extremely active. They also evolved naturally with blueberries and so the native bees tend to do a better job than honey bees, which are not native to North America.

Another consideration in fruit quality is the scar that the fruit has after it is picked. On some cultivars, the area around the pedicel (fruit stem) is very watery when picked, or worse, some of the skin around the pedicel may actually be torn off when the berry is pulled off the plant. Both conditions can result in a shorter shelf-life for the fruit. This is primarily of concern in commercial operations.

Fruit scarring is of little consequence for the backyard producer, as long as the grower is aware of it and does not try to store the fruit for too long. As usual, my solution to fruit that is not eaten quickly is to freeze or can the stuff. Ah, the benefits of being small.

CULTIVAR SELECTION

You can select a variety of blueberry cultivars for your garden to provide fruit from midsummer through fall, if desired. (See Table 5.1 for approximate harvest dates in your area.) Prospective growers should consult with other growers in their area and/or contact their local county extension personnel or other consultants for the most up-to-date information on cultivars for their location. For best fruit production, plant at least two cultivars, though you can still get a significant crop if only one cultivar is planted.

Table 5.1. Typical Blueberry Harvest Times by Region

Region	Harvest Time
New England	late July–September (highbush); August (lowbush)
Mid-Atlantic	mid-July–late September
Midwest	mid-July–late September
South Central	late May–mid-July
Southeast	April–May
Pacific Northwest	July–August

Many noteworthy blueberry cultivars are described here; a list of recommended cultivars by region is given at the end of this chapter. Table 5.2 provides information on season, hardiness, and productivity for the highbush cultivars. Rabbiteye and southern highbush blueberries are adapted to the southern climes of the United States and are too cold tender to survive in colder climates.

Table 5.2. Highbush Blueberry Cultivars by Season, Hardiness, and Productivity

Cultivar	Harvest Season*	Hardiness	Relative Productivity
Northern Highbush Blueberries			
'Berkeley'	midseason	hardy	medium
'Bluecrop'	midseason	very hardy	high
'Bluegold'	late	very hardy	high
'Bluejay'	early	very hardy	medium
'Blueray'	early	very hardy	high
'Bluetta'	very early	hardy	medium
'Brigitta'	midseason	hardy	high
'Collins'	early	very hardy	medium
'Coville'	late	hardy	medium
'Duke'	very early	very hardy	high
'Earliblue'	very early	hardy	medium
'Elizabeth'	late	very hardy	medium
'Elliot'	late	very hardy	very high
'Jersey'	late	very hardy	high
'Lateblue'	late	very hardy	high
'Patriot'	early	very hardy	medium
'Rubel'	midseason	very hardy	medium
'Sierra'	midseason	very hardy	high
'Spartan'	early	very hardy	high
'Toro'	midseason	very hardy	high
'Weymouth'	very early	very hardy	medium
Southern Highbush Blueberries			
'Cape Fear'	early	tender	high
'Flordablue'	early	tender	medium
'Gulfcoast'	early	tender	medium
'Ozarkblue'	late	tender	high
'Sharpblue'	early	tender	medium
'Summit'	midseason	tender	high
Half-High Blueberries			
'Northblue'	midseason	very hardy	medium
'Northcountry'	midseason	very hardy	medium
'Northland'	early	very hardy	very high
'Northsky'	midseason	very hardy	low
'St. Cloud'	midseason	very hardy	medium

*The blueberry harvest season extends from mid-July through late September in most regions. See Table 5.1.

NORTHERN HIGHBUSH BLUEBERRIES

'Berkeley'. Bush is tall, open, and spreading but tends to drop fruit. Berries are very large, light blue, and firm. Flavor is only fair. Production can be inconsistent. Clusters tend to be hidden by heavy foliage, which slows hand picking. The berries store well in spite of a large stem scar. This cultivar is a poor shipper unless the berries are picked early in the ripening period. Susceptible to fungal diseases in wet seasons.

'Bluecrop'. Best early-midseason variety presently available. Bush is vigorous and upright, but canes tend to be slender and whippy. Fruit is medium-sized, firm, small scarred, and resistant to cracking. It has good flavor. Shows consistently high production and good winter hardiness. Season tends to be prolonged. Berries appear to be ripe (completely blue) well before full sweetness is achieved, so they need to be picked 5 to 7 days after the full blue color is present. Resistant to shoestring and red ringspot virus; moderately resistant to mummy berry and powdery mildew.

'Bluegold'. Medium-sized berries with small, dry scars. Good flavor and firmness. A low-growing plant with many branches.

'Bluejay'. Bush is vigorous, upright, and open. Long-stemmed berries hang in loose clusters, remaining on the bush without loss of quality until most are ripe. Fruit is medium-sized, firm, and light blue, and they have small stem scars. Wood and buds are resistant to low winter temperatures, but flowers are less resistant to frost than those of 'Bluecrop'. Resistant to mummy berry and field resistant to shoestring virus. Production is sometimes erratic.

'Blueray'. Plant is vigorous and propagates easily. Fruit is borne on small, tight clusters that can cause berries to drop, especially in hot weather. Berries are large, firm, and dark blue, with a medium scar and good flavor. Consistently productive, but may overproduce if not pruned properly. Upright-spreading habit. Very hardy.

'Bluetta'. Forms a short, compact, low-spreading bush of medium vigor. Fruit is medium-sized, soft, and blue-black with fair flavor. Stem scars tend to be broad; fruit can hang on for a long period. Consistency of production may be a problem. Winters well, and does not break dormancy too early.

'Brigitta'. Bred in Australia from a cross of 'Lateblue' and 'Blue-crop'. Upright, vigorous bush with production similar to 'Blue-crop' in Australia. Fruit is large and firm with a small, dry scar. Very light blue in color. Clusters are loose, and ripening is concentrated. Excellent fruit quality and shelf-life. Limited availability in the United States.

'Collins'. Bush is vigorous and upright with some spreading canes. May not sucker freely. Fruit is large, firm, light blue, and has very good flavor and a small scar. An early cultivar, it ripens about 5 to 7 days after 'Earliblue'. Susceptible to winter injury and has narrow soil adaptation. Produces only moderately.

'Coville'. Very vigorous, moderately spreading bush with open fruit clusters. Berry is large, medium blue, highly aromatic, and tart. Requires bee concentration for best pollination. Fruit-set problems can limit productivity. Fruit is susceptible to anthracnose disease. Narrow soil adaptation. Moderate producer.

'Duke'. A vigorous, upright bush that bears medium-sized, light blue, firm fruit with a small, dry scar. Blooms late, avoiding early frosts, but ripens relatively early. Plant has numerous canes that are stocky and moderately branched. Buds and wood tolerate fluctuating winter temperatures well. Harvest can be completed in two or three pickings. Flavor is mild-sweet.

'Earliblue'. Forms a vigorous, upright-spreading bush. Early season fruit is large, firm, and light blue with fair flavor. Fruit does not drop easily when ripe. Plants have some resistance to powdery mildew.

'Elizabeth'. Purported to be extremely flavorful, with very large berries. No longer commercially important because of inconsistent productivity, but of interest to home gardeners because of excellent flavor. May be difficult to find in nurseries.

'Elliot'. Latest of all cultivars. Bush is vigorous and upright. Very productive, hardy, and resistant to mummy berry disease. Berry is medium-sized and light blue in color, with firm flesh and only fair flavor; late, small fruit can be tart. Berry may be fully blue when not fully ripe. Interplanting with another late-blooming cultivar provides cross-pollination and improved size and flavor.

'Jersey'. Vigorous and erect bush with open fruit clusters. Medium-sized, firm fruit with good color and fair flavor. May have fruit-set problems; tends to set fruit parthenocarpically (without pollination), but this fruit remains small. Considered by some to have the sweetest flavor of the cultivars. 'Jersey' also has very wide soil adaptation, so it is highly recommended for backyard use.

'Lateblue'. Bush is erect, vigorous, and very productive. Berries are firm, light blue in color, have small stem scars, and are fine flavored but tart. High temperatures during harvest may lead to excessive stemminess.

'Patriot'. Plant is upright, small to medium in height. Fruit is large, firm, and has a small, dry scar. Excellent flavor, though fruit must be completely ripe. Ripens with 'Collins' early in the season. 'Patriot' was developed in Maine and has excellent cold hardiness; early bloom is susceptible to frost damage. Plants are resistant to root rot.

'Rubel'. A wild selection with small, firm fruit. Bush is erect and very productive. Flavor is fair.

'Sierra'. A vigorous, upright, productive bush. Fruit is medium-sized and has good color and excellent flavor and firmness. It forms a small, dry scar. 'Sierra' is an interspecific hybrid of four species, and its cold hardiness is unknown; it has performed well in central Pennsylvania and central Ohio (USDA zones 5 and 6).

'Spartan'. Plants are vigorous, upright, and open; fruits are large, firm, light blue, and highly flavored. Plant performs poorly on amended soils that diverge from the blueberry's naturally preferred soil (acidic, high organic matter). Partially resistant to mummy berry. Blooms late, but ripens relatively early. Late bloom date helps prevent frost injury.

'Toro'. A vigorous, upright bush that has consistently high production. Fruit is medium-sized with small, dry scars. Good color and flavor. Begins ripening with 'Bluecrop', but unlike that cultivar, 'Toro' has a concentrated ripening, and harvest can be completed in two pickings. Tolerates fluctuating winter temperatures well.

'Weymouth'. Primarily planted for its early season, since the plant is low and spreading with relatively low productivity and fruit quality.

SOUTHERN HIGHBUSH BLUEBERRIES

The southern highbush cultivars are appropriate for the Southeast and warmer areas of the south-central United States only.

'Cape Fear'. Productive with excellent growth. Early fruit is large and of fair to good quality. Very heat tolerant.

'Flordablue'. A medium-sized bush with very large early fruit. Firmness is average and scar is wet.

'Gulf Coast'. Vigorous plants with medium productivity. Chilling requirement is higher than that for 'Sharpblue', limiting its development in the deep South.

'Ozarkblue'. High, consistent producer. Blooms relatively late, avoiding late frosts and freezes. Excellent fruit quality. Fruit is late ripening. Vigorous, heat-tolerant plant.

'Sharpblue'. Early ripening (mid to late April in Florida). Fruit is medium-sized with good flavor. Susceptible to root rots.

'Summit'. Excellent flavor and quality, best among the southern highbush cultivars. Productive, midseason plant. Heat tolerant.

HALF-HIGH BLUEBERRIES

Half-high blueberries are cultivars of *Vaccinium corymbosum* developed in Minnesota for production in very cold regions. The success of these cultivars, however, depends on a consistent snow cover to protect against cold injury; if exposed, they are no more hardy than their highbush cousins. Half-high blueberries are low-growing bushes. Fruit quality and yield is not as good as that of the northern highbush cultivars, although the half-highs are a wonderful alternative in harsh climes. Where standard highbush blueberries can be grown, they are preferable to the half-highs.

'Northblue'. Short variety with low to moderate yields. Fruit is dark blue and firm with good flavor. Leaves are particularly ornamental in the fall, turning a lovely dark red.

'Northcountry'. Medium-sized fruit is sweet and mild. Bush reaches only about 3 feet (1 m) in height.

'Northland'. Very productive with medium-sized fruit. Fruit can be soft. Canes are flexible and can be weighted down by snow. Generates a large number of canes. 'Northland' is the most established and tested of the half-high cultivars.

'Northsky'. Pronounced "north sky." Bush is less than 3 feet (1 m) in height and has dense branching. Fruit is light blue and stores well. Also has lovely dark foliage in the fall.

'St. Cloud'. The tallest of the half-highs at about 4 feet (1.2 m). Fruit is medium-sized and has good flavor. Particularly firm, and stores well.

LOWBUSH BLUEBERRIES

The commercially produced lowbush blueberries are naturally appearing clones and are actually many different genotypes mixed together. Only a few lowbush cultivars are available, primarily in New England at specialty nurseries that carry novelty fruits. These plants hold promise for the backyard grower, though. Available cultivars include 'Putte' and 'Tophat', but little is known about their characteristics or potential.

A word on taste (and size). Our culture has long insisted on fruit size as a criterion for commercializing cultivars of fruit species. In our rush for size, however, we often neglect flavor as a selection criterion, at least on a commercial scale. The berries of many cultivars are, therefore, large but not nearly as flavorful as their native counterparts. In addition, wet years often result in larger fruit with less flavor. Be careful with your irrigation. You need enough water to size the fruit and alleviate stress on the plant, but not so much that it dilutes the flavor. I have known commercial producers who irrigated their plants enough to weaken the wonderful berry flavors.

As a backyard grower, you can choose to focus on taste rather than size by selecting cultivars that are reputed to have better than average flavor. So, which cultivars are best for flavor? 'Elizabeth' is hard to beat for rich, aromatic blueberry flavor, but it can be hard to find in catalogs. 'Jersey' and 'Nelson' are also terrific, as is 'Sierra', a relatively recent release. Keep in mind that all blueberries will taste better if they are left on the bush until fully ripe, rather than harvested at the first sign of blue.

Unfortunately, some of the better tasting cultivars may have other limiting characteristics to contend with, such as lower fruit yield or a less favorable growth habit (more spreading or even drooping). A bit of good news is that blueberry breeders are increasingly sensitive to the flavor issue. Many are working on improving flavor, not only by using the more flavorful selections of the highbush species but also by using other species that are inherently more flavorful, such as *Vaccinium darrowii*, a southern native with a spicy, aromatic taste.

HOW TO GROW HIGHBUSH BLUEBERRIES: PLANTING THROUGH HARVEST

Site Selection and Preparation

You may think that because blueberries, particularly the highbush type, grow naturally in or around bog areas, they can tolerate standing in water. If you take a closer look, however, you will find that even though they may be growing in a bog area, the plants are actually situated on small hills of soil that are high and dry, and the plants' shallow roots are often dangling just above the water table, which is usually shallow in these bog areas. In this way, the blueberry plant can absorb water when it wants to, yet still enjoy adequate soil aeration.

In many traditional growing areas, such as Michigan and southern New Jersey, blueberries are grown on sandy soils high in organic matter where the water table is very shallow. In most areas with more typical agronomic (mineral) soils, however, the soil will need to be amended heavily for plant survival and adequate fruit production.

In cultivation, the best soils for blueberries are moist, porous, and acidic. All noxious weeds should be eliminated one to two years prior to planting, and if necessary, the soil's organic matter should be increased before planting by applying manure and/or cover crops. Organic matter increases the soil's aeration, nutrient supply, and water-holding capacity.

Blueberries require a pH between 4.5 and 5.0; they should never be planted in soils with a pH higher than 5.0 without first amending the soil. A low pH can result in manganese or aluminum toxicity, whereas a high pH makes certain nutrients, most notably iron, unavailable. Sulfur is frequently added to high pH soils before planting in order to lower the pH (increase the acidity). Sulfur does not move through the soil readily, and so applying it to the soil surface after the plants are in place is slow to lower the pH; the plants will not thrive and may die. The finer the grind, the more quickly it will act, though the finer grinds (such as wettable sulfur, also used as a pesticide) are also more difficult to handle—be sure to put them down on a windless day. Sulfur and phosphorus (if needed) should be added the summer or fall before planting. Potassium can be added either in the fall or when nitrogen is applied in the spring.

Guidelines for adding sulfur to acidify the soil are provided in the following chart. Some older publications suggest using aluminum sulfate to acidify soils, but this is no longer recommended. Though aluminum sulfate is effective at rapidly reducing soil pH, blueberry plants are quite sensitive to high levels of aluminum in the soil, and once it is added, it does not leave but is bound up in the soil. Iron sulfate is an acceptable means of lowering the soil pH, but it is much more expensive than elemental sulfur, so you are better off using straight elemental sulfur, if you can find it.

Blueberry plants are also sensitive to fluctuating soil moisture. A 4-inch (10-cm) deep, low-pH mulch and consistent irrigation are essential for a healthy planting and consistent yields in nontraditional sites. Blueberries require at least 1 inch (2.5 cm) of water per week during the growing season, and up to 4 inches (10 cm) per week during fruit ripening. Soils that are sandy will require more water than those with a higher water-holding capacity. An application of mulch is one of the best ways of conserving water and minimizing fluctuations in soil water. Hardwood bark mulch (such as that used for landscaping), rotted sawdust, and chopped corncobs

Amount of sulfur needed to acidify soil to the desired pH for blueberries.

Present pH of soil	Desired pH					
	4.5			5.0		
	sand	loam	clay	sand	loam	clay
	(pounds per 100 sq. ft.)			*(pounds per 100 sq. ft.)*		
4.5	0.0	0.0	0.0	–	–	–
5.0	0.4	1.2	1.4	0.0	0.0	0.0
5.5	0.8	2.4	2.6	0.4	1.2	1.4
6.0	1.2	3.5	3.7	0.8	2.4	2.6
6.5	1.5	4.6	4.8	1.2	3.5	3.7
7.0	1.9	5.8	6.0	1.5	4.6	4.8
7.5	2.3	6.9	7.1	1.9	5.8	6.0

are all good mulches for this purpose. Do not use uncomposted leaves or wood chips, as these can result in plant burning and nutrient deprivation.

Although either overhead or trickle irrigation can be used for blueberries, trickle both conserves water and supplies the plant with adequate water. The trickle line can be placed on the soil or under mulch so that it is out of the way and, in some cases, semipermanent. Overhead irrigation has the advantage of cooling the plants and the berries during times of extremely high temperatures, but wetting the fruit and foliage can result in higher incidences of disease. Overhead irrigation can also be used for frost protection if your site is prone to frost during bloom times. Overhead irrigation may be more practical for larger acreages on frost-prone sites.

Planting and Establishment

As we have seen, blueberry plants have very particular soil requirements and limited soil adaptation. If you are lucky enough to have the ideal blueberry soil, then you do not need to amend beyond what is recommended by your soil test. However, most backyards have soils with higher pH and lower organic matter than is preferred by blueberries, and these require amendments and mulching at planting.

If the soil needs amending, you can place peat moss in the planting hole, replacing about one-half of the original soil with the organic material. After watering and fertilizer application, the plants should be heavily mulched along the length of the row with about 4 inches (10 cm) of rotted sawdust or other organic matter. ("Rotted" means it has been sitting in a pile somewhere out in the rain and weather for at least 2 years.) Other great mulches for blueberries include grass clippings, chopped corncobs, and straw. These mulches are somewhat less desirable than rotted sawdust because they have to be replaced more often, but if that is not a limitation for you, there's no reason not to use them. It is possible to do damage with mulch, though. Green sawdust can burn the tender green stems and will compete with the plant for nitrogen. Even sawdust that looks well rotted can rob nitrogen from the plant when it is put in the planting hole, which is why I recommend peat moss instead of sawdust as a preplant soil amendment. I have seen plants mulched with raw, chopped municipal waste (usually chopped branches from road pruning crews) that burned the blueberry plants as though a blowtorch had hit them. Chopped, uncomposted leaves can have the same effect. There is a lot we don't know about mulches, so stick with what is known, or experiment on a small scale. One final thought: my sheep-owning friends have told me that sheep fleece that is unusable for hand-spinning makes a great mulch. That will be my next experiment.

The best organic amendment that I have experimented with, in terms of increasing plant growth and overall happiness, is leaf litter collected from the floor of a forest that has blueberries growing in it. I can hardly recommend that commercially, since it is both hard to get and limited in supply, but if you know of such a forest, procuring a bit of the litter to put in the planting hole with your blueberry plants is certainly acceptable. Another benefit of growing small.

If you are planting 2-year-old bare-root plants, which are preferred, 50 to 60 percent of the wood should be removed immediately after planting. Removing the flowers from 2-year-old plants will help the plant become established. Some of the crop should also be removed in the following year, again to encourage sound establishment. Sacrificing this small amount of fruit is well worth the dividend of establishing a planting that will fruit for 50 years or more if well maintained. For a large-scale site, a planting design in which four rows of one cultivar are alternated with four rows of another cultivar encourages cross-pollination. On a smaller scale, you can simply alternate plants in a row. I have a six-plant blueberry planting in which the cultivars 'Sierra' and 'Bluecrop' are staggered, making for an artistic-looking grouping.

Potted blueberry plants are available in some parts of the country. They are often more expensive than bare-root plants but work well in home-garden situations. When planting a potted plant, the planting hole should be prepared in the same way as for bare-root plants, but the top portion of the plant does not have to be cut back since the root system is only minimally disturbed. If the plant is pot bound, treat it as you would any pot-bound plant, breaking up the roots with your hands and spreading them outward as you plant them.

Establishing permanent sod between rows of blueberries is recommended in nontraditional sites with high pH, mineral soil. Hard fescues *(Festuca)* perform extremely well as permanent sod covers, since they are slow growing, relatively noncompetitive, and tough enough to withstand foot traffic. You can also just mow whatever grows between the rows. Be sure to control dandelions, though. They may harbor a virus that can be transmitted to the blueberry plant by nematodes in the soil.

Plant Nutrition and Fertilization

If the soil is properly prepared prior to planting, only nitrogen fertilizer is required on an annual basis. Do not fertilize with straight nitrogen in the first year, as the root system is susceptible to root burning at this stage. You can apply a water-soluble starter solution for acid-loving plants at planting. In subsequent years, always fertilize with ammonium sulfate in March or April. For each plant, apply 4 ounces (112 grams) of ammonium sulfate in year two, 5 ounces (140 grams) in year three, 6 ounces (168 grams) in year four, 7 ounces (196 grams) in year five, and 8 ounces (224 grams) in year six and subsequent years. If nutrient-deficiency symptoms (light green or red leaves in the summer, poor growth, poor yield) develop in the planting, retest the soil to make sure the pH is at the recommended 4.5–5.0. Never apply nitrate-containing fertilizers, such as ammonium nitrate and calcium nitrate, which are toxic to blueberries. If you suspect a nutrient deficiency that is not related to soil pH, use a tissue analysis kit (available through your extension office) to determine the specific deficiency.

In my experience, common nutrient deficiencies include magnesium, zinc, and boron. Low magnesium causes a yellowing around the leaf edges, which if left untreated can get so bad that the yellow edges turn brown and die. Application of Epsom salts (magnesium sulfate) will take care of this; a tissue analysis will recommend a precise amount of Epsom salts to add.

With boron, blueberries have a fairly narrow range of tolerance. Too little is bad, usually causing stunting and poor fruit set, but too much is worse, causing tissue burning and, in some cases, plant death. Some growers will have a near-religious experience with boron—they apply it to boron-deficient plants and miraculous improvement occurs almost overnight—and decide that if a little is good, more is better. Not good. Blueberries are susceptible to injury from high levels of this element, as most plants are.

As discussed earlier, excess aluminum can also cause problems, including overall stunting of the plant. Though not common, it can occur in heavy clay soils where the soil has been acidified, because the acidification process releases the aluminum that naturally resides in clay particles.

Pruning

The philosophy behind pruning blueberries is to constantly renew the plants by cutting out the older, less productive canes and forcing new ones to develop from the base of the plant. Pruning not only controls crop load and thus increases fruit quality, it also invigorates the plant as a whole. Canes are most productive when they are between 3 and 6 years old, offering a balance of abundant fruit and good fruit size. When the canes are more than 6 years old, berry size tends to dwindle, and the canes of some cultivars get so tall or highly branched that they are difficult to manage. If properly pruned, the plant will replace old canes with new canes, while the majority of the canes are in a productive intermediate stage. The center of the plant is also more open after pruning, and criss-crossing twigs are removed (Figure 5.2).

Pruning is best accomplished toward the end of the dormant season in late winter or early spring. Fall pruning is not recommended, as it can force the plant to produce new shoots that will be killed by winter cold. In the plant's first year in the field, all fruit buds should be removed in order to force vegetative growth. The fruit buds are easily recognizable during late dormancy, as they are plumper than the vegetative buds and are found on the tips of the branches. The first year or two should be spent establishing the plant's frame and root system, which, if properly cared for, will bear fruit for many decades. Once the plant is mature (6 years old), it should produce at least three to five new shoots per year and bear two to three canes each of new, 1, 2, 3, and 4 years in age, or 10 to 15 canes total. The production of new shoots is somewhat cultivar dependent; some may not respond as well to pruning as others.

Following are some recommendations for specific blueberry pruning situations:

Plants with an open or spreading growth habit. Examples: 'Berkeley', 'Bluetta', 'Coville', 'Weymouth'. Try to keep these plants growing more erectly than is their tendency. Concentrate pruning on the outer edge of the bush, pruning drooping lateral branches back to the main stem.

Plants with an erect or upright habit. Examples: 'Bluecrop', 'Blueray', 'Collins', 'Earliblue', 'Elliot', 'Jersey', 'Lateblue'. These plants tend to become very dense in the center, causing shading that reduces shoot formation and flower bud initiation. Remove the older central canes, and prune excessive inward-pointing laterals back to the main canes of the plant. In other words, keep the centers from becoming too dense.

a

b

Figure 5.2. Pruning blueberry plants: a) unpruned blueberry bush, with small arrows indicating where major cuts are made; b) pruned blueberry bush.

Plants that are very vigorous. Examples: 'Blueray', 'Collins', 'Coville', 'Earliblue'. For these cultivars, focus on removing whole canes at the base, rather than detail pruning. While removing some canes is needed on all cultivars, do so more "vigorously" with these.

Plants that are weak or slow growing. Example: 'Bluetta'. Treat weak-growing cultivars the opposite of how you would the vigorous ones. Specifically, focus on detail pruning, rather than removal of whole canes at the base. Where many laterals ("twiggy" growth) have formed, remove half of them at pruning. Systematically removing the weaker laterals (those less than ⅛ inch in diameter) will improve berry quality.

Old unattended plants. Perhaps you find these on a property you have just purchased, or perhaps you have not been able to keep up with pruning. Old overgrown plants can be rejuvenated by cutting back all the canes and allowing regrowth, or by cutting back half the canes in one year and half in the following year. The latter method is preferred, since it avoids a complete lapse in the crop.

Harvest and Postharvest

A mature blueberry plant will easily produce 7 to 10 pounds (3–4.5 kg) of fruit per year. Harvest begins in early summer with cultivars such as 'Earliblue' and may continue through mid-autumn with 'Elliot' (see Table 5.1). Berries turn blue 3 to 4 days *before* they attain maximum sweetness and flavor, so let them hang. Commercial growers often wait until a few berries fall to the ground before they begin harvest. It's not easy to resist the temptation to pick such luscious-looking fruit, but remember that the great thing about growing fruit in your backyard is that you *can* wait and time the harvest to your best advantage. The fruit should be blue all the way around when ripe for picking. The area around the stem (pedicel) that connects to the fruit will be the last to ripen. As you harvest, make sure to glance at the back of the fruit before you roll it off the plant. If the fruit is not quite ripe, the stem end will be either green or reddish in color rather than blue—come back in a few days to try again. If blueberries are placed in the refrigerator immediately upon harvest, they will store well for 7 to 10 days. They can also be put directly into the freezer (ziplock bags or other plastic containers work perfectly) and made into jams or pies at some later, colder, more convenient date.

Propagation

If you buy your plants from a reputable nursery you may well avoid the embarrassment and headache of bringing viruses into your yard. If, however, you find that you need to propagate in order to get more plants, or you simply want to try your hand at it (and what horticulturist doesn't enjoy a little propagation?), here's the best way to go about it. Remember that there is *huge* variation in how well blueberry plants root, and it primarily depends on their genetic makeup. In other words, some cultivars root quite well, and others are really tough. Expect a rooting percentage of about 50 percent— with this conservative expectation you will rarely be disappointed and often be joyous at your success.

Softwood cuttings. If you have access to a mist system, propagating blueberries with softwood cuttings is the quickest method, though it is also the technique most fraught with difficulty. Timing is extremely important. Collect 4-inch (10-cm) shoot-tip cuttings during the first flush of growth. Leave two or three leaves on each cutting, then stick them in a propagating medium of equal parts peat moss and perlite to a depth of 2 inches (5 cm). Rooting hormones, such as indole-butyric acid (IBA), can be used to increase rooting percentage. The mist should be kept adequate but not excessive— this takes close attention, since the cuttings will need more mist on sunny days and considerably less on cloudy days. The cuttings should root in 4 to 6 weeks, at which point they can be moved directly to the garden, planted close together in good soil in a location where you can watch them daily (this arrangement is known as "nursery rows"); alternatively, the rooted cuttings can be held in a greenhouse over the winter to produce more growth prior to planting the following spring.

Hardwood cuttings. If you are like most home gardeners, you probably do not have access to intermittent-mist systems or a greenhouse—but despair not. Even without this sophisticated equipment, you can still try your hand at propagating blueberries. A propagation frame can be constructed of treated wood with chicken wire underneath. It should be about 8 inches (20 cm) tall and filled with a propagation medium of equal parts sphagnum peat and coarse white play sand. Dormant shoots that are roughly pencil-sized in diameter, or a little bigger, can be cut anytime from December through March. Remove the top portion of the shoot (which harbors the flower buds) and cut the remaining shoot into sections about 5 inches (12.5 cm) in length, keeping the bottom cut just above a vegetative bud. (If you live in a cold climate, it is best to take your cuttings in mid-December, before any winter injury may have occurred. The cuttings should be wrapped in a paper towel, placed in a plastic bag, and stored in the refrigerator until March.)

The propagating medium should be watered well before you stick the cuttings. (The peat may take a while to absorb the water.) Stick the cuttings into the medium vertically, allowing only the top bud to remain above the surface. Always make sure to keep the cuttings right side up—they won't root otherwise. Water thoroughly after sticking the cuttings, and keep the medium moist but not wet. If cuttings are stuck in early spring, vegetative buds will first leaf out in about 6 weeks later. The cutting is not rooted at this time, but after about another 4 weeks, a second flush announces that the little cane has finally rooted. Transfer the new plants to a nursery row. The young plants should be tended to assiduously in the first year. Apply a soluble fertilizer for acid-loving plants weekly through midsummer. The next spring, move plants to their permanent home.

NICHES IN THE LANDSCAPE

Blueberry plants are beautiful. There is simply no other way to describe them. Their primary limitation in the landscape is their requirement for acidic soils, but with the amendments described earlier, they can be utilized in many garden situations. The form of

blueberry plants varies from the lowbush blueberry, which makes
an effective groundcover and propagates by stolons, to the highbush blueberry, which often reaches 10 feet (3 m) in height in its
natural habitat, to the rabbiteye blueberry, which can attain a
height of 20 feet (6 m) in southern locations. All these blueberries
have lovely bright green, sometimes glossy leaves that turn fire red
in the fall (Plate 19). The red color is so intense that it can rival the
much-used landscape plant burning bush *(Euonymus atropur-
purea)*. The twigs of most cultivars also turn red, making a wonderful winter contrast to the surrounding dull colors of most vegetation
and to the snow (Plate 20). And if all this isn't enough, in spring the
blueberry offers clusters of bell-shaped blossoms (much like its
cousin andromeda, *Pieris japonica*) that are white to pink in color
when grown in adequate sunlight (Plate 18). Once pollinated, those
flowers give rise to our luscious blueberries (Plate 21).

The development of blueberries specifically for ornamental use
is still in its infancy, but I expect to see more in the future. Bear in
mind that all significant blueberry breeding to date has been with
the objective of improving plant and fruit quality for *commercial*
producers. The aesthetic beauty of the plant is a by-product of the
practical commercial breeding objectives (fruit size, plant habit,
fruit quality, pest resistance, among others). Increasingly, however,
blueberry breeders are figuring out that there is a terrific market in
backyard gardens, and selections that were once thrown away because of low production, or a darker-than-light-blue color, are being
considered for release as ornamentals. Planted in an appropriate
location, these plants have few pest problems and offer a range of
forms for use in landscaping.

PESTS IN THE PLANTING

When blueberries are grown in a sunny site with soil that pleases
them, they have relatively few insect and disease pests—unless you
happen to be located near a large population of blueberries in commercial production. The large monocultures are too attractive for
the pests to ignore, and if your planting is within an easy jaunt,

either by wind or wings, the pests will come. Weeds are likely to be a problem one way or the other, but you can easily escape the disease and insect affront if you are gardening in an isolated area. New and healthy plantings have the best success rate when it comes to avoiding pests. Weakened plants are much more likely to succumb to the numerous cane diseases that afflict blueberries, and they are also more likely targets for mites and aphids.

Some diseases of blueberry plants, including some of the cankers and leaf infection of the shoots, can be mimicked by frost injury. Frosts can rob you of your fruit and damage your plants, and although you can take some action to prevent damage (see Chapter 3), often it is simply not possible to control frost. In order to avoid a misdiagnosis and possible panic, you should at least be aware of when a frost has occurred, so you know the reason why the new blueberry foliage is brown, or why you didn't get any fruit. Though frost usually is toughest on opened flowers, in the case of blueberry it can also cause injury to the small green fruits.

Most of the disease and insect pests documented to plague blueberries are outlined in Tables 5.3 and 5.4. For recommended chemical and cultural controls, contact your local extension office or consultants. Also be sure to read Chapter 1 of this book for extensive recommendations on controlling pests using cultural management.

Birds

There is a pest that makes any blueberry grower shudder. It can completely consume a crop before it is ripe, or even more dishearteningly, the crop can be devoured a few days or minutes before harvest. The heinous criminal? *Birds.* Birds simply adore blueberries. They consume them with greedy delight. The species of bird wreaking this havoc vary by location, but the most common culprits are starlings, robins, and cedar waxwings. Netting is the one and only solution to controlling this damage. Nothing else has worked well enough in our experience to consider merit. I have seen birds sitting on the bird alarm devices as they are going off. I have seen them sit on the heads of suspended owls with aplomb; likewise on balloons with eyes painted on them. The only creatures that have been scared off by the inflatable snakes I put in my planting are the human occupants; even the dogs are oblivious. So, bite the bullet and buy some netting. Put it on as the fruit starts to ripen. A few temporarily happy birds may find themselves caught between the netting and the bush, but hopefully they won't get all your wonderful fruit.

Weeds

Weeds can be a problem in blueberry plantings, particularly if they are not tended to regularly. The blueberry has an advantage over the lowly strawberry here by virtue of its height; it takes a tall weed to compete with a 6-foot (1.8-m) blueberry plant for sun. On the other hand, blueberries are not particularly adept at taking up water, particularly when the soils are cold, and weeds can easily rob them of the continuous supply of water upon which they thrive. Weeds may also harbor viral diseases that can be transmitted to the plant by nematodes.

Because mulch is used on blueberries grown in mineral soil conditions, many growers make the mistake of thinking that they will not have any weed problems if they mulch. It is true that mulch is generally good for suppressing weeds, but it is also often the case that the mulch contains weed seeds. This is a reason to avoid using straw mulch, even though its mulching properties are fine. Most straw has either weed seeds or seeds from straw crop that will rapidly become weeds if brought into your blueberry planting. As with strawberries, there is a herbicide that you can use if you become overrun with grasses. I consider this a last resort, but often it is nearly impossible to remove all the grasses that can infest the blueberries, so it is best to deal with the problem as soon as possible. The product of choice is called Poast (sethoxydim), and the labeled instructions should be followed.

Diseases

Canker diseases. *Fusicoccum*, *Phomopsis*, and *Botryosphaeria* cankers can all damage blueberries. They most often affect plants that are

Table 5.3. Common Blueberry Diseases and Causal Organisms in the United States

Name of Disease	Plant Parts Affected	Causal Organism
Alternaria fruit rot and leaf spot	leaves, fruit	*Alternaria alternata* (fungus)
anthracnose	fruit, leaves	*Colletotrichum gloeosporioides* (fungus)
Botrytis blight	flowers, fruit, leaves	*Botrytis cinerea* (fungus)
Fusicoccum canker	stems, canes	*Fusicoccum putrifaciens* (fungus)
mummy berry	stems, fruit	*Monilinia vaccinii-corymbosi* (fungus)
Phomopsis canker and twig blight	stems, canes	*Phomopsis vaccinii* (fungus)
Phytophthora root rot	roots	*Phytophthora cinnamomi* (fungus)
powdery mildew	leaves	*Microsphaera penicillata* (fungus)
stem blight	stems	*Botryosphaeria corticis* (fungus)
witches broom	stems, canes	*Pucciniastrum goeppertianum* (fungus)
blueberry scorch	systemic	probably aphid-vectored carlavirus
blueberry shock	systemic	pollen-vectored ilarvirus
leaf mottle	systemic	virus vectored by pollen
mosaic	systemic	virus vectored by blueberry aphid and by diseased propagation wood
necrotic ringspot and tomato ringspot	systemic	virus vectored by dagger nematode and by diseased propagation wood
red ringspot	systemic	virus probably vectored by mealybug and by diseased propagation wood
Sheep Pen Hill disease	systemic	unknown virus; carlavirus suspected
shoestring disease	systemic	virus vectored by blueberry aphid
stunt	systemic	mycoplasma vectored by sharp-nosed leafhopper

already weak from other stresses, but these cankers can also harm healthy plants. The best control is to remove canes that show symptoms at pruning or as they appear and take the prunings out of the area and burn them. *Fusicoccum* canker manifests itself as small red spots that may enlarge into bull's-eye-like marks on the canes. Look for the signs when you are dormant pruning, and remove affected canes. *Phomopsis* and *Botryosphaeria* can cause wilting of new shoots as the new growth emerges in the spring, causing the shoots to dry up and often curl. Prune and burn any canes that show these symptoms, being sure to cut the canes down to where the pith is no longer brown.

Mummy berry. A fungal disease, mummy berry afflicts new shoots, flowers, and fruit. Shoots and leaves will turn brown and wilt as they emerge, and flowers may also appear to be brown and water soaked. Infected flowers that are left to fruit will form fruit that is tan in color. These will shrivel, become hard, and are completely inedible. If you see any mummy berry in your planting, be sure to rake up the soil below the plants in early spring. This will cover the overwintering fruiting structures of the fungus, which are on the ground under the plant. If the problem is severe, you may need to apply a fungicide; recommendations should be available through your local extension service.

Insects

Many insects that attack a wide range of plants also attack blueberries. Japanese beetles are much fonder of roses, raspberries, and grapes, but given the chance, they may zero in on your blueberries. Gypsy moths, in years when they are abundant, may also become problematic. A few of either of these insects will not cause much difficulty for the plant, but if numbers become very high, insecticides such as B.T. *(Bacillus thuringiensis)*, Sevin (carbaryl), or malathion can be used. A few insect pests are more specific to blueberries. Though not frequently a problem, if they become entrenched in your planting you will want to know who they are and what can be done about them. (See Table 5.4.)

Blueberry maggot. Though not often present, blueberry maggot *(Rhagoletis mendax)* wins the "grossness" award when it surfaces. These small larvae are white maggots. Only one larva will attack each fruit, but unfortunately the infected fruit stays on the plant, and you may have the extreme displeasure of biting into it. If you have a heavy infestation of these guys, by all means spray. Living with the anxiety of the constant question "Does *this* berry have a maggot in it?" is just not an option.

Cranberry fruit worm and cherry fruit worm. Both of these worms render the fruit useless. Cranberry fruit worm *(Acrobasis vaccinni)* damage is characterized by fruits that are webbed together and the presence of its frass (excrement) in the webbing. The cherry fruit worm *(Grapholitha packardi)* is a little more insidious. This worm enters the fruit and systematically consumes all the contents inside the skin, leaving only its frass in exchange. Fruit will turn blue prematurely, and it may also have some webbing on it. If you open this fruit with your fingers (please don't bite into it), you will find only dry frass. If either of these insects become a problem, they can be controlled with labeled insecticides at petal fall and 10 days later. For specifics, contact your local extension office.

FREQUENTLY ASKED QUESTIONS

My blueberry plants are growing just fine, but why aren't they producing any fruit? A couple of things can cause this. First, if the blueberries are in deep shade, they may not receive enough sunlight to initiate flower buds. The plants need about 20 percent full sunlight for flower bud initiation, but remember that the wood on the interior of the plant can be shaded by the plant as well as by things beyond it. You can also experience an intermediate situation where the light is low but not low enough to completely eliminate flowering, in which case there will be few flowers or fruit. Blueberries evolved as understory trees, so they can tolerate low levels of sunlight. They just will not fruit well in such situations.

A more likely cause of lack of fruiting is frost or freezing tem-

Table 5.4. Major Blueberry Insect and Mite Pests in the United States

Common Name of Pest	Scientific Name of Pest	Pest Class
blueberry bud mite	*Acalitus vaccinii*	attacks buds
cutworms	*Lepidoptera*	attacks buds
spanworms	*Palenacrita vernata, Alsophila pometaria, Cingilia catenaria*	attacks buds
winter moths	*Operophter brumata, Lepidoptera*	attacks buds
blueberry maggot	*Rhagoletis mendax*	attacks flowers and fruit
carpenter bee	*Xylocopa virginica*	attacks flowers and fruit
cherry fruit worm	*Grapholitha packardi*	attacks flowers and fruit
cranberry fruit worm	*Acrobasis vaccinni*	attacks flowers and fruit
cranberry weevil	*Anthonomus musculus*	attacks flowers and fruit
green fruit worms	*Lepidoptera*	attacks flowers and fruit
plum curculio	*Conotrachelus nenuphar*	attacks flowers and fruit
scarab beetles		attacks flowers and fruit
Japanese beetle	*Popillia japonica*	
false Japanese beetle	*Strigoderma arboricola*	
rose chafer	*Macrodactylus subspinosus*	
yellow jackets	family Vespidae	attacks flowers and fruit
blueberry aphids	*Illinoia pepperi, Myzus persicae, Finbriaphis fimbriata*	attacks leaves and shoots
blueberry leafminer	*Gracilaria vacciniella*	attacks leaves and shoots
blueberry stem gall wasp	*Hemadas nubilipennis*	attacks leaves and shoots

peratures. If the flowers or the little green fruit are subjected to such low temperatures, they will not develop fully into fruit.

Why are my blueberries so small? Size of blueberries is controlled by several factors. The first is the genetics of the plant. Some plants are just programmed to produce smaller fruit, just as some people are shorter than others. The fruit of the lowbush blueberry is always small relative to that of its highbush cousins. Most commercial blue-

Common Name of Pest	Scientific Name of Pest	Pest Class
blueberry tip borer	*Hendecaneura shawiana*	attacks leaves and shoots
leafrollers	*Argyrotanenia velutinana, Archips argyrospilus, Choristoneura rosacenna*	attacks leaves and shoots
orange tortrix	*Argyrotaenia citrana*	attacks leaves and shoots
sawflies	family Hymenoptera	attacks leaves and shoots
sharpnosed leafhopper	*Scaphytopius magdalensis*	attacks leaves and shoots
blueberry stem borer	*Oberea myops*	attacks stems, canes, crowns, and roots
lecanium scale	*Lecanium*	attacks stems, canes, crowns, and roots
putnam scale	*Diaspidiotus ancylus*	attacks stems, canes, crowns, and roots
root weevils	*Otiorhynchus ovatus, O. rugostriatus, O. sulcatus*	attacks stems, canes, crowns, and roots
white grubs	*Popillia japonica, Macrodactylus subsinosus, Maladera castanea, Phyllophaga,* others	attacks stems, canes, crowns, and roots

berry cultivars have good fruit size. If you are lucky enough to have a native population of highbush plants to observe, you will see that the fruit tends to be much smaller than that of the cultivated counterparts.

Flower blossoms do not appear until spring, but they are actually initiated the previous summer. If the plant's resources are limited at that time (due to drought or a nutrient stress, for example), the flowers may only have the capacity to produce smaller fruit.

Still, even after the flowers have been initiated, water availability during both flowering and fruiting will have a dramatic impact on ultimate fruit size. Any blueberry plant will have smaller fruit if it does not have enough water, so make sure that the plants have adequate water during these key stages.

Finally, blueberries are one of the few small-fruit plants that benefit from cross-pollination between different cultivars. Larger fruit will result if the flower was pollinated by pollen that came from a different cultivar, so interplanting several cultivars is an excellent means of increasing fruit size.

Why are my blueberry plant's leaves so yellow (or red) in the early spring? Blueberry plants have relatively inefficient water pumping systems. Remember that they evolved in situations where they grow on hillocks in areas with low water tables, and the plant effectively "dangles" its roots just above the water table and feeds from it as needed. So, given their natural evolutionary strategy, blueberry plants have no need for efficient pumping systems. If the soil is still cold when the plant starts to leaf out in early spring, however, the root system cannot pump the water as well and thus cannot transport all the necessary nutrients. This results in yellowish or reddish leaves between the veins. I had a grower call me up to tell me that an entire acre of blueberries was off-color in this way. It had been a particularly cool spring, and knowing that we were due for some warm weather, I told him to wait a week, and if it was still a problem, we would do a tissue analysis. He called four days later to tell me that the leaves colored up after three days of 70°F (21°C) temperatures. Voila—the soil warmed, the roots got going, and so did the nutrients.

Some commercial growers apply a foliar spray of nutrients (usually zinc, boron, and iron) to alleviate the situation. This nutrient spray does green up the foliage, but there is no evidence that it helps the plants in the long run—it just gives the grower a little peace of mind, which is not to be undervalued.

Why are the leaves of my blueberry plants yellow (or red) throughout the growing season? Ah, well. This situation is a little different than yellow or red leaves early in the season. If leaves are notably discolored between the veins after the cool days of spring have passed, it is an indication of iron deficiency, known as iron chlorosis. (Chlorosis means a lack of chlorophyll, which is the green pigment in the leaves.) So, you add iron, right? Wrong. Iron is abundant in almost all soils. The problem is that, if the soil pH is too high, the blueberry plant is unable to extract the iron from the soil. (This is a problem for some street trees, too. Have you even seen a yellow-looking pin oak? It's suffering from the same phenomenon.) The first thing to do is test the pH of the soil. Nine times out of ten, you will find that the pH level is well above the preferred level of 5.0, so you need to apply sulfur to bring that pH down again. Many folks also add iron shavings, but this is unnecessary. Bring the pH down, and the iron will come.

My fruit seems to be disappearing just as it is almost ripe. What could cause this? Those sneaky vertebrates. Blueberry disappearance is usually due to birds, and you can often catch them doing the dirty deed. However, squirrels and chipmunks are also known to chow down on almost-ripe blueberries, and they are more likely to do it when you're not looking. Netting is the only solution that I am aware of, and you have to make sure the netting is tied securely around the base of the canes to exclude the rodents. I have been told that spreading mothballs will also discourage the critters. The smell certainly discourages me, so it may be worth a try.

Is it possible to transplant a large blueberry plant? As long as the blueberry plants are not inordinately large, they can be transplanted quite successfully. Transplanting is best done in the early spring, after the soil has thawed but before bud break. First, remove half of the canes at the base of the plant. Prune any remaining canes back to 3 to 4 feet (1–1.2 m) in height. Dig around the root ball, taking as big a ball as you can reasonably move. Be sure to prepare the space that you are moving the plant to before you dig it up. Follow the soil-amendment instructions given earlier in the chapter. It is always a good idea to have the new hole significantly larger than the root ball so that you can ensure good root-to-soil contact by putting loose soil firmly around the new inhabitant. Remember to water the plant in well and keep the soil moist, not wet, for the first few weeks in its new home.

It is possible that a blueberry plant can be too large to move, practically speaking. I have seen root systems that were a few feet deep and several feet in diameter. The plant may survive if you try to divide it, but it will struggle for years. If you need additional plants, it might be better to try cutting propagation, or just order some new ones.

How should I treat the ancient blueberry plants on the land I just purchased? If the blueberry plants are tall (more than 6 feet or 1.8 m), or have a lot of gray or dead wood in the center, or have a lot of branching of the twigs, or have no new growth coming up from the base, chances are they need some rejuvenating. The best approach is to cut back about half of the canes at the base, then prune the remaining canes to a height of no more than 6 feet (1.8 m). This work is best done at the end of the dormant season, usually around February. If the remaining canes have a lot of fine, highly branched wood, selectively prune out the smallest shoots (always cutting them back to the larger shoot to which they are attached), thus allowing the remaining shoots greater access to water, nutrients, and sunlight. In early spring (March or April), fertilize with 8 ounces (224 grams) of ammonium sulfate per plant, mulch the plants with 4 inches (10 cm) of rotted sawdust (or other suggested mulch), keep them watered, and you're off and running. You should see considerable new shoot production that same year. After that, remove one to two of the old canes per year until you have established the desired plant form, as described earlier under "Pruning."

RECOMMENDED BLUEBERRY CULTIVARS BY REGION

The following lists suggest the cultivars most suitable for various regions of the United States; more descriptive information is given earlier in the chapter.

MID-ATLANTIC AND MIDWEST

Northern Highbush Blueberries
'Berkeley'
'Bluecrop'
'Bluejay'
'Blueray'
'Bluetta'
'Coville'
'Duke'
'Elliot'
'Jersey'
'Lateblue'
'Patriot'
'Sierra'
'Spartan'
'Toro'
'Weymouth'

Half-High Blueberries
'Northblue'
'Northcountry'
'Northland'
'Northsky'
'St. Cloud'

NEW ENGLAND

Northern Highbush Blueberries
'Bluecrop'
'Blueray'
'Jersey'
'Nelson'
'Patriot'

Half-High Blueberry
'Northland'

SOUTH CENTRAL

Northern Highbush Blueberries
'Bluecrop'
'Blueray'
'Coville'

'Duke'

Southern Highbush Blueberries
'Cape Fear'
'Legacy'
'Ozarkblue'
'Summit'

Rabbiteye Blueberries
'Brightwell'
'Premier'
'Tifblue'

SOUTHEAST

Southern Highbush Blueberries
'Gulf Coast'
'Sharpblue'

Rabbiteye Blueberries
'Beckyblue'
'Bluebelle'
'Bluegem'
'Bonita'
'Brightwell'
'Chaucer'
'Climax'
'Powderblue'
'Premier'
'Snowflake'
'Tifblue'
'Windy'
'Woodard'

PACIFIC NORTHWEST

Northern Highbush Blueberries
'Bluecrop'
'Blueray'
'Chandler'
'Earliblue'
'Jersey'
'Patriot'
'Spartan'
'Toro'

CHAPTER 6

Grapes

FAMILY: VITACEAE, THE VINE FAMILY

PRIMARY SPECIES:

Vitis aestivalis Michx.—summer or pigeon grape
Vitis labrusca L.—fox grape
Vitis riparia Michx.—riverbank grape
Vitis rotundifolia Michx.—muscadine or southern fox grape
Vitis vinifera L.—European grape

Grapes are a wonderful crop to grow in the backyard. Many species are natives of North America, and they are extremely well adapted to conditions there (translation: they are easy to grow), whereas others, primarily the wine grapes, are natives of Europe and can present a daunting horticultural challenge to the most ardent grower in the United States. North America is home to about 30 species of grapes, only a few of which are used in the development of cultivars, although many more, such as *Vitis berlandieri* and *V. rupestris*, have been used to impart pest resistance to rootstocks. Because grape plants are vines, the form that they take is limited only by the grower's imagination—from arbors to fences to standard trellis systems, grapes can be trained into a variety of shapes and sizes.

It is hard to find a fruit crop with more uses than grapes. Table grapes are the most consumed fresh fruit in the world. Juices and jams made from grapes fill the shelves of grocery stores. Of course wine, both ancient and contemporary, is most often made from the grape. The pleasures of drinking wine have long been acknowledged, but it is only in recent years that the health benefits of moderate wine consumption have been defined. Though the ancients were probably well aware of the benefits, we are now able to name and explain them. So, a toast! To the ancient, modern, and noble grape.

HISTORICAL BACKGROUND AND OTHER INTERESTING FACTS

Grapes are an ancient crop. The tombs of the Egyptian pharaohs have depictions of grape harvests. The crop has been cultivated for so long that the origin and ancestry of some of our most common cultivars ('Cabernet Sauvignon', 'Zinfandel') are only now being sorted out by tools of DNA analysis. These cultivars were being grown and propagated long before the science of breeding was developed by Gregor Mendel in the nineteenth century. Though modern breeding has added certain useful characteristics to grapes, including cold hardiness and pest resistance, breeders have been unable to reproduce the wine quality inherent in many of the classic cultivars, which were presumably selections from the wild or chance seedlings found in old vineyards.

Currently, California accounts for 93 percent of the total grape production in the United States. New York, Washington, Pennsylvania, and Michigan also produce significant quantities of grapes, with much of the production in the Midwest and East devoted to juice grapes such as 'Concord' and 'Niagara', selections of the native *Vitis labrusca*. Other leading grape-producing nations include Italy, France, Spain, and Russia.

Volumes could be written on the history of grapes and viticulture (the culture of grapes) around the world, but I will limit my comments to fairly recent history, and with a decidedly Western slant.

Grapes for Wine

When Europeans first came to settle on the eastern shore of the Americas, they were duly impressed by the wealth of grapevines that covered the land. One could imagine that this abundance signaled wealth and prosperity, both for consumption and for the export value of the raw product and its wine. Unfortunately, they found that the wine made from the native North American grapes did not approach the quality of what they were used to in Europe. The common *Vitis labrusca* had a pungent or "foxy" flavor (hence the common name fox grape), which made the wine less than pleasing to their palates. Furthermore, although the native grapes flourished, all the grape plants that were brought from Europe and planted in the New World died. Records show that Thomas Jefferson, Benjamin Franklin, and numerous lesser-known growers tried and failed to grow European grapes repeatedly, until they finally gave up.

By the mid-1800s, more palatable grapes for eating and wine making, such as *Vitis labrusca* 'Catawba', were found amongst the natives. In the latter quarter of the nineteenth century, grapevines were shipped from North America to France—an event that was to have a lasting effect on the world grape industry. These rooted American grapevines most likely were imported to France because they were resistant to powdery mildew, a problematic fungal disease on both continents. Unbeknownst to all involved, however, the imported vines were infested with the grape phylloxera, a root louse, and the entire French wine industry was decimated within a few years. The presence of this pest also explains why the European vines were not able to survive in the Americas. The native grapes, which had co-evolved with the vermin, had developed resistance to phylloxera, but the unsuspecting European plants were like lambs brought to the slaughter. Though it was known at the time that the European grapevines could be grafted onto resistant rootstocks, the French growers felt that the rootstock imparted bad flavors to the wine, and they embarked on a massive effort to marry the high quality of the European wine grape with the insect and disease resistance of the American grape through hybridizing. Many North American species were used in this effort, but the one that proved most useful was *V. riparia*, the riverbank grape. The breeding work had an unforeseen benefit as well: though they are relatively cold tender, the European grapevines are able to produce crops from adventitious buds, so if the flowers are killed by frost, all is not lost. Today, many of the minor wine-growing regions in the United States depend on the cultivars that resulted from the hybridization of the European and American grapes. As a group, they are called the French-American hybrids, and the hybridization efforts continue to this day.

The West Coast of the Americas has a completely different viticultural history. In the early 1500s, the Spanish conquistadors brought viticulture from Spain. The success of the New World plantings was so great, however, that the Spanish crown forbade the planting of new vineyards in 1595 because it feared that the competition from this new land would be too great. In the late 1600s and 1700s, grapevines traveled with the missions being established up the coast of what is now California. The principal purpose of these vineyards was to produce wine for the church, but in the early nineteenth century, as more ships frequented California ports, wine came to be increasingly in demand. The first commercial planting of vines in California was established in the early 1800s, in the Los Angeles area. Subsequently, more vineyards were planted, and by the late 1850s, California grape growing was a substantial industry. The discovery of gold in northern California elicited an increase in the consumption of grapes and wine, and an unprecedented expansion of the wine industry ensued in the area. Though growers had been importing European grape varieties all along, in 1862 Colonel Agoston Haraszthy was commissioned by the California governor to go to Europe and bring back the grape varieties best suited for California, as well as knowledge about grape culture from the established European wine makers. This marked the beginning of a new industry, based primarily on the best wine grapes of Europe.

The California wine industry experienced many booms and busts throughout its history, but perhaps the most notorious was the bust brought about by Prohibition. In the years leading up to Prohibition, from 1912 to 1919, commercial wine production dropped by almost one-half, until it ceased altogether with the ratification of the Eighteenth Amendment to the Constitution, prohibiting the production and sale of all alcoholic beverages in the United States. In California, however, the reality was that instead of decimating the industry, Prohibition moved wine making into the basements and bathrooms of private homes, and bootleggers paid top prices for fresh grapes. Shipments of grapes out of state also increased, and the higher prices for the illegal end-product resulted in the planting of many new vineyards. The largest acreage in the history of California (648,000 acres) was reached in 1927, still 6 years before Prohibition was repealed. Unfortunately, this expansion was dominated by money-seeking businessmen who knew little about grapes, which brought instability to the industry in spite of the prosperity. The repeal of Prohibition in 1933 brought some sanity back to the growing of wine grapes in the region, but it was many years before the inappropriate cultivars were culled out, the dilapidated vineyards replaced, and the industry regained solid footing.

Unlike in California, the wine industries in the rest of the country were decimated by Prohibition, although they have recovered in the last few decades. Today, local wineries can be found in most of the 50 United States as a result of winery acts passed in the 1970s and '80s.

An important development of the last century in the international wine industry is the protocols established by the major wine-producing nations of western Europe regarding the naming of wines. The term "Chablis," for example, is set aside to denote wines made from a particular cultivar (*Vitis vinifera* 'Chardonnay') and from a particular region in France (Burgundy). To this day, if you purchase a French wine labeled a Chablis, it must meet the stringent, government-controlled standards that seek to ensure reliably consistent, good to excellent wines with particular definable characteristics. The United States was not party to this agreement, a situation that has led to great confusion in wines and wine labeling. Specifically, American wine makers (as well as Australian wine makers) do not follow these rules of nomenclature, and so terms such as "Chablis" or "Burgundy" are used generically rather than in reference to the specific French wine types.

Grapes for Juice

The development of the nonalcoholic-grape-juice industry in the United States can be traced back to the discovery of a single grape, the 'Concord'. In 1843, E. W. Bull of Concord, Massachusetts, planted seeds from a wild grape, which had likely cross-pollinated with *Vitis labrusca* 'Catawba'. The new grape selection was introduced in 1854, and the popularity of this variety grew enormously from then on, though it was primarily grown for fresh market in the early years. The discovery of the Concord grape heralded a sort of golden age of grape production in America. The industry flourished between 1854 and 1880, particularly in the East. By the early 1900s, the Concord grape juice industry was developing along the Great Lakes in western New York and Ohio, and it remains stable today. As an aside, I've often thought that Concord grape juice (and jelly) are to Americans what black currant juice and jelly is to Europeans. Both are purple, strong-flavored juices, though most Europeans seem to like their currant juice even stronger than we do our Concord juice.

Grapes for Fresh Consumption

Grapes that are grown for fresh consumption are referred to as table grapes. While many people in other countries happily consume seeded grapes, Americans as a group are rather insistent on the seedless varieties. The original seedless table grape was a cultivar of the European grape *Vitis vinifera*, 'Thompson Seedless' (known as 'Sultana' in most of Europe and Asia). It is the everyday grocery store green grape that we have come to know and expect. It is also the grape cultivar from which most raisins are made. Its juice is often used as a filler for wine making, and though the juice lacks the character of that of wine grapes, 'Thompson Seedless' has high yields and a high sugar content, which translates into alcohol in wine making. Originating in Asia Minor, this grape is ancient, and little is known about its origin. It is well adapted to the hot areas of California. Several other cultivars of table grapes are produced in California, including 'Perlette', 'Ruby', and 'Tokay', but 'Thompson

What About Raisins?

The word *raisin* comes from the French words for "dry grape" *(raisin sec)*. Early peoples likely dried all sorts of fruits as a means of preserving them, but the raisins we know today were only developed after suitable grape varieties became available. Two selections of Muscat grapes, which have a strong, characteristic aroma (primarily of *Vitis vinifera* background), were introduced in 1856, spurring development of the raisin industry in California. Raisin production really took off, however, when the 'Thompson Seedless' ('Sultana') grape was introduced in 1878. Only 110 tons of raisins were produced in California in 1875; by 1890, 10,000 tons were being produced, and today production is at 200,000 tons.

Most raisins are dried under natural conditions in the field. Before harvest, soil between the east- and west-oriented vines is smoothed to form an incline to the south. The grapes are put in flat pans made of heavy paper, one cluster deep, and the trays are placed on the south-facing slope between the rows. The grapes are usually turned after about a week. When the grapes are so dry that no juice can be extracted by squeezing them, they are rolled up in the heavy papers on which they are drying and left in the vineyard for curing until they are ready for boxing. A raisin that keeps well will have a water content between 13 and 15 percent.

Raisins that are golden in color are not dried in the same way but are dipped in special solutions prior to drying. The grape clusters are dipped for 2 to 3 seconds in a hot solution of 0.2–0.3 percent sodium hydroxide (caustic soda) and then, while still moist, exposed to fumes of burning sulfur in a sulfur house for 2 to 4 hours. The grapes are dehydrated in a dehydrator, rather than naturally.

Seedless' dominates grape plantings there for both raisins and fresh consumption.

The seedless table grapes just mentioned will only grow in California or areas with similar climates. The good news for those of us who don't live in such Mediterranean (or desert) climates is that wonderful seedless table grapes have been developed for colder climes as well. Several breeding programs in the eastern United States have produced a lineup of hardy seedless table grapes. They are different from their European cousins, and in some ways superior. Their flavor is rich, full, and aromatic, making the common grapes found in the grocery store taste like little more than bags of sugar water. They have varying degrees of cold hardiness. As a result of this breeding work, excellent-flavored seedless table grapes can be grown in most backyards throughout the country.

BIOLOGY OF THE PLANT: KNOWING IT AND USING IT TO YOUR ADVANTAGE

The grapevine *(Vitis)* is the only member of the family Vitaceae that is a food-bearing plant. It is a perennial woody vine (or liana) that is described botanically as having nonshowy flowers and true berry fruits. Grapevines are also characterized by their tendrils, which allow them to grab on to other surfaces to climb toward that most important energy source, the sun. The tendrils are found opposite many of the leaves on the plant (Figure 6.1). Grapes grow primarily in the temperate areas of the world, but there are a few subtropical and tropical species. Although species have been designated and described among the Vitaceae, many grapes found in nature are actually hybrids of several species that may reside in close proximity to one another in the North American woods.

The aboveground portion of the grapevine is divided into the trunk and its branches, which are called shoots when they first emerge, canes when they mature and drop their leaves, and cordons when they are trained horizontally and are more than one year old. Because grapes are vines, their height or length is somewhat indeterminate. They can grow to the tops of 30-foot (9-m) trees in

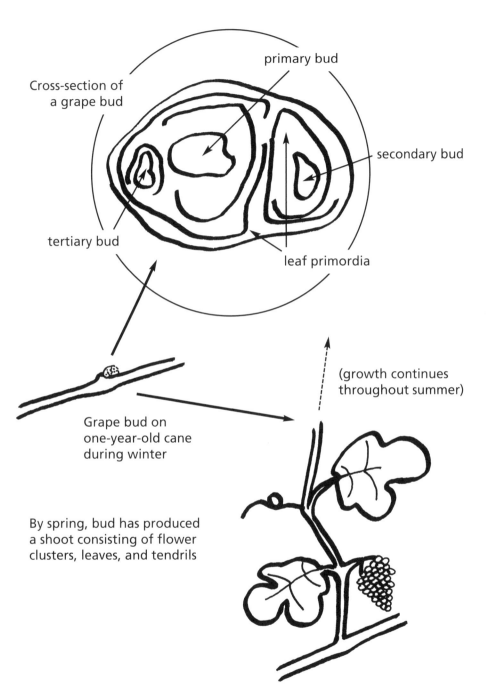

Cross-section of a grape bud

primary bud

secondary bud

tertiary bud

leaf primordia

Grape bud on one-year-old cane during winter

(growth continues throughout summer)

By spring, bud has produced a shoot consisting of flower clusters, leaves, and tendrils

Figure 6.1. The grape bud and shoot.

the woods—though you probably won't ask them to do that in your garden. Bear in mind that grapevines can be trained to a much taller height than the traditional 6 to 8 feet (1.8–2.4 m).

Grape leaves are alternate, and the tendrils and inflorescences (flower clusters) are borne opposite the leaves. The leaves are always simple, lacking multiple leaflets. They are relatively large, often the size of an extended hand or larger, and lobed to varying degrees. The leaves on many of the American species are covered with a soft pubescence ("fur") that gives them a fuzzy appearance. Grape cultivars are often identified by their leaves, via a science called ampelography that was developed in France. The leaf's shape, surface, color, contour, sinus depth, and margin characteristics can be used to identify the plant.

Buds develop in the axils of the leaves. These buds, which will be next year's leaves and fruit, form during the summer while the plant is growing and working on the current year's crop. (Busy plant!) A mature bud has three distinct growing points (see Figure 6.1). Under normal conditions, only the largest (primary) bud grows. However, the primary bud is also the most susceptible to cold injury. If the primary bud is damaged, the secondary bud will grow. The fruit crop on this smaller bud will also be smaller, but some fruit usually develops. If both the primary and secondary buds are killed by cold temperatures, then the tertiary bud will develop, though it usually produces no fruit and only a vegetative shoot. This neat arrangement allows the plant to survive marginal temperatures. It is an evolutionary strategy that protects the existing individual, sacrificing the current year's progeny for that of future years.

The bud that develops in the summer will overwinter and then start to grow the following spring. Each bud contains primordia (the beginning structures) for both shoots and flowers. The flowers of the grape can best be described as discreet and unusual. The cluster is readily observable, but the flowers themselves are very small, often green, and have a fused set of petals (the corolla) that are attached upside down on the flower cluster. When the grape flower blooms, the corolla peels back from its attachment at the base of the flower and falls off, exposing the anthers and the stigma. Peak bloom is when 50 percent of the fused petals have fallen. Grapes are self-fruitful, meaning that a flower can be pollinated by pollen from the same cultivar—and therefore more than one cultivar is not required for pollination—though pollination by foreign pollen occurs frequently.

Grapes differ from other small-fruit crops in that they are wind-pollinated and do not require insects for pollination. Problems with pollination can occur under certain circumstances, however, such as if the temperature is unusually cool during pollination, in which case the pollen tube will not grow quickly enough to fertilize the egg. The resulting cluster will tend to drop many newly developed little berries, making the cluster look "straggly" and lacking the fullness of a normally developed cluster. Growers can do little in this situation other than sigh, shrug their shoulders, and look forward to next year. The beauty of perennial crops is that there will be a next year.

The fruit of grapevines vary considerably in size, depending on the cultivar. Individual berries range from marble-sized (about ½ inch or 1 cm) to almost the size of a quarter (1 inch or 2.5 cm) in diameter. Berry shape is most often spherical, but certain cultivars are quite ovoid. Commercially, gibberellic acid or cane girdling is used to increase both size and length of the individual berries. The fruit cluster, likewise, is quite variable in both size and density. Extremely large clusters, up to 3 pounds (1.4 kg) in weight, are produced by such cultivars as 'Remailly', whereas other cultivars, such as 'Canadice', have clusters in the half-pound (227 grams) range. The looseness of the cluster can be a problem in some varieties, because berries loosely strung together with big open spaces between the fruit are considered unattractive. On the other hand, too tight a cluster creates a great micro-environment for the development of fungal diseases—also not desirable. In addition, some cultivars produce bunches that are so tight as to cause individual berries to be deformed as they develop in such close contact with one another.

The root system of a grapevine varies according to the genetic background of the plant, but generally the roots reside in the top 2 to 5 feet (0.6–1.5 m) of the soil. It should be noted, however, that grapevine roots have been found down to 40 feet (12 m) in sandy soils.

CULTIVAR SELECTION

Aside from choosing an appropriate site (see "How to Grow Grapes," later in the chapter), the most important decision a prospective grape grower must grapple with is the selection of appropriate cultivars. Cultivar selection is determined by two primary factors. The first is the purpose of the grapes. While 'Concord' makes wonderful juice and jelly, it produces a wine of limited appeal, and many people dislike the seeds when consuming the grapes fresh. The seeded juice grapes 'Concord' and 'Niagara' are wonderfully adapted to many North American climates, however, offering good resistance to pests and good cold hardiness. On the other hand, many cultivars of the European grape *(Vitis vinifera)*, such as 'Cabernet Sauvignon' or 'Chardonnay', have excellent winemaking qualities but are susceptible to a whole host of diseases and are more cold tender than many native North American grapes. In many cases, using the French-American hybrid grapes offers a good compromise for wine production because they have better winemaking characteristics than their American parents and better horticultural traits than the Europeans.

Grapes are generally more cold tender than most other small-fruit crops. Muscadine grapes *(Vitis rotundifolia)* belong to a different botanical group than the other grape species, which are known as "bunch grapes." The muscadine grapes can only been grown in hot climates, regions where bunch grapes generally do not thrive due to lack of chilling.

To determine which cultivars are appropriate for the climate of your site, the following rules of thumb, developed by Michigan State University, provide a useful starting point. You can obtain long-term local weather information from county, state, or national weather services.

1. If the long-term (50-year) minimum temperature is −10°F (−23°C) or higher, AND the frequency of −5°F (−21°C) temperatures is three times or less over 10 years, AND the frequency of −10°F (−23°C) is once or less over 10 years, any of the cultivars listed can be grown on your site.

2. If the long-term minimum temperature is –15°F (–26°C), AND the frequency of –5°F (–21°C) temperatures is four times or less over 10 years, AND the frequency of –10°F (–23°C) is once or less over 10 years, you can grow any of the cultivars listed, although those listed as "tender" or "very tender" will be injured in some years.

3. If the long-term minimum temperature is –15°F (–26°C), AND the frequency of –5°F (–21°C) temperatures is annual, AND the frequency of –10°F (–23°C) is no more than four times in 10 years, you can only grow those cultivars listed as "medium hardy" or "hardy."

4. If your site experiences temperatures of –10°F (–23°C) five or more times in 10 years, AND/OR winter temperatures drop to –15°F (–26°C) three or more times in 10 years, your site is not suitable for grape production of any kind.

The typical harvest season for grapes is shown in Table 6.1. A list of recommended cultivars by region is given at the end of this chapter. Information on season, hardiness, and fruit quality of grape cultivars in provided in Table 6.2.

Table 6.1. Typical Grape Harvest Times by Region

Region	Harvest Time
New England	September
Mid-Atlantic	August–October
Midwest	August–October
South Central	late July–mid-September; late August–early October for muscadines
Southeast	July–August
Pacific Northwest	mid-September–mid-October

Table 6.2. Bunch Grape Cultivars by Season, Hardiness, and Fruit Quality

For the purposes of this table, "fruit quality" refers to the size of the berry for table and juice cultivars and to the wine-making qualities for wine grape cultivars.

TABLE AND JUICE CULTIVARS

Cultivar	Harvest Season	Hardiness	Fruit Size
Seedless Red			
'Canadice'	early	hardy	small-medium
'Einset'	early	hardy	medium
'Reliance'	early	hardy	large
'Suffolk Red'	mid	tender	small
'Vanessa'	mid	hardy	medium
Seedless White			
'Himrod'	early	medium	very small
'Interlaken'	very early	tender	small
'Lakemont'	early-mid	medium	medium
'Marquis'	mid	medium	large
'Remailly'	late	medium	large
'Skookum'	early-mid	medium	large
'Sooke'	early-mid	medium	medium
Seedless Blue/Purple			
'Glenora'	mid	medium	small
'Mars'	mid	medium	large
Seeded White			
'Golden Muscat'	late	hardy	large
'Niagara'	mid	hardy	large
Seeded Blue/Purple			
'Alden'	late	medium	very large
'Beta'	early	very hardy	small
'Bluebell'	early	very hardy	medium
'Buffalo'	early	medium	large
'Concord'	mid	very hardy	large
'Steuben'	late	medium	large

WINE GRAPES

Cultivar	Harvest Season	Hardiness	Wine Quality
White			
'Aurore'	early	hardy	fair
'Catawba'	late	hardy	good
'Cayuga White'	early	hardy	good–excellent
'Chardonel'	late	medium	good–excellent
'Chardonnay'	early-mid	tender	excellent
'Delaware'	early	hardy	fair
'Gewürztraminer'	early-mid	very tender	excellent
'Melody'	late-mid	medium	good
'Muscat Ottonel'	late	tender	excellent
'Niagara'	mid	hardy	good
'Seyval'	mid	medium	good
'Traminette'	late-mid	tender–medium	good–excellent
'Vidal'	late	medium	good
'Vignoles'	late-mid	hardy	good–excellent
'White Riesling'	late	tender	excellent
Red			
'Cabernet Franc'	mid	tender	excellent
'Cabernet Sauvignon'	late	tender–very tender	excellent
'Chambourcin'	mid	medium	good–excellent
'Chancellor'	mid	medium	good–excellent
'Cynthiana' ('Norton')	late	medium	good–excellent
'DeChaunac'	mid	very hardy	good
'Léon Millot'	very early	hardy	good
'Maréchal Foch'	very early	very hardy	fair
'Rougeon'	mid	medium	good
'Steuben'	late	medium	good

Table and Juice Cultivars

The eastern table grapes deserve special mention. Though seedless table grapes that perform well in cooler climates have been around for at least 20 years (including such older cultivars as 'Interlaken' and 'Lakemont'), they are a fairly well-kept secret. It is hard to beat the flavor of a 'Canadice' grape, full of the aromatic *labrusca*-type flavors and rounded off with just enough sweetness. The fruit of 'Remailly' looks just like that of 'Thompson Seedless'—an elongated, large green berry in large clusters—but the flavor is far superior. 'Remailly' is not just a sweet berry, it is a berry with character. Many of these seedless berries have thicker, tougher skins that slip off the berry, a trait referred to as "slip skin." Don't like that? Try 'Einset', which forms a dark pink berry with a crisp texture and nonslip skin. Pay close attention to the hardiness ratings in the cultivar table (Table 6.2). It will be the most limiting factor in your selection of a seedless table grape. All the cultivars listed here are selections of the North American native *Vitis labrusca*.

SEEDLESS RED

'Canadice' (Plate 25). Relatively winter-hardy pink grape with a wonderful aromatic flavor. Clusters are small to medium, and vines can be very productive. Because the berries grow tight in the cluster, 'Canadice' is particularly susceptible to some fruit rots.

'Einset'. Good hardiness and pink to red, seedless fruit; flavor is strawberry-like and unusual. Berries are more oval in shape than those of 'Canadice', and they have a crisper texture and nonslip skin. Plant is susceptible to fungal diseases, but it has great promise if diseases are controlled.

'Reliance'. Fruit has a sweet *labrusca* ('Concord'-like) flavor, with flesh of a melting texture. The berries are large and quite round but do not always color well. They may crack in wet seasons.

'Suffolk Red'. An older cultivar that produces fairly large clusters of small, delightfully flavored fruit. Clusters tend to be loose, a good trait for disease avoidance, but not always the most attractive-looking cluster. Winter injury can be a problem in northern climes.

'Vanessa'. Excellent quality grape, from Canada. Vine is only moderate in vigor, though it is particularly hardy. Seed remnant is usually large and soft. Flavor is mild and fruity; clusters well filled. Among the best of the seedless grapes.

SEEDLESS WHITE

'Himrod'. Produces large bunches of small, spherical white fruit with excellent flavor. Cane girdling can increase berry size and cluster fullness. May develop small or loose clusters.

'Interlaken'. An early ripening cultivar with a strong grape flavor. Develops clusters that are usually small and often loose. Birds nail these early cultivars.

'Lakemont'. Milder in flavor than 'Himrod'. Tends to overproduce, and bunch rot can be a problem. Often develops loose clusters.

'Marquis'. Large-clustered, large-fruited white grape with excellent flavor. Not widely tested, but very promising.

'Remailly'. Large clusters bear large, elongated berries with crisp texture and nonslip skins. Clusters can be damaged by exposure to direct sunlight. Flavor is more neutral than that of most eastern seedless cultivars.

'Skookum'. A recent release from Canada, this cultivar has not been sufficiently tested in the United States. The name means "large" in Chinook trade language. Reported to have good fruit size and delicate flavor, with a high degree of vigor. Yields in Canada have consistently been higher than those of 'Himrod', 'Interlaken', or 'Lakemont'.

'Sooke'. Another recent release from Canada. 'Sooke' is a Coastal Salish word that is the name of a coastal town on Vancouver Island. As with 'Skookum', yields are reported to be quite high, and winter hardiness is reportedly comparable to medium-hardy cultivars such as 'Seyval' (a white wine grape). Flavor is mild and delicate.

SEEDLESS BLUE/PURPLE

'Glenora'. Delicately flavored berries with a tender skin. Quite cold tender.

'Mars'. Can develop soft seed traces when grown in cooler climates.

SEEDED WHITE

'Golden Muscat'. For the connoisseur of grapes. Produces very large clusters of large, amber-colored grapes. Flavor is complex, combining the flavors of the fox grape *(Vitis labrusca)* and the European Muscat. Requires a particularly long ripening season.

'Niagara' (Plate 26). A standard for the industry. Produces large berries on well-developed clusters. Makes a nice white juice or jelly with 'Concord'-like flavor, but without the staining capacity. It fruits a bit earlier than 'Concord' and is not quite as cold hardy.

SEEDED BLUE/PURPLE

'Alden'. A reddish blue cultivar with large clusters of large, firm berries. Cluster thinning is necessary to increase compactness and to aid uniform ripening. Berries have mild *labrusca* and Muscat flavors.

'Beta'. Dark blue berry is small and seedy, with a strong 'Concord'-like flavor. Seems to have good disease resistance, too. Can be grown in cooler (but not terribly cold) regions where other grapes cannot survive the winter. New England only.

'Bluebell'. Later than 'Beta', but has large fruit and more attractive clusters. Best for fresh eating. Can be grown in cooler (but not terribly cold) regions where other grapes cannot survive the winter. Warm regions of New England only.

'Buffalo'. Loose clusters and a fruity *labrusca* flavor. Susceptible to powdery mildew. Brittle rachises can also be a problem.

'Concord'. The standard juice grape for the Great Lakes industries. Large berries with rich flavor and slip-skins. Well adapted and easy to grow.

'Steuben'. Bluish black grapes form on long, compact clusters. Very attractive. Flavor is sweet and spicy, and vines are hardy and vigorous. Great for the home garden for its multiple uses: fresh eating, wine, juice, or jam.

Wine Grape Cultivars

WHITE

'Aurore'. Fruit matures early, extending the wine grape season. Vine is vigorous and productive. Bird damage and fruit rot can be a problem. Though not of great quality, the wine is used for blending.

'Catawba'. North American native with good adaptation to local conditions. Used for dessert wines and occasionally a champagne-type drink.

'Cayuga White' (Plate 27). Grows well and produces a dry wine that can be made in many styles. Well-adapted and disease resistant, but can have problems with new shoot breakage in windy sites.

'Chardonel'. A French-American hybrid developed at Cornell University to fill the niche of a more cold-tolerant Chardonnay-type wine grape.

'Chardonnay'. One of the great European wine grapes. Susceptible to bird predation and fruit cracking after heavy rains.

'Delaware'. Forms small clusters and berries with a mild flavor of the American *labrusca* species. May crack with too much rain. Not overly vigorous, so should be planted on fertile soils.

'Gewürztraminer'. A European cultivar famous in the French region of Alsace. The wine has a wonderful spicy quality. North American growers often have problems getting a consistent crop from year to year. Plant is often overly vigorous, resulting in shaded fruit.

'Melody'. Very productive, vigorous vine that produces mild-flavored fruit for a neutral-tasting wine that is excellent for blending. Good disease resistance.

'Muscat Ottonel'. Used for a dessert-type wine. Very rich and pungent.

'Niagara'. Strong grape flavor. For wines with a *labrusca* flavor, this cultivar is preferred.

'Seyval'. Widely planted wine grape east of the Rocky Mountains. Wine can be thin, but it can be improved by certain wine-making techniques. Very susceptible to *Botrytis* rot, and tends to fruit prematurely. Remove fruit for the first year of growth.

'Traminette'. Cold hardiness is better than that of its parent 'Gewürztraminer', but its wine does not have as spicy a flavor. Good in areas where conditions are too cold for 'Gewürztraminer'. Plants are not particularly productive. Moderate disease resistance.

'Vidal'. Very productive white grape. Tends to overcrop and crop prematurely. Remove flower clusters in early years, and thin fruit annually. A standard French-American hybrid that makes a good dry white table wine.

'Vignoles'. Makes a nice, spicy dessert or late-harvest wine. Well adapted culturally, but fairly susceptible to disease. Vines are moderately vigorous. Late bloom avoids spring frosts.

'White Riesling'. The classic wine of Alsace. Can be made in a sweet or drier style. Plant tends to be susceptible to disease, particularly *Botrytis*. Though cold tender, it is among the hardier of the European *(Vitis vinifera)* cultivars. Fairly late to mature.

RED

'Cabernet Franc'. Though rarely grown as a varietal wine in Europe, this cultivar has performed well in the eastern and midwestern United States. Wine quality approaches that of 'Cabernet Sauvignon', but plants are better adapted and fruit much earlier.

'Cabernet Sauvignon'. The classic red wine grape of France. Often difficult to grow and highly susceptible to disease. Late season may limit production in colder regions.

'Chambourcin' (Plate 28). Makes a dark red wine with lots of tannin and a hint of black pepper or spiciness.

'Chancellor'. Good to excellent wine quality, but clusters are quite susceptible to downy mildew, and foliage to powdery mildew.

'Cynthiana'. Also known as 'Norton', 'Cynthiana' is the only wine grape cultivar selected from the species *Vitis aestivalis*. With medium hardiness and a fairly long growing season, it makes a dark, complex wine that has been called the "Zinfandel of the east." Crop load and vigor need to be controlled.

'DeChaunac'. Like 'Chambourcin', a very dark red wine grape with lots of tannin.

'Léon Millot'. Produces very early, blackish grapes. More vigorous than 'Foch', a sister seedling and close relative.

'Maréchal Foch'. Makes a fruity, light red table wine. Like many early cultivars, it is highly susceptible to bird predation. Medium vigor.

'Norton'. See 'Cynthiana'.

'Rougeon'. Often inconsistent yield if not grown on rootstocks.

'Steuben'. Makes a light, semi-sweet wine, similar to red Zinfandel. Cropping can be erratic.

Muscadine Grapes

Muscadine grapes are suitable for growing only in the south-central and southeastern United States.

'Albermarle'. Medium-sized black berries borne on a vine with medium hardiness. Self-fertile.

'Carlos'. Bronze fruit that is small to medium in size. Plant is very hardy and productive. The leading cultivar for processing in the south-central U.S. It is self-fertile.

'Cowart'. Medium-sized, black fruit. Plant is productive, though of only moderate vigor. Self-fruitful. Midseason.

'Darlene'. Very vigorous plant with large, midseason fruit.

'Doreen'. Bears bronze fruit late in the season. Very productive with medium-sized berries. Plant is self-fertile.

'Fry'. Bronze fruit is large. Plant is productive and of high quality. Plant is pistillate (has only female flowers) and requires a male of another cultivar for pollination. Midseason.

'Jumbo'. Extremely large, black fruit. Vine has medium vigor. Plant is pistillate (has only female flowers) and requires a male of another cultivar for pollination.

'Nesbitt'. Midseason. Fruit is black, plants are self-fertile. High quality.

'Southland'. Medium-sized, black fruit borne on a vine of medium vigor. Self-fertile.

'Sugargate'. Early, black fruit has excellent flavor and is very sweet. Moderate yields. Plant is pistillate (has only female flowers) and requires a male of another cultivar for pollination.

'Summit'. Large fruit is bronze and very sweet. Early and very productive. Plant is pistillate (has only female flowers) and requires
a male of another cultivar for pollination

HOW TO GROW GRAPES: PLANTING
THROUGH HARVEST

Site Selection and Preparation

Grapevines are broadly adapted to a variety of soils, thriving and
producing fruit on a surprising range of types and pH's. The American grapes tend to favor a lower pH (5.0–6.0) and can be found in
rich forest soil, slightly acidic soils, and sandy soils. The European
and French hybrid grapes—which are used primarily for wine grape
production in climes that are not conducive (for example, too cold
or too wet) to growing European grapes—prefer a more neutral pH
of 6.0–7.0, but these grapes, too, grow on soils ranging from those
that look like little more than chunks of rock to sandy soils to more
typical agronomic soils. As usual, soil testing is the vital first step,
followed by amendment of the soil according to the recommendations before putting the plants in the ground. The soil should be
tested and amended a year prior to planting.

Probably the most important issue when selecting a site for
grapes is the temperature of the site in winter. Grapes tend to be
much more cold tender than most of the other plants in this book,
though American cultivars such as 'Concord' and 'Niagara' thrive in
most locations of the eastern and midwestern United States. Eval-
uation criteria for site temperature are outlined in the section on
"Cultivar Selection."

Planting and Establishment

Grapes may be purchased as rooted cuttings (referred to as "own-
rooted" plants) or as grafted plants. Both types are usually offered as
bare-root dormant plants, which should be planted in the spring as
soon as the soil can be worked. Only the European grapes (*Vitis*

vinifera and its cultivars) require grafting, since they are susceptible to the root louse known as phylloxera, which is ubiquitous in most North American soils. Some French-American hybrids also need to be grown on rootstocks, not for phylloxera resistance but to increase uniformity among the individual plants.

Grapevines should be planted in a large hole with the roots 4 to 6 inches (10–15 cm) below the soil surface. Prune off damaged roots and spread the remainder within the planting hole. Each plant should be pruned back to one cane with two to three nodes. After shoot growth begins and danger of spring frost has passed, remove all but the two strongest shoots. Be sure to keep the new vines watered and weeded, and remove all flower clusters in the first year. On some French-American hybrids, the flower clusters are extremely prolific and should be partially removed in the second year as well, leaving about one cluster per lateral.

Remember that your first goal is to establish the plant. A well-established grapevine that is well adapted to its climate will produce fruit for 50 years or more. Vines can be staked as needed, and the desired trellis system can be erected in the summer or the fall. How the plants are supported is up to the individual grower, of course, and the grape plant adapts graciously to most forms. Several common trellis systems are described later under "Pruning and Training Systems." Insect and disease pests should be monitored and, if necessary, controlled during the first year and subsequent years.

Plant Nutrition and Fertilization

Two to three weeks after planting, apply 2 ounces (56 grams) of 33-0-0 fertilizer per plant, taking care to keep the fertilizer 1 foot (30 cm) away from the vine. In subsequent years, apply 4, 6, or 8 ounces (112–224 grams) of 33-0-0, or 1 to 2 pounds (450–900 grams) of 10-10-10 fertilizer, per plant before the buds start to swell in the spring. If the vines are too vigorous, omit nitrogen for 1 or 2 years. Test the soil periodically (every 3 to 5 years), and maintain the soil pH between 5 and 7.

Propagation

Grapes are easily propagated from dormant cane cuttings. To propagate your plants, collect dormant wood (pencil thickness, exposed to full sun) in December and store it in a cold, but not freezing, place until spring, making sure to note which end of the cuttings is up—the cuttings will not root if put in the soil upside down. In the spring, place the cutting two nodes deep in friable, moist, well-drained soil, and keep them watered. Rooting generally will occur in 4 to 8 weeks or so. Transplant to the desired site the following spring. In vineyard situations with such fox grape cultivars as 'Catawba', 'Concord', or 'Niagara', I have often trained a long cane 6 to 8 feet (1.8–2.4 m) from the vine, buried a node, and propagated a new vine right there. (A U-shaped piece of wire can be used to hold the cane in place initially.) Few plants allow you the luxury of such easy propagation.

Pruning and Training Systems

Grapevines can be grown to conform to numerous shapes—arbors, fences, and decorative trellises are only a few of the possibilities. Since many home gardeners may opt for less traditional training systems, a few general principles should be kept in mind when pruning and training your grapevines. As with all fruit crops, this primary pruning should be done in the dormant season.

1. The grapevine should be trained to reasonably fill the structure but not become overgrown. This is easier said than done, since initially the vine grows fairly slowly, but as it matures, it may become a monster of vegetation. One to two layers of leaves for any area on the canopy is best for flower bud and fruit development.

2. Mature grapevines, by their nature, produce much more wood than they can support. Think of the wild grapevine growing in the forest: it produces a huge amount of wood just to climb up to the sunlight. Your garden grapevines will not need to do that, but they still produce much more wood than is necessary or de-

sirable. Typically during dormant pruning you need to remove as much as 90 percent of the new growth on a mature grapevine. Plan on leaving about three or four buds per foot of cordon (the horizontal trunk on a grapevine) length. Dormant pruning is usually done in late winter or early spring (February or March in Pennsylvania).

3. Grapes bear their fruit on one-year-old wood. Figure 6.1 shows the shoot that is formed from a single bud on a one-year-old cane.

4. Different grape cultivars have different growth habits. The canes of American cultivars tend to grow in a willowy, downward direction, whereas those of the European cultivars and many French-American hybrids tend to grow directly up. Choose your training system with this in mind.

5. Grapevines vary considerably in their vigor, due to both inherent (genetic) and environmental factors. Because of this variation, it is difficult to make exact recommendations as to how many buds (how large a crop) to leave on the vine in any given year. Vigorous vines can support and ripen a larger load of fruit than less vigorous vines. In other words, you can leave more buds for next year's fruit development on a big and robust vine than you can on a little waif of a thing. Makes sense. Therefore, you need to make a judgment about how many buds to leave during pruning based on how much growth the plant achieved in the previous growing season, which can be estimated by the amount of wood you have to remove during dormant pruning. As a general rule, plants that are relatively weak growing should have 2 buds per foot of cordon (row) or 30 buds per plant retained, whereas vigorous vines should have 3 to 4 buds per foot of cordon or 40 to 45 buds per plants retained. This concept is called "balanced pruning" because it balances the crop for next season with last season's growth.

Remember that although our methods of pruning and training are based on science and experimentation, much of grape pruning relies on experience and, for lack of a better word, art. These instructions seem a little befuddling at first glance, but as you engage in the process of pruning, you will understand them more fully and come to appreciate the time spent in your vineyard in winter, in sweet anticipation of the summer to come.

By way of guidance, some traditional training systems employed by commercial and backyard viticulturists (grape growers) are described here. All the figures illustrating the various trellis systems depict a vine in the early spring after dormant pruning.

High-wire cordon (Figure 6.2, Plate 23). American cultivars such as 'Concord' or 'Niagara' tend to produce shoots that grow in a downward direction, so it generally makes sense to put the permanent horizontal branch (the cordon) on a high wire and let the plant drape toward the ground. In the high-wire cordon system, also known as the Hudson River Umbrella, a single horizontal wire is secured at a height of 6 feet (1.8 m), and another is placed at a 3-foot (1-m) height. The lower wire will be used to hold the vine up during early training, and later, after the plant is trained, it will only be used to secure the trunk in place.

In training a vine to this system, select two strong canes and train them up to the top wire; then, as the canes grow, place them along the top wire, in opposite directions. Be careful not to wrap the canes around the wires, since they will expand in girth over time and can girdle themselves on the wire. It is better to tie the canes to the top wire at first. They will eventually send out tendrils to secure themselves to the wire, but they will need a little help initially. Make sure that you keep an eye on the string that is securing the canes to the wire, since the string can also girdle the canes as they grow. Cordons from one vine should not overlap with those of adjacent vines. Ideally, you would like to train up the first two canes in the first year of growth, but realistically it often takes two years to get the cordons trained to the upper wire. Have patience—they will eventually get there, provided that they are in the appropriate climate. As is the case with growing many other perennial small-fruit crops, your training and patience in the first years will pay off in future decades.

Once the cordons are established, they should be pruned so that you are left with several shoots (spurs) that are five to seven buds long, for a total of 30 to 45 buds per plant, depending on the vigor of the plant, as discussed earlier. These spurs should be spaced 6 to 12 inches (15–30 cm) apart on the cordon. In addition, for each seven-bud spur, leave one two-bud renewal spur. The smaller spurs will provide the shoots for the following year.

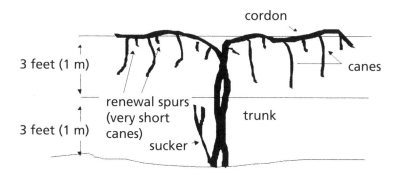

Figure 6.2. High-wire cordon (Hudson River Umbrella).

The fruiting shoots will hang like a curtain in groups from the spurs that originate from the arms along the top wire. Shoots should be carefully separated and placed vertically downward from the top wire for a distance of 18 to 24 inches (45–60 cm). Positioning should be carried out as soon as the shoots have toughened, usually two to three weeks after peak bloom (when 50 percent of the fused petals have fallen). Extreme care must be exercised during shoot positioning, as any shoot lost at this time can result in a poorly filled trellis.

In subsequent years, select new canes and leave new renewal spurs from the shoots that developed from the previous year's buds. Remember to balance the number of buds with the vigor of the plant: a higher number of buds should be left on vigorous plants than on weaker ones.

Low-wire cordon (Figure 6.3). The idea behind the low-wire, or low-bilateral, cordon training system is similar to that of the Hudson River system just described. The low-wire system, however, is used for grapevines that have a tendency to grow up rather than down, as is the case with the European grapes and most of the French-American hybrids. If you put these forms on a Hudson River system, the shoots would grow up from the top, 6-foot (1.8-m) high wire—not a good thing. The low-wire cordon system takes advantage of the plant's natural tendency to grow up, allowing the shoots from the permanent cordons on the lower, 3-foot (1-m) high wire to fill in the trellis from the bottom up. Of course, gravity tends to work against you, so as the shoots grow up, you need to "help" them by using catch wires that sandwich the new shoots between them as they grow up. Usually, two sets of catch wires are adequate.

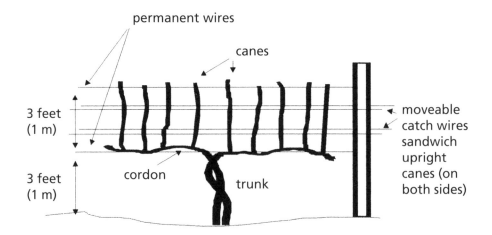

Figure 6.3. Low-wire cordon.

Umbrella Kniffin system (Figure 6.4). In the Umbrella Kniffin system, the plant's trunk is brought up and tied to a 6-foot (1.8-m) high wire, with four or more canes left near the top of the trunk (head) bearing a total of 50 to 60 buds. All other wood except for two renewal spurs (short canes of one or two buds) is removed from near the head. After pruning to the desired number of buds, retie the trunk to the top wire. The canes should be bent rather sharply over the top wire so that the outer bark cracks, and the tips are tied to the lower, 3-foot (1-m) high wire. The renewal buds will develop into shoots that probably will not be fruitful but should be allowed to grow. They are there to be used for next year's fruiting canes. The buds on the main canes will form fruiting shoots that do not need to be tied because the vine has already been trained. Some of those shoots may be well located and can replace the original canes the following season, in which case the renewal shoots are not needed.

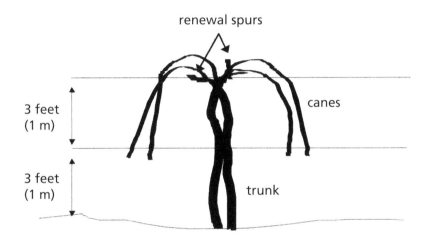

Figure 6.4. Umbrella Kniffin trellis.

Four-Cane Kniffin system (Figure 6.5). The Four-Cane Kniffin system is a variation on the Umbrella Kniffin system in which the canes are selected from both the top and the middle of the trunk. It is most often used on low-vigor cultivars. The lower canes are shaded by the upper canes, and the lower ones often produce later-maturing fruit that may be lower in quantity and/or quality than that on the cordons trained on the top wire.

Other training systems. The production of 'Thompson Seedless' grapes in California and similar climates requires cane-pruning systems, since the buds closest to the base are not fruitful, yet those are

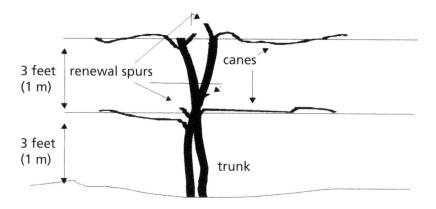

Figure 6.5. Four-Cane Kniffin trellis.

the only buds that are left on the vine in cordon systems. If you trained 'Thompson Seedless' to, say, a low-wire cordon, you would get a lot of leaves and no fruit. The most commonly employed training system for this cultivar is head training (Figure 6.6). Head training involves tying the main trunk to a vertical post.

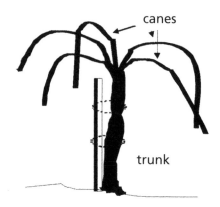

Figure 6.6. Head training.

Another common training system is the Geneva Double Curtain (Figure 6.7). This system is good for extremely vigorous vines since it allows the plant to achieve its potential yield in a relatively small space. Weaker growing vines would not fill such a large trellis system.

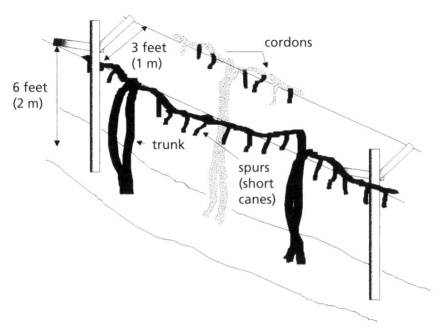

Figure 6.7. Geneva Double Curtain.

Harvest and Postharvest

Grapes should be harvested when they taste good or are ready for wine making. The first criterion applies to table grapes. You will notice that they change color (a stage called verasion) several weeks before they obtain maximum sweetness. The eastern seedless cultivars will develop not only sugars but all sorts of complex flavors as well. Remember to be patient and let the grapes hang, unless you see rot beginning and fear losing them. They will pucker your mouth for some time after they color.

Grapes for wine making need to obtain a sugar content of 22 percent (measured on the Brix scale) to ferment to an alcohol level of 10 to 12 percent, which is normal for table wine. Unfortunately, most mouths cannot measure sugar percentage, so you will need to purchase a refractometer (the expensive route) or a hygrometer, which is much cheaper and perfectly adequate for this purpose. In cooler climates it is not always possible to ripen the grapes to 22 percent sugar. If your season is too short, don't worry. You can add sugar to the wine to make up the difference. The references section at the back of this book lists a few helpful books for the hobbyist wine maker.

Grapes usually keep well in the refrigerator for a week or two after harvest. They vary considerably in their susceptibility to rots, however. As with all small fruits, refrigeration is crucial for maximizing shelf-life. Grapes also make wonderful juices, jams, jellies, and pies, in addition to wine. Grapes that are called "wine grapes" also make some lovely jams and juices, so don't hesitate to experiment in the kitchen.

NICHES IN THE LANDSCAPE

Because grapevines can be trained to any form, their use in the landscape is limited only by your imagination, innovation, and engineering. Traditional uses for grape plants include growing them along fences, rose trellises, and arbors—they provide a great source of shade under an arbor—but you can also train them to any imaginable shape. For example, three trunks can be loosely braided and trained into a tree form. I have one great vine of the cultivar 'Cayuga', an extremely vigorous French-American hybrid, trained up to a second-story trellis, where it provides a screen on our small bedroom deck. The privacy afforded by the trellised grape allows us to drink wine in the evenings unnoticed by the world or our suburban neighbors. To create this screen of vines, I removed all the lower branches and trained the vine over 2 years to reach the second-story trellis, which is about 8 feet (2.4 m) off the ground. The lower portion of the plant consists of a couple of trunks with all the laterals removed, and I trained several higher laterals along the screen on the second floor. This required some ladder work, particularly in the first few years, but now I simply remove any newly sprouted branches on the lower portion of the vine and prune the upper portion from the deck.

Growing grapes as landscape plants does warrant some caveats. Using cultivars that are well adapted to your situation and have relatively good disease resistance is the easiest approach, but even so, most grapevines will require some fungicide application in wet years. If you fail to do this, the grapes are prone to rot—and if the vine is growing on an arbor above a table or bench, rotten grapes hanging over your head is not exactly appealing. Even less appealing are the yellow jackets that will be attracted by the rotting fruits if you do not remove them promptly. This is obviously less of a problem where the grapevines are trained to a fence or a trellis, but most backyard gardeners want to enjoy the fruit from their plants, so it is well worth the effort of fungicide applications.

Also be aware that grapes, along with blackberries and raspberries, can be Japanese-beetle magnets. Applications of a labeled material such as malathion or Sevin (carbaryl) may be in order if beetles become a problem. Fortunately, Japanese beetle infestations usually come well in advance of fruit ripening, so you should have plenty of time between spray application and harvest. For specific recommendations for insecticide sprays, consult your local extension office.

PESTS IN THE PLANTING

So, what pests are you likely to encounter in your grape plantings? The primary pests are probably birds (especially for early bearing cultivars) and fungal diseases. Most grapes require some fungicide application, particularly in wet years. Insect pests can be devastating, but they tend to be isolated, both in location and year. Alas, for birds, the only solution is netting. Be ready to net the plants at veraison (when grapes start to change color). Netting is a pain, but it's better than losing your crop.

Many of the disease and insect pests that have been documented to plague grapes are outlined in Tables 6.3 and 6.4. For recommended chemical and cultural controls, contact your local extension office or consultants. Also be sure to read Chapter 1 of this book for extensive recommendations on controlling pests using cultural management.

Weeds

Weeds can always present a problem for small-fruit crops and should be controlled in the area around the base of the plants. However, because grapes are trained high and are deep-rooted, weeds are not nearly the challenge to grapes that they are to the more diminutive berry crops. They can be controlled by hand pulling or hoeing, and if grasses become a problem, the herbicide Poast (sethoxydim) can be used, as described in Chapter 3.

Diseases

As mentioned earlier, when you grow grapes, you should simply expect some disease problems in wet years. The best way to minimize disease infestations (other than by spray applications) is to keep the plants well pruned so that air circulates well through the canopy. The importance of this simple cultural management technique cannot be overemphasized. Think of the mildew that grows on your shower curtain. Nothing encourages it like the still, moist air that surrounds the curtain after you take a shower (if you're like me, you like long, hot ones that steam the place up); moving that moist air out of the shower area limits the growth of the mildew. Likewise, when the leaf canopy on a plant is too thick, the moisture inside cannot get out because air circulation is limited. All the wind in the world may not be able to penetrate the layers of leaves on an unpruned grape canopy, thus making an ideal environment for many fungi. Allow air to circulate by creating a more open canopy, and the fungi all of the sudden are not so comfortable. (Don't worry. They'll probably find someone else's grapes to enjoy.) And fungi are not good "sharers"—once in your canopy, they can quickly decimate the entire crop.

Table 6.3. Common Grape Diseases and Causal Organisms in the United States

Name of Disease	Plant Part Affected	Causal Organism
anthracnose	shoots, leaves, fruit	*Elsinoe ampelina* (fungus)
Armillaria root rot	trunks, cordons, canes, shoots, leaves, systemic	*Armillaria mellea* (fungus)
bitter rot	fruit	*Greeneria uvicola* (fungus)
black rot	canes, flowers, fruit, leaves	*Guignardia bidwellii* (fungus)
bunch rot, *Botrytis* blight	leaves, shoots, flowers, fruit	*Botrytis cinerea* (fungus)
downy mildew	canes, flowers, fruit, leaves	*Plasmopara viticola* (fungus)
Eutypa dieback	trunks, leaves, shoots, systemic	*Eutypa lata* (fungus)
macrophoma rot	fruit	*Botryosphaeria dothidea* (fungus)
Phomopsis cane, leaf, and fruit rot	canes, fruit, leaves, cordons	*Phomposis viticola* (fungus)
powdery mildew	canes, flowers, fruit, leaves	*Uncinula necator* (fungus)
ripe rot	fruit	*Colletotrichum gloeosporiodes* (fungus)
Verticillium wilt	leaves, shoots, canes,	*Verticillium dahliae* (fungus)
crown gall	trunks, cordons, roots	*Agrobacterium tumefaciens* (bacterium)
Pierce's disease	leaves, trunks, flowers, fruit, canes, systemic	*Xylella fastidiosa* (bacterium)
corky bark	systemic (causes an incompatibility to develop at the graft union)	virus transmitted by insects
fanleaf	systemic	virus transmitted in soil by certain nematodes of the genus *Xiphinema*
tomato black ringspot	systemic	virus carried by a nematode *(Longidorus elongatus)*

Black rot. The most common disease in the East and Midwest, black rot (caused by *Guignardia bidwellii*) can affect all parts of the vine. The fungus resides on old prunings and on berries that have dropped off and become "mummified" (dark, shriveled, and certainly not appetizing). Symptoms are circular, or somewhat angular, tan to brownish spots that appear on the leaves anytime during the growing season. These spots eventually develop a very light brown center, followed by the emergence of small, black pinpoints, which are the spore-bearing bodies of the fungus. You may only notice the symptoms on ripening fruit in the first year of black-rot infection, but take time to look at the plant earlier in the season. Infections can occur from bloom through the end of the season.

A combination of wet leaves and temperatures between 50 and 90°F (10–32°C) is optimal for fungal development. Along with thinning the canopy by pruning, all prunings and mummified berries, both on the plant and on the ground, should be removed from the area. If you have had problems with this disease in the past, or if you have a particularly rainy spring, start applying fungicide sprays early in the season—nip it in the bud, in other words. Specifics on spray applications for your area can be obtained through local extension consultants.

Bunch rot or *Botryris* blight. Bunch rot in grapes is caused by the same species of the fungus *Botrytis* that nails raspberries and strawberries with gray mold. *Botrytis cinerea* is not a picky fungus—it enjoys an enormous range of hosts and is ubiquitous the world over. Bunch rot disease favors temperatures between 60 and 70°F (16–21°C) and, like black rot, the presence of water. It has two primary fruit symptoms. Early in the spring, *Botrytis* will cause the buds and young fruit to turn brown and dry out. You may also see large, reddish-brown necrotic (dead) patches on the edges of some leaves. The second fruit symptom occurs from fruit ripening onward. Once the sugar content in the fruit is high enough, the fungus will cause it to rot. Cultivars that have compact fruit clusters suffer from this disease more than those with loose clusters. Infected white grapes will turn a tannish brown color, whereas darker grapes will take on more of a reddish cast. Eventually, the grayish-white mycelium (fungal mass) will take over the whole cluster. No question, you have lost the whole cluster once this guy gets going. Again, applying fungicides early in the season, during bloom, will do a lot to control the disease. The sprays are applied early enough that any residue will be long gone by the time you harvest your pristine, lovely fruit.

***Phomopsis* cane, leaf, and fruit rot.** Another fungal disease, the rot caused by *Phomopsis* is frequently seen in humid regions. Look for reddish spots that are about ¹⁄₁₆ inch (1–2 mm) in diameter on new shoots. If the infection is really bad, these lesions run together and form dark blotches that crack. Leaves will develop small, light green, irregular spots with dark centers. They may also pucker along the veins near the edge of the leaf, or the edge may be turned under. The stems of the clusters can also get lesions, which will damage water flow to the developing fruit. When the fruit is infected, it turns brown, looks sort of wet, and has black fruiting bodies on it; it eventually shrivels and drops. Early applications of fungicide are the key here.

General notes on rots. From the preceding discussions, it is probably becoming clear that several rots can cause grief for the backyard grower of grapes. These diseases are usually only a problem in especially wet years, but if you miss controlling them in the wet years, the inoculum from the diseases will take up residence in your vineyard and may cause problems even when the weather is not conspiring against you. To make matters worse, several other minor fungal diseases can affect our grapes from time to time, so disease control can get even more complicated. Take heart. The keys to prevention are keeping the plants well pruned, applying fungicides early in the season when it is wet, and staying on top of plant maintenance. A wonderful publication is also available for folks who are interested in pictures and more in-depth information on grape diseases: *Compendium of Grape Diseases* by R. C. Pearson and A. C. Goheen, published by the American Phytopathological Society.

Insects

A few insect pests affect grapes, but with the exception of Japanese beetles, I have had little trouble with insects on my backyard plantings.

Japanese beetles. If you have raspberries or roses in your garden, Japanese beetles will probably go for those crops first, but they are also fairly fond of grape leaves. See the discussion of Japanese beetles in Chapter 4 for control recommendations.

Grape berry moth. I have never seen grape berry moths *(Endopiza viteana)* on my home plantings or my research plots, but they can cause devastating damage on commercial vineyards. These tiny moths feed on buds, flowers, and newly set fruit. The second generation feeds on the berries themselves. If you see a reddish spot on the fruit, proceed with caution. Sometimes the red discoloration can extend over a fair portion of the green berry. Injured berries will ripen prematurely, split, and shrivel. This also opens up infection sites for the various rots. If the infestation is light, remove injured berries by hand. If you get a bad infestation, though, consult local extension personnel for pesticide recommendations.

Grape cane girdlers. These are small weevils (insects with snouts) that girdle the grape cane by chewing two rings of holes around the shoot several inches apart. These girdles are usually beyond the last grape cluster, so fruit is not lost. Canes that have been girdled will break off. If you see broken shoots hanging down from your vines, grape cane girdlers *(Ampeloglypter ater)* are the likely culprit. The broken shoots are most obvious in the early portion of the season. Cutting them off below the lower girdle, before the adult insects emerge in summer, should control the damage. If the infestation becomes too bad, call in the Marines . . . I mean, pesticides. As usual, local recommendations are best.

Phylloxera and erineum mites. Though often found in grape plantings, the phylloxera root louse *(Daktulosphaira vitifoliae)* and eri-

Table 6.4. Major Grape Insect and Mite Pests in the United States

Common Name of Pest	Scientific Name of Pest	Pest Class
climbing cutworms	many species; *Amathes c-nigrum* most common in eastern United States	attacks buds
grape flea beetle	*Haltica chalybea*	attacks buds
fruit fly	*Drosophila melanogaster*	attacks flowers and fruit
grape berry moth	*Endopiza viteana*	attacks flowers and fruit
grape blossom midge	*Contarinia johnsoni*	attacks flowers and fruit
grape curculio	*Graponium inadequalis*	attacks flowers and fruit
rose chaffer	*Macrodactylus subspinosus*	attacks flowers and fruit
European red mite	*Panonychus ulmi*	attacks leaves and shoots
grape cane gallmaker	*Ampeloglypter sesostris*	attacks leaves and shootsi
grape cane girdler	*Ampeloglypter ater*	attacks leaves and shoots
grape curculio	*Craponius inaequalis*	attacks leaves and shoots
grape erineum mite	*Colomerus vitis*	attacks leaves and shoots
grape flea beetle	*Altica chalybea*	attacks leaves and shoots
grape leafhopper	*Erythroneura*	attacks leaves and shoots
grape phylloxera	*Daktulosphaira vitifoliae*	attacks leaves and shoots
grape tumid gallmaker	*Janetiella brevicauda*	attacks leaves and shoots
grapevine aphid	*Macrosiphum illinoisensis*	attacks leaves and shoots
Japanese beetle	*Popillia japonica*	attacks leaves and shoots
two-spotted spider mite	*Tetranychus urticae*	attacks leaves and shoots
grape cane borer	*Amphicerus bicaudatus*	attacks trunks, cordons, and canes
grape phylloxera	*Daktulosphaira vitifoliae*	attacks crowns and/or roots
grape root borer	*Vitacea polistiformis*	attacks crowns and/or roots
grape rootworm	*Fidia viticida*	attacks crowns and/or roots
root knot nematode	*Meloidogyne incognita*	attacks crowns and/or roots

neum mites *(Colomerus vitis)* have to be present in very high numbers before they do any real harm to the plant. I include them here mainly because they are so alarming to see. Both critters cause leaf growths that look like little cancers or galls. The gall of the erineum mite blisters on the top surface of the leaf and forms a felty brown patch beneath the blister on the underside of the leaf. Phylloxera leaf infections cause spherical galls that protrude on the lower surfaces of the leaves. Though the root form of phylloxera is devastating to nonresistant plants, the leaf form only makes the leaves look bad. A good rule of thumb is that if 15 percent of the shoots become infected, you may want to spray. If you have a light infestation, by all means remove and destroy the infected leaves. That removes the creature living inside the gall and allows you to view your plants without horror.

FREQUENTLY ASKED QUESTIONS

My grapes always look fine until they are about to ripen, then they get a mold on them. What's the problem? Several fungi attack grapes. The most common ripe rot is *Botrytis*, but there are several others (as discussed under "Diseases"). The most important thing to remember is that wet weather contributes enormously to the development of fungi. The solution? In particularly wet years, apply fungicides (follow local recommendations), and in all years keep your grapevines well pruned to avoid moister-than-necessary conditions within the canopy. Also, pull out any tall weeds that are growing up into the canopy. You will be amazed at how much longer the grape canopy stays wet when it is overly dense, whether a result of its own leaves or those of an intruder.

Why are my grape clusters so straggly looking? Some cultivars tend to produce long, thin clusters, including 'Concord Seedless', 'Himrod', and 'Suffolk Red'. Straggly clusters often occur as a result of poor pollination. Think back to when the grapes were in bloom: Was it a cool, wet period? If so, pollen tube growth may have been inhibited, so less fruit was set than usual. Another cause of straggly fruit can be boron deficiency. If you suspect this, have a tissue (leaf or leaf pedicel) sample taken for analysis. Be sure to sample the tissue, not the soil, since soil analyses are often less telling for boron.

Is it worth keeping the old abandoned vineyard (or grapevine) on the property I just bought? If so, how should I manage it? The first thing to do is determine if the grapevine bears grapes that you want. People have varied preferences—some like seedless table grapes, some wine grapes, some the classic 'Concord'. Ask the people you bought the place from, or sample the grapes yourself. If you decide you want to keep the vine, and it is growing on its own roots, the best approach is to remove one-half to three-quarters of the vine in the first year, preferably when it is dormant. You can do some one-cut pruning—that is, remove the entire top portion of the plant—but this will encourage canes that are excessively large in diameter. These so-called bull canes are overly vigorous and difficult to manage. As it is, you will force plenty of new growth in the first season after removing half of the vine. As the canes grow out during that first season, select a couple of strong, upright-growing canes and tie them to your trellis. Then, during dormant pruning the following winter, remove the rest of the old plant, and prune and train according to the directions provided earlier in this chapter.

I have a cultivar that I don't want. Is there anything I can do with the existing plant? Grapes can be successfully top-grafted to new cultivars, and you can do this as long as the root portion is in good shape. Greatest success is achieved when cleft grafts are used. Obtain disease-free, pencil-sized wood of the cultivar you desire (called the scion), and graft in the early spring. Note that grafting is both an art and a science. Many folks fail many times before they get the hang of it. For a good reference on grafting, see *Plant Propagation* (Hartmann et al., 1997), listed in the reference section at the back of this book.

Why didn't my grapevine produce any fruit this year? There are several likely culprits for this problem. One is frost. If a frost comes when the flowers are open, it can damage all the flowers and prevent them from forming. Cold temperatures, too, can injure the primary and secondary buds, leaving only the vegetative tertiary bud to develop. It could have been worse—the cold could have killed the entire plant. Another possible culprit is excessive nitrogen, which can cause plants to become extremely vegetative. Once the plant becomes overly vegetative, it pours its energy into leaf production instead of fruit production. I have only seen this happen on a few French-American hybrids, but if you have eliminated the other potential causes, you may want to check your nitrogen levels.

Why do the leaves have funny-looking growths all over them? Two insects can cause abnormal galls (usually about ⅛–¼ inch in diameter). The first is the aerial form of phylloxera *(Daktulosphaira vitifoliae)*, the root louse that decimated the European grape-growing industry in the mid-nineteenth century. Although this pest can be devastating if you have susceptible vines, the aerial infections usually are not a serious problem (other than cosmetically), and if the vines are resistant or growing on resistant rootstocks, you do not have to worry about the root louse. The other critter that can cause abnormal leaf growths is the erineum mite *(Colomerus vitis)*. Again, though ugly or even alarming to look at, this mite rarely causes significant damage. Remove and dispose of the afflicted leaves, and things will be fine.

Very rarely you will come across another insect problem on your grape leaves: the galls caused by the grape tumid gallmaker *(Janetiella brevicauda)*. These galls are much bigger than those caused by phylloxera or erineum mites, deforming the entire leaf. They look more like cancerous growths and have a good bit of red pigmentation in them. Again, the best control is to remove and destroy the affected tissue.

RECOMMENDED GRAPE CULTIVARS BY REGION

The following lists suggest the cultivars most suitable for various regions of the United States; more descriptive information is given earlier in the chapter.

MID-ATLANTIC AND MIDWEST

Seedless Table Grapes
'Canadice'
'Einset'
'Himrod'
'Interlaken'
'Lakemont'
'Marquis'
'Reliance'
'Remailly'
'Suffolk Red'
'Vanessa'

Seeded Table Grapes
'Alden'
'Buffalo'
'Concord'
'Golden Muscat'
'Niagara'
'Steuben'

Wine Grapes
'Aurore' (white)
'Cabernet Franc' (red)
'Cabernet Sauvignon' (red)
'Cayuga White' (white)
'Chambourcin' (red)
'Chardonel' (white)
'Chardonnay' (white)
'Cynthiana' (red)
'DeChaunac' (red)
'Melody' (white)
'Riesling' (white)
'Seyval' (white)
'Traminette' (white)
'Vidal' (white)
'Vignoles' (white)

NEW ENGLAND

Grapes can only be grown in the warmest sites in New England.

Seedless Table Grapes
'Canadice'
'Reliance'

Seeded Table Grapes
'Beta'
'Bluebell'
'Delaware'
'Fredonia'

SOUTH CENTRAL

Seedless Table Grapes
'Mars'
'Reliance'

Red Wine Grape
'Cynthiana'

Muscadine Grapes
'Carlos'
'Cowart'
'Darlene'
'Doreen'
'Fry'
'Nesbitt'
'Sugargate'
'Summit'

SOUTHEAST

Seedless Table Grape
'Orlando Seedless'

Seeded Table Grapes
'Blanc Dubois'
'Blue Lake'
'Conquistador'
'Daytona'
'Lake Emerald'
'Stover'
'Suwannee'

Muscadine Grapes
'Albermarle'

'Cowart'
'Jumbo'
'Nesbitt'
'Southland'

PACIFIC NORTHWEST

Seedless Table Grapes
'Canadice'
'Einset'
'Himrod'
'Interlaken'
'Remailly'

'Suffolk Red'
'Venus'

Seeded Table Grapes
'Concord'
'Golden Muscat'
'New York Muscat'
'Niagara'

Wine Grapes
'Chardonnay' (white)
'Pinot Gris' (white)
'Pinot Noir' (red)
'Riesling' (white)

CHAPTER 7

Minor Crops

"Minor crops"—the term seems so judgmental. "By whose judgment?" asked my illustrious consort and spouse one day. By mine, of course. And by the extent to which they are grown. And though it should be remembered that most "major" horticultural crops were once minor—the ever-common blueberry was a complete novelty as recently as 60 years ago—most of these crops are minor for a specific reason. That is not to say they are without merit. I know folks who have 60 cultivars of gooseberries, for example, simply because they love gooseberries. To them, gooseberries are not minor, they are merely misunderstood or underappreciated.

The limitations of these crops may include slowness to fruit (my hardy kiwi planting was 6 years old before it bloomed for the first time), excessive thorniness (many of the gooseberries), bland flavor (gooseberries), and outrageous flavor that must be processed to be appreciated (black currants, elderberries). The point is that there are reasons why these crops haven't hit the big time. Of course, many of us are waiting to be discovered too, for all our thorns or tartness— perhaps that is part of the appeal of these interesting plants.

The other consideration that makes gooseberries, hardy kiwis, elderberries, and the others minor is our collective inexperience with them. For the most part, these guys have not been researched as thoroughly, so we do not know as much about them. It's an opportunity for you to learn more than the so-called experts.

I discuss in detail a number of these crops, and a section at the end of this chapter presents others that are "most minor." Often these fruits can only be obtained if one grows one's own. A challenge: Try growing something that you can't buy.

CURRANTS AND GOOSEBERRIES

FAMILY: SAXIFRAGACEAE, THE SAXIFRAGE FAMILY

PRIMARY SPECIES:

Ribes americanum Mill.—American black currant, wild currant
Ribes aureum Pursh.—golden currant
Ribes grossularia L.—English or European gooseberry
Ribes hirtellum Michx.—gooseberry
Ribes nigrum L.—black currant, European currant
Ribes odoratum H.—Buffalo currant, Missouri currant
Ribes rubrum L.—red currant, northern currant
Ribes sativum Syme—red currant, common currant, garden
   currant
Ribes uva-crispa L.—English or European gooseberry

Gooseberries and currants have enjoyed great popularity, particularly in Europe. In the 1800s, as many as 722 cultivars of gooseberry were available on the continent, and gooseberry clubs were established by enthusiasts. Most of the European cultivars were large fruited and sweet as a result of centuries of selection and breeding, whereas American types had less desirable flavor but more disease resistance. The gooseberries grown today are primarily hybrids of these two types, offering good flavor as well as varying degrees of resistance. Northern Europe is the main region of production.

Though seldom eaten fresh due to their tart flavor, currants (black, red, and white) make excellent jams and jellies. Some people say that if you let them hang on the bush long enough (or if you have a taste for the tart), currants are just fine for fresh eating, so feel free to give it a try. In any case, surely no fruit is more beautiful than red currants. They truly look like little jewels hanging on their hosts. I find the visual appeal reason enough to grow red currants (Plate 31).

Regarding Illegal Plants

There is often confusion as to the legality of growing gooseberries and currants, since up until 1966 a federal ban prohibited their production in the United States. The ban was established because gooseberries and currants can serve as alternate hosts to white pine blister rust *(Cronartium ribicola)*, a fungus that needs both *Ribes* and white pine *(Pinus strobus)* to complete its life cycle. After the federal legislation was rescinded in 1966, it was up to the states to decide whether to accept these potential Typhoid Marys in their provinces. The picture got even more complicated because counties and townships often made their own rulings as well. Many localities limited the import and/or growing of *Ribes* but later decided not to enforce the laws.

If you want to grow currants or gooseberries, first find out what the local ordinances are. If they do not prohibit growing *Ribes*, go ahead and plant. If you have white pines nearby, however, you should consider growing species or cultivars that are less susceptible to white pine blister rust. Black currant *(Ribes nigrum)* is by far the most susceptible, and for this reason many areas prohibit growing this species. Cultivars of black currant that are resistant to the blister rust fungus have been developed, including 'Consort' and 'Crusader'. Red and white currants are less susceptible, and gooseberry is the least susceptible. The issue of *Ribes* and the proliferation of white pine blister rust is currently being revisited by plant scientists. I would not be surprised to see more information available in the near future.

Plant Biology

Gooseberries and currants are woody perennial shrubs that reach a height of 3 to 6 feet (1–1.8 m) when mature. The two types are often considered together because they are so closely related, but there are some noteworthy differences between the species. The fruit of gooseberries are larger, ranging from pea-sized to the size of a large grape, and borne singly along the stems of the plant (Plate 30); most have a crisp texture. As mentioned earlier, even fruit wimps can eat these little morsels fresh, though gooseberries are often processed into jams or pies. Currant fruits are smaller (usually pea-sized or a little smaller), borne in small clusters, and have a more melting texture. They are also too tart for all but the most courageous palate, and adding sugar is a requirement for most folks. The black currants have some extremely strong flavors that many of us find unpalatable until the fruit has been processed. Gooseberry plants are spiny, though this characteristic varies with the cultivar, whereas currants are spineless. The two types of *Ribes* also differ in leaf shape, with gooseberries having fairly small, slightly frilly leaves, while currant leaves are much larger, with three distinct lobes and coarse serrations.

Unlike other fruiting plants, gooseberries and currants tolerate and even produce fruit in partial shade. Plants are self-fruitful and therefore do not require more than one cultivar for adequate pollination. An additional attribute of currants and gooseberries is that they are very winter hardy, tolerating temperatures as low as −22 to −31°F (−30 to −35°C).

Cultivar Selection

Prospective *Ribes* growers should consult with other producers in their area and/or contact local consultants for the most up-to-date information on cultivars for their location. Though I do not have a lot of experience with the various *Ribes* cultivars, I am lucky enough to live within a few hours of Ed Mashburn, executive secretary of the International Ribes Association. (For more information, see "References and Other Resources.")

In general, powdery mildew is less of a problem on currants compared to gooseberries, but currants are more susceptible to white pine blister rust (as discussed earlier). Choose your poison.

GOOSEBERRIES

The gooseberry cultivars listed here tend to weather powdery mildew and leaf spot diseases better than others. Those with a mostly North American background have more natural resistance but, unfortunately, also less interesting fruit flavors. In addition to those mentioned, several other European cultivars are available from specialty nurseries. The European types usually have larger and better flavored fruit than the American cultivars, but they generally are not as resistant to mildew.

'Achilles'. An old European cultivar that has fruit with great flavor, red color, and good size. It is unfortunately quite susceptible to the mildews and grows in a wide-spreading habit. Because of the mildew susceptibility, 'Achilles' should be grown only in open areas with good drainage.

'Downing'. Often used for commercial processing. Hardy and productive, it produces small green fruit that is, frankly, only useful for processing. The flavor is quite tart and quite abundant. Makes a beautiful chartreuse-colored jam. North American background.

'Glenndale'. An old and vigorous variety with serious spines, but also good disease resistance. The fruit is dark red and has good flavor. Also best for processing rather than out-of-hand eating. North American background.

'Hinnonmaki Red'. One of the best flavored and highest yielding gooseberries. True to its name, it is a deep red color. Some mildew resistance.

'Hinnonmaki Yellow'. Has performed well in trials in central Pennsylvania. The fruit is large and yellow and has good flavor. The bush is substantial.

'Hoening's Earliest'. An early, large, and vigorous plant. It also has formidable spines on the branches, but the fruit is quite large, yellow, and simply delicious. A word of warning, though. The fruit has little, brushlike spines on it, which may surprise you the first time you eat it. Learn to ignore them. The spines are quite soft, and the fruit flavor is worth the initial surprise. The plant yields well but is also somewhat susceptible to powdery mildew.

'Invicta'. A relatively new introduction that bears large green gooseberries. It is resistant to mildew and late frosts, and has ponderous spines. North American background.

'Pixwell'. The most commonly sold gooseberry cultivar. It is very productive, but the fruit is of fair quality. Similar to 'Downing', it is tart and useful mainly for processing. North American background.

'Poorman'. Red-fruited, large, and flavorful. 'Poorman' is the best American cultivar for the home garden. It forms a sturdy, vigorous, and thorny bush and is highly productive. North American background.

'Red Jacket'. A very strong, upright-growing plant with some mildew resistance. The spines are less obtrusive than some. Fruit is easy to harvest because it hangs well below the branches. It is of medium size and decent flavor.

RED CURRANTS

For most folks, red currants are not for fresh eating, but for eye-candy and for processing.

'Red Lake'. A vigorous, hardy, and productive cultivar. The good quality fruit is large and bright red when mature. The long-stemmed clusters are easy to pick.

'Red Start'. A relatively new release from England. Its primary advantage over 'Red Lake' is that it blooms later and yields fruit later, thus avoiding spring frosts in cooler regions.

'Wilder'. Very much like 'Red Lake'—high yielding and good quality berries—but 'Wilder' has greater resistance to leaf spot.

WHITE CURRANTS

'White Grape'. Produces light amber, large, mild-flavored fruit.

'White Imperial'. Purported to be a better cultivar than 'White Grape', but it is not as readily available from nurseries.

BLACK CURRANTS

A small story about black currants. I was touring the Plant Repository in Corvallis, Oregon, with a large group of my colleagues. A couple of them pulled me aside and asked if I had ever tasted black currants. I responded in the negative, and they practically dragged me to a bush in full fruit and said, "Boy, are you in for a treat!" I should have suspected their motives (they were too enthusiastic). The fruit has such a strong, skunky flavor that I had to spit it out (and glare at my fellow professionals). The short explanation is that black currants are an acquired taste, and eating them a little on the green side is simply a dreadful experience. Let them ripen, then use them to make the wonderful juice or jelly of which the Europeans are so fond.

'Ben Lomond'. A cultivar from Scotland with excellent fruit quality and good resistance to mildew and leaf diseases. It is susceptible to white pine blister rust, though, so plan accordingly. This cultivar forms a large, robust plant with good yield and relatively large fruit.

'Consort'. Has great rust resistance but apparently not a lot else. Its productivity is low, and the berries tend to tear at the stem ends when harvested. In addition, these plants are quite susceptible to powdery mildew and some of the leaf spots. If you have a white pine in your yard, and you really need the resistance to that disease, 'Consort' is worth a try. Two other rust-resistant cultivars are also available: 'Crusader' and 'Coronet'.

'Crandall'. Not a cultivar of the typical black currant *Ribes nigrum* but of a different American species, *R. odoratum*. It ripens relatively late (August) and is productive with glossy black fruit. Ed Mashburn claims that this one can be eaten right off the bush (I remain suspicious) and is disease resistant. Might be a good one to try.

'Titania'. A large black currant that is immune to white pine blister rust and has good mildew resistance, too. Plants are large and vigorous, and fruit quality is excellent for juices.

Though of limited use either commercially or for the landscape, the golden currant *(Ribes aureum)* is a very hardy shrub with showy yellow blossoms that hang in clusters. The fruit is fair in quality but not abundant in quantity.

How to Grow Currants and Gooseberries: Planting Through Harvest

Planting and establishment. In fall or early spring, plant well-rooted 1- or 2-year-old dormant plants, cutting back the top portions of each plant to 6 to 10 inches (15–25 cm). Space plants 3 to 4 feet (1–1.2 m) apart in rows 6 to 8 feet (1.8–2.4 m) apart. Remove the flower blossoms in the first year to encourage plant establishment and growth for future years. Well-established plants can fruit for 10 to 15 years or more. To fertilize, apply 6 to 8 ounces (168–224 grams) of 10-10-10 annually in an 18-inch (45 cm) ring around each plant in early spring. Plants can be vegetatively propagated by stem cuttings.

Pruning. For all gooseberries and currants, prune dormant plants in early spring just before growth resumes. Remove canes that drop on the soil or those that shade out the center of the plant. After the first season of growth, remove all but six to eight of the most vigorous shoots. Red and white currants and gooseberries produce fruit at the base of 1-year-old wood, with the greatest production on spurs of 2- and 3-year-old wood. After 3 or 4 years, the older wood becomes less productive and therefore should be replaced gradually with young shoots by a thinning and renewal process. Black currants produce the best fruit on wood that is one year old, though this wood is supported by the 2- to 3-year-old shoots.

After the second season, four or five 1-year-old shoots and three or four 2-year-old canes should be retained on gooseberries and red or white currants. Following the third season, keep three or four canes each of 1-, 2-, and 3-year-old wood. In subsequent years, remove all the oldest canes, replacing them with new canes annually. For black currants, maintain 10 to 12 shoots per mature bush, about half of which should be 1-year-old shoots. All canes that are more than 3 years old should be removed to encourage growth of new canes.

Harvesting. Well-colored fruit should be harvested as they appear, generally in early to midsummer. Each plant will produce between 5 to 7 pounds (2–3 kg) of fruit when mature, usually by the third or fourth year.

DIGRESSION

On Scale of Production

Fruits that are virtually unheard of or, at best, novelties here in North America are often commonplace in other parts of the world. Black currants are an example. In the United Kingdom, Poland, and New Zealand, black currants are grown on a large scale for processing. Juices are the primary products, however jams and jellies are also commonly produced. As mentioned in Chapter 6, black currant juice fills the niche in those countries that Concord grape juice fills in the United States, though it is probably even more widely consumed than our grape juice. In New Zealand, growers begin their plantings with 8- to 18-inch (20–45 cm) long cuttings spaced 6 to 12 inches (15–30 cm) apart in rows 8 to 10 feet (2.5–3 m) apart. This results in 11,000 to 26,000 plants per hectare. More typical plantings, such as those in the United Kingdom, provide 3 to 4 feet (1–1.2 m) between plants and 10 to 12 feet (3–3.5 m) between rows. The plantations are machine harvested, and most of the large plantations are completely mechanized.

Niches in the Landscape

Gooseberries and currants are spreading shrubs that range from nearly spherical to more upright in habit, though they are always somewhat spreading. Height varies from about 3 to 4½ feet (1–1.4 m), and the circumference tends to be slightly less than the height. These shrubs work well clustered irregularly around foundations or in the center of a larger island planting. Some dense and thorny gooseberries, such as 'Glenndale' or 'Poorman', form a thick hedge that does not spread via root suckering. Remember that gooseberries are among the few fruiting plants that bear fruit in partial shade—something to take advantage of.

During a visit to Poland, I had the privilege of seeing a method of growing gooseberries and currants that is not currently employed in North America but which has great promise for the backyard grower. Scion wood from gooseberry or currant cultivars were budded high on a tree form of *Ribes (Ribes arboreum)*, resulting in a small tree of gooseberries or currants (Plate 32). Not only does this elevated version offer better fruit exposure and easier harvest, but it makes a lovely landscape plant. Such plants are not available commercially, as far as I know, but they may pose an achievable challenge for the resourceful backyard propagator.

Pests in the Planting

Powdery mildew *(Sphaerotheca mors-uva)*, leaf spot *(Mycosphaerella ribis)*, and anthracnose *(Pseudopexixa ribes)* are common fungal diseases found on currants and gooseberries, and as mentioned, all *Ribes* can fall prey to white pine blister rust *(Cronartium ribicola)*, with gooseberries being the least susceptible and black currants the most susceptible. Ferbam is a labeled fungicide for gooseberries and currants, but it is only effective on leaf and fruit rots. Liquid lime sulfur can be used for controlling mildew. It should be applied when the plants are at the green-tip stage of bud development (this is just what it sounds like: when the leaf tips are just showing green) and again 2 to 3 weeks later, after bloom. Again, consult local authorities for complete recommendations. Raking leaves out from under the plants in the fall will remove the inoculum for leaf spots, so this is a good practice, as is the careful pruning off of any injured or weak wood during dormancy.

A product called JMS stylet oil has recently been tested on numerous crops for its effectiveness against mildews. Though it can be phytotoxic (causing damage to leaves), it offers great promise for gooseberries that have good fruit quality but poor disease resistance. At this writing, JMS stylet oil is not yet legal for use on gooseberries (though it has been approved for grapes and cane berries). Contact local consultants for the latest information on this product.

The currant borer *(Synanthedon tipuliformis)* and imported currant worm *(Nematus ribesii)* are among the more serious pests of currants and gooseberries. The currant borer tunnels through the pith of the cane, causing foliage on afflicted canes to turn yellow. The imported currant worm is a small, spotted, caterpillar-like insect that consumes foliage vociferously. Both pests can be controlled by applications of malathion. Any canes infected with the currant borer should be removed and destroyed. Currant stem girdlers act much as the grape and raspberry stem borers do. If you see new shoots drooping and wilting in the spring, you will likely find evidence of small larvae in the cane below the flagging shoot. Removal and destruction of infected shoots is the best control.

HARDY KIWI

FAMILY: ACTINIDIACEAE, THE ACTINIDIA FAMILY

PRIMARY SPECIES:

Actinidia arguta Planch.—hardy kiwi
Actinidia deliciosa Planch.—common kiwi
Actinidia kolomikta Maxim.—Arctic kiwi

Actinidia is abundant on the hills of southwestern China. All members of the genus have a distinctive female flower (usually borne on plants that have only female flowers) that has many styles radiating out from the top of the ovary. The best known of the actinidias is the so-called kiwi fruit, *Actinidia deliciosa*. Though the kiwi fruit, once referred to as Chinese gooseberry, has been grown and collected from the wild for centuries in Asia, it has only recently become commonly available in the Western world. It was first developed as a commercial crop in New Zealand (hence the new name, kiwi) and is becoming an increasingly important fruit crop throughout the world. The hen's-egg-sized fruit is covered with a brown, fuzzy skin and has a melting and tasty green pulp. This type of kiwi, which can be readily purchased at our grocery stores, cannot be grown in most temperate areas of North America, due to its cold tenderness and its requirement of a long growing season. A cousin of the common kiwi, though, the hardy kiwi *(A. arguta)*, is much more cold hardy. Also referred to as kiwiberry or baby kiwi, this crop is the subject of considerable interest in cooler temperate regions due to its lovely flavor, its relatively smooth and quite edible skin, its convenient size for eating (the fruit is about the size of a large grape), and its good shelf-life. Commercial plantings are established in several locations in North America, most notably Oregon and Pennsylvania, but the growing of hardy kiwi remains an experiment—which makes it a perfect choice for the backyard grower. Be forewarned, however, the hardy kiwi does not look nearly as good as it tastes. The skin can have a dull brownish green color, though a few cultivars are reddish (Plates 35 and 36). In addition, the pedicel adheres to the fruit, so when you eat the fruit you need to bite off the stem. Likewise, if you process hardy kiwi, remove the stems before putting the fruit in the pot.

Hardy kiwis have some horticultural limitations that need to be addressed by the prospective grower.

1. Male and female flowers are borne on different plants, so both males and females must be planted. The ideal ratio of males to females is roughly 1:6.
2. The plants often take several years to mature, and fruit is usually not borne until the plants are 5 to 9 years old.
3. Though the plants are extremely winter hardy, tolerating temperatures as low as −30°F (−34°C), they develop shoots early in the spring that are extremely sensitive to frost. In most years,

my hardy kiwi shoots experience some "burning" from frost, but they usually survive and fruit in spite of some natural shoot removal in spring. If the flowers are damaged by frost, fruit will not develop that year.

4. Pollination can be a problem even when both male and female plants are planted. This may be because the male plants obtained from the nursery are not really male—labeling errors, unfortunately, are easy to make in nurseries. A second possible explanation is that pollen borne by the male plants is easily injured by chilling, even if an outright frost does not occur.

5. Hardy kiwis are extremely vigorous-growing vines, requiring a substantial trellis for support.

In spite of these challenges, once you have sampled the fruit, hardy kiwi seems well worth the trouble. The fruit is aromatic, with flavors of the fuzzy kiwi, banana, strawberry, and pear all wrapped up in one delightful package.

Plant Biology

The hardy kiwi plant, like its cousin the common kiwi, is a deciduous liana that climbs by wrapping itself around things; it does not bear tendrils like grapevines. The vines are dioecious (male and female flowers are borne on separate plants) and are extremely vigorous in even modestly fertile soils (Plate 33). The plants may live and be productive for 50 years or more. Shoots start growing in the spring, and new buds for the following year begin to form as the shoots extend. Unlike most perennial fruit plants, the hardy kiwi does not form its flower buds at this time, even though the stimulus or evocation has been received by the bud. Actual flower bud development does not happen until spring, 10 days or so before the new shoots emerge. As a result, full bloom occurs fairly late in the season, since flowers are borne on the current season's growth. Like some apple cultivars, kiwi can fall into a biennial, or alternate-year, fruiting cycle. Specifically, they may fruit heavily in one year and lightly the next. Light fruiting may stimulate even more vegetative growth than usual.

Pollination is required for fruit production, and yet kiwi flowers are not particularly attractive to bees since they lack nectar. Further, as already mentioned, male flowers are borne on different plants than female flowers (save one exception, the cultivar 'Issai'). Most commercial producers move honeybee hives into their area to facilitate pollination. A small percentage of the flowers are wind-pollinated.

Cultivar Selection

Development of hardy kiwi cultivars is in its infancy due to the newness of this crop. A few cultivars are available and can be obtained from the nurseries listed in the Appendix.

'Ananasnaya'. A Russian cultivar, the name means "pineapple-like." Because of the tongue-twisting name, many nursery catalogs refer to this cultivar as "Anna" or "Ana." The fruit is of good quality, with a sweet aroma and intense flavor. Skin color is green and develops a purple-red blush in the sun. A very vigorous vine. 'Ananasnaya' is currently the standard to which we compare the others.

'Geneva'. Several selections of 'Geneva' are available through nurseries, but they have not been widely tested. The fruit ripens earlier than that of either 'Anna' or 'Issai' and has a good flavor.

'Issai'. The only self-fertile cultivar, 'Issai' is less vigorous than other hardy kiwis. It has small fruit with good flavor. Harvesting is a challenge because the fruit ripens unevenly within a cluster. Originating in Japan, it has not performed well in Pennsylvania.

'Meader'. Available as both a male and a female; be sure to order the female if you want fruit. The fruit is medium-sized.

How to Grow Hardy Kiwis: Planting Through Harvest

Planting and establishment. Hardy kiwi vines are usually available from nurseries as rooted cuttings or as potted plants. Purchase male and female plants that flower at the same time. The male plants should be distributed throughout the planting for best pollination results. Plant dormant rooted cuttings as soon as the soil can be worked in the spring. Space plants 10 feet (3 m) apart. The width of the planting row, if rows are used, will depend on the type of trellis and the equipment used in the planting. Containerized plants may be planted in the spring after danger of frost has passed. The roots may need trimming at planting. Plant the vines just deep enough to cover the roots well with soil, and water well. Irrigate throughout the season as needed, and monitor for insect and disease pests.

Propagation. Softwood cuttings taken from new growth can be rooted by using a rooting compound (such as IBA, indole-3-butyric acid) and mist propagation. Rooting usually takes 6 to 8 weeks. If you do not have mist propagation (not something that I have in *my* backyard), try putting polyethylene tents over the area, being careful not to have the tent touch the cutting tops. Another clever approach that I have seen uses 2-liter plastic bottles with the bottoms cut off and the tops used as individual "mini-greenhouses" over each cutting. Do this in a sheltered environment if you try it. Remember to cut each cutting just below a node and remove the bottom two leaves before sticking the cutting in a well-drained medium, such as equal parts peat and perlite or equal parts soil, peat, and perlite.

Fertilization. Because hardy kiwi roots burn rather easily, apply fertilizer cautiously. No fertilizer is necessary in the year of planting. In the spring of the second year, apply 2 ounces (56 grams) of 10-10-10 fertilizer per plant, and increase this amount by 2 ounces each year until each plant receives a total of 8 ounces (224 grams). If growth is excessive, by all means cut back on the fertilizer.

Pruning and training. In order to manage the high level of vigor of the hardy kiwi vine, you must prune and train your plants. As with most perennial fruit plants, they require dormant pruning. However, they also need to be pruned several times during the summer by cutting back the terminal growth to four to six leaves beyond the last flower. Also remove watersprouts (vigorous upright shoots originating from older wood) and shoots from the trunk, as well as vines that become entangled. This removal may be substantial in the summer.

Dormant pruning is usually done sometime between December and March in the eastern and midwestern United States, and whenever plants have dropped their leaves and gone into dormancy elsewhere. The flowers of *Actinidia arguta* develop on current-season shoots that come from one-year-old canes (last year's growth). Shoots from older wood rarely produce flowers. As with grapevines, a large percentage of the wood is removed at dormant pruning—as much as 70 percent. New fruiting canes will have developed at the base of the previous year's growth. Leave some renewal canes for future fruiting. Fruiting canes should be spaced at 8- to 12-inch (20–30 cm) intervals on the cordons.

Training should begin in the first year of planting. Like grapes, these flexible vines can be trained to a number of forms, though a pergola (Figure 7.1) is the most common training system in commercial plantings since it accommodates the kiwi's vigor. Establishing the trunks and structure of the vine early in its development will ensure fruit for many years to come. The training systems described for grapes in Chapter 6 may provide further inspiration, but keep in mind that hardy kiwi is more vigorous than most grapevines.

Harvest and postharvest. A single mature hardy kiwi plant will yield between 50 and 100 pounds (23–45 kg) of fruit per year. Hardy kiwi fruit can be vine-ripened; at ripening they will contain about 18 to 25 percent sugar. A single harvest, rather than selective harvest over several pickings, is acceptable. Unlike the other small fruits, however, hardy kiwi will "after-ripen"—specifically, they can be harvested at less-than-optimal ripeness (tart but flavorful) and then placed in cool storage to ripen. When picked in this manner, hardy kiwi fruit will hold in a cooler for up to 2 months. The fruit is also sensitive to the fruit-ripening hormone ethylene. If harvested early, the fruit can be placed close to ripe bananas (which naturally release ethylene) to increase the rate of ripening.

Niches in the Landscape

Another vine! Yea! This one is even more vigorous than grape, but it can be used in the same niches. Remember that hardy kiwi plants

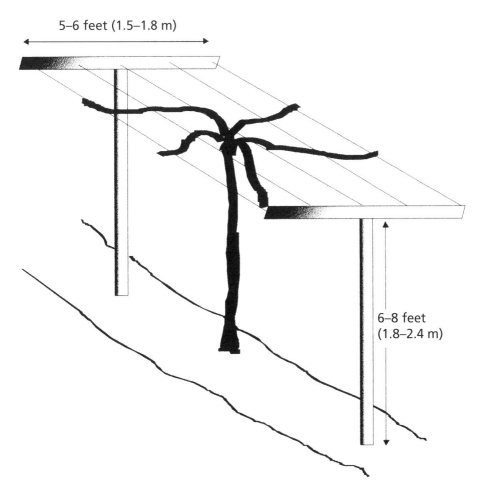

5–6 feet (1.5–1.8 m)

6–8 feet
(1.8–2.4 m)

Figure 7.1. A mature hardy kiwi plant on a pergola trellis.

do not have tendrils, so they need to be "shown" or tied to their support structure initially, and then they will happily grow around it. The vines twine around every thing within their reach—and watch out! Sometimes they seem like they're growing so fast you can see them extending, wrapping themselves around everything in their grasp.

Pests in the Planting

This plant is so new to us that pest complexes are not well known for North America. In my own work, I have seen western flower thrips *(Franklinella occidentalis)* and aphids injure the leaves. Root knot nematodes *(Meloidogyne)*, two-spotted spider mites *(Tetranychus urticae)*, and Japanese beetles *(Popillia japonica)* have also been reported on hardy kiwi. Several diseases have affected *Actinidia arguta*, including powdery mildew *(Uncinula necator)*, gray mold *(Botrytis cinerea)*, and *Phytophthora*. Extrapolating from what we know about other crops, we can assume that maintaining good aeration in the canopy through recommended pruning practices will help control these diseases.

ELDERBERRIES

FAMILY: CAPRIFOLIACEAE, THE HONEYSUCKLE FAMILY

SPECIES:

Sambucus canadensis L.—American elder

Elderberries are underestimated plants with myriad uses. The stems of the elderberry are hollow tubes from which the pith is easily removed, and the hollow stems were often used as pipes, straws, and flutes. In fact, the genus name *Sambucus* derives from the Latin word *sambuce*, which was an ancient flute. In addition to their aesthetic uses, the pipes made from the elderberry plant were used to tap sugar maples. Elderberry bark and roots are rich in a tannin that was used for tanning leather, and the flowers and fruit have been used to make both dyes and wine. Is this a plant or what? And the fruit is great, too. Well, let's define "great." The individual fruits are quite small, but they are borne on large, umbrella-like inflorescences called cymes (Plate 38). When ripe, they are dark purple in color, hence their usefulness in dyeing. Elderberries are rarely eaten fresh because of their tartness and relative seediness. Most people use them in pies or jams; I have made and enjoyed both. Some folks may prefer to remove some or all of the seeds in these products, a task easily accomplished by straining the cooked fruit through four layers of cheesecloth. I am told that elderberries also make a great juice and a very interesting wine, using the flowers or the fruit. The ascorbic acid (vitamin C) content in elderberries is the highest of any garden fruit except for black currants. One of the greatest things about these plants is that they are particularly easy to grow. Given a sunny site and decent soil, these North American natives have few pest problems, are vigorous, and give freely of their many bounties.

Plant Biology

The American elder *(Sambucus canadensis)* is a shrub that grows in clumps of individual canes and reaches 4 to 15 feet (1.2–4.5 m) in height (Plate 37). It is indigenous to North America, with a range from Nova Scotia to Minnesota, south to Florida and Texas. The leaves are pinnately compound, with 5 to 11 leaflets averaging 5 inches (12.5 cm) in length with finely serrate margins. The inflorescence, or cyme, is a cluster of flowers ranging from 3 to 10 inches (7.5–25 cm) in diameter. The flowers are pleasantly scented. Unlike most other small-fruit crops, the crop of elderberry is borne on the current season's growth, on the terminus of new shoots. Therefore, winter injury to the flower buds is not a concern. The plants are extremely winter hardy.

Elderberries require well-drained soil with a pH between 5.5 and 6.5. The root system is fibrous and shallow, so cultivation should be shallow. Plants come into full production after 3 or 4 years, with berries maturing in late August to early September.

Plants are propagated easily by stem cuttings (hardwood or softwood), but viruses are sometimes a problem in the wild, so it is best to purchase plants from a nursery. All cultivars are only partially self-fertile, so they benefit from planting two or more cultivars together.

Cultivar Selection

Though relatively little breeding work has been done with the American elder, there are several readily available cultivars from which to choose. Plant at least two cultivars no more than 60 feet (18 m) apart to aid in cross-pollination.

'Adams #1' and 'Adams #2'. These are the oldest cultivars. Vigorous and productive, with large fruit clusters and berries. Ripen in early September.

'Johns'. Also very vigorous, producing 10-foot (3-m) canes on fertile soils. It ripens about 10 days earlier than the 'Adams' cultivars.

'Nova'. Berries are larger and sweeter than those of 'Adams #1' and 'Adams #2'. It lacks the astringency of some varieties.

'Scotia'. Yields berries with a higher sugar content than others, though the bushes are somewhat smaller.

How to Grow Elderberries: Planting Through Harvest

Planting and establishment. In early spring, plant rooted cuttings 5 to 7 feet (1.5–2.1 m) apart in the row, with a minimum of 10 feet (3 m) between rows. Apply 2 ounces (56 grams) of ammonium nitrate per year of the plant's age (up to no more than 1 pound or 0.5 kg per plant) in a ring around the plant in early spring.

Pruning. Healthy elderberry plants usually produce several new canes each year that attain their full height during the first year. Two-year-old canes with several lateral branches are most fruitful, so you want to be sure to retain plenty of these. Older trunks lose vigor and become weak after 2 to 3 years and should be removed, along with any dead, broken, or weak canes. Remove canes at ground level during the dormant season, leaving an equal number of 1-, 2- and 3-year-old canes.

Harvest and postharvest. Elderberry plants produce a small crop in the first year after planting. They should reach full production in 3 to 5 years, offering about 12 to 15 pounds (about 5–7 kg) of fruit per plant per year. To harvest, the clusters should be cut, and the berries stripped from the stems and either frozen or processed shortly thereafter.

Niches in the Landscape

Elderberries make for useful ornamentals in the garden. The plants thrive in full-sun locations but tolerate some shade. It forms an upright shrub that can be planted in tall, 6- to 10-foot (1.8–3 m) hedges or scattered as a background or foundation planting behind shorter plants. Leaves turn an attractive red in the fall.

Pests in the Planting

Because tomato ringspot virus can be a problem on elderberries, it is especially important to control weeds around the root zone. Tomato ringspot virus naturally resides in such common weeds as the dandelion and is transmitted by soil nematodes, so removing the weeds removes a primary source of infection.

Fungal diseases such as stem and twig cankers *(Cytospora, Nectria,* and *Sphaeropsis)* can infect elderberries, but they can be effectively controlled by removing and burning afflicted wood. Likewise, the elder shoot borer *(Desmocerus dalliatus)* may cause dieback and cane loss, but infested canes can be simply removed and burned. No insecticides or fungicides are labeled for use on elderberry in the United States.

HIGHBUSH CRANBERRY

FAMILY: CAPRIFOLIACEAE, THE HONEYSUCKLE FAMILY

SPECIES:

Viburnum trilobum Marsh.—highbush cranberry, American cranberry

The name highbush cranberry is much more appropriate than the other common name for *Viburnum trilobum,* American cranberry. Though this plant is a native of North America, so is the low-bush cranberry *(Vaccinium macrocarpon),* from which our familiar

DIGRESSION

About Pesticide Labeling

Why is it that some crops have no pesticides labeled for them? It is not because they do not have pests, but rather it is primarily because, in most cases, the costs associated with getting a pesticide approved (often in excess of a million dollars) are borne by the chemical company that manufactures them. This makes perfect sense, of course, since the chemical companies stand to gain the most by the sale of these products. However, while it may be worthwhile to research, test, and label a product for corn, or cotton, or wheat, it simply is not cost-effective for chemical companies to go through the trouble of labeling a product for, say, elderberries. As an optimistic estimate, there are perhaps 100 acres of commercial elderberries in the entire country. So the lack of a labeled product for elderberries is not because it isn't safe but because the research and legal costs are simply too great and the sales potential too low to justify the expense.

Exactly how much acreage is necessary to make labeling worth the manufacturer's investment? I don't know of a magic number, but all the crops in this book, as well as most vegetable and tree-fruit crops, are considered minor. Fortunately, several alternative—and legal—means can be employed for labeling pesticides for minor uses.

cranberry sauce is made. So the name highbush cranberry avoids confusion.

This species is a real "sleeper." It is a simply gorgeous bush, with bright red fruit (Plate 39) and beautiful red foliage in the fall. The difficulty is that the fruit tastes simply dreadful when fresh, much like the lowbush cranberry. It is tart, acidic, and stringent—what an

A federal program, the Interregional Committee 4 or IR4, takes on the costs of researching and testing existing pesticides for use on minor crops, or minor uses on major crops. This research is done in cooperation with the chemical company that manufactures the pesticide, but the cost is borne by the government. It is a good investment for the average taxpayer, because it allows for the safe, legal use of tested pesticides on these minor crops. Research is revealing that all sorts of healthful chemicals reside in many fruit crops, such as ellagic acid, a potent anti-tumor chemical found in high levels in strawberries, raspberries, and blueberries. Nature, in her eloquence, has evolved many hidden means of sustaining her subjects. Another example that has gotten much press is the antioxidants found in red wine.

Unfortunately, requests move through the IR4 program at an unbelievably slow pace. Another alternative for labeling pesticides on a minor crop is third-party labeling. In this arrangement, a group of people in the industry, usually growers, take on the liability of using a product in exchange for the support of the chemical company and specific labeling for their product. Third-party labeling is not often used, primarily because it is expensive—and growers of minor crops are rarely wealthy—and accepting liability presents a threat to the grower. Ah. The world is ruled by the lawyers, make no mistake.

endorsement. The processed fruits are very nice, however. They can be used for jelly, in pies, or if the large seeds are removed, as a substitute for lowbush cranberries in sauce. The fruit is particularly high in pectins, making it jell nicely.

Plant Biology

The highbush cranberry is a deciduous shrub that ranges from 8 to 12 feet (2.4–3.6 m) in height. Its broad, ovate leaves are 2 to 5 inches (5–12.5 cm) long and have coarsely toothed lobes. The fruit is borne on cymes 3 to 5 inches (7.5–12.5 cm) across. The fruit is bright scarlet and will begin to color in late summer, and if left unharvested, it will retain the color until the following spring.

Cultivar Selection

Highbush cranberry is most often sold as species plants in nurseries, though several cultivars are available. The tall cultivars—to 9 feet (2.7 m) in height—'Andrews', 'Hahs', and 'Wentworth' were released in the 1920s. Fruiting among these selections spans the fall harvest season (mid-September through late October in Pennsylvania): 'Wentworth' is early, 'Andrews' late, and 'Hahs' midseason. A smaller, 6-foot (1.8-m) shrub called 'Compactum' is also available. It has denser foliage and a broader form than the others and excellent fall foliage color. All are beautiful.

How to Grow Highbush Cranberries: Planting Through Harvest

Plant well-rooted shrubs in well-drained loam or silt-loam soil. The plants prefer moist, but not wet, conditions, so the soil should have good water-holding capacity. Soil pH is best kept at 6.0–7.5, though there has been little research on this crop. Highbush cranberry is a widely adapted plant, but it is sensitive to extended drought and may die under such conditions. It is tolerant of partial shade.

Plants should be spaced 6 to 8 feet (1.8–2.4 m) apart in the row. Maintain an adequate water supply to the plants, and fertilize as for elderberries. As the plants mature, dormant pruning, which consists of removing about one-third of the mature shoots and leaving five or more stems, should improve yield. Some fruit production will occur during the third season after planting, with full production realized in the fifth year. Fruit will be ready to harvest when fully mature in mid-September through early October.

The plant can be propagated fairly easily by softwood cuttings taken in midsummer, or by layering.

Niches in the Landscape

The plant form of the highbush cranberry is similar to that of the elderberry. It is a little taller and bushier and will fill in as a tall hedge beautifully. I view highbush cranberry first as an ornamental and secondly as a plant with interesting, usable fruit. Several cultivars have brilliant fall foliage, and the fruit is simply gorgeous. When it looks this good does it have to taste good, too? Well, we would prefer it that way, but looks alone justify this species, in my opinion.

Pests in the Planting

Few diseases and insect pests seriously compromise this *Viburnum*. Bacterial diseases such as bacterial leaf spot *(Pseudomonas viridflava)* and crown gall *(Agrobacterium tumafaciens)* can infect it, and among fungal diseases, both powdery mildew *(Uncinula necator)* and a shoot blight caused by *Botrytis cinerea* may cause injury. If you are not using the fruit of these plants, you can use fungicides that are labeled for ornamental viburnums. Tarnished plant bug *(Lygus)* may feed on blossoms and young shoots, but it is rarely a serious problem.

AMELANCHIERS

FAMILY: ROSACEAE, THE ROSE FAMILY

PRIMARY SPECIES:

Amelanchier alnifolia Nutt.—Juneberry
Amelanchier asiatica Siebold & Zucc.—Chinese serviceberry, shadblow

Amelanchier canadensis L.—running serviceberry, Chinese
    serviceberry
Amelanchier laevis Wieg.—Allegheny serviceberry
Amelanchier stolonifera Wieg.—running serviceberry

The amelanchiers—variably called currant tree, Indian pear, juneberry, sarvis, sarvistree, saskatoon, serviceberry, shadblow, shad-
bush, snowy mespilus, and swamp sugar pear—are well adapted to
the temperate to cold climes of middle and northern North America. These species have masses of beautiful, showy flowers in early
spring and are thus widely planted as ornamentals, but the edible
fruit is useful too. The fruit can be eaten fresh (though some types
are bitter or sour) or made into pies and jams. Historically, amelanchier fruit was used as a primary ingredient in pemmican, a semi-
dry mixture of the fruit and meat consumed by early native and
nonnative North Americans.

Plant Biology

Amelanchier is a genus of tall, slender shrubs that range from 6 to 15
feet (1.8–4.5 m) in height and have coarsely toothed oblong leaves
about 1½ inches (3.8 cm) long. The flowers are typical of the rose
family, with five petals arranged around a center of anthers and stig-
mas. The fruit is green when unripe (Plate 40), and when ripe is
more reminiscent of a blueberry (though this bush is not closely related to blueberry). The dark blue-purple-black fruit has a waxy
bloom on the surface.

Amelanchiers occur extensively in native populations across
North America, and they have wide adaptability to climates and soils.
The only soils in which amelanchiers do not grow well are those that
are poorly aerated or poorly drained. *Amelanchier alnifolia* is the dom-
inant species among the named cultivars. They are adapted throughout Canada and the northern and north-central United States.

Numerous cultivars of *Amelanchier* are available, and most are
dual-purpose plants that have improved fruit size and quality but
also can be used as ornamentals for their showy white flowers and
beautiful fall color. I have tasted the fruit of amelanchiers, and they

are, quite honestly, a little nondescript in flavor, but apparently there is a lot of variation among species. Like the fruit of most other members of the rose family, they tend to be quite tart (and high in pectin) early in the ripening period, with sugar accruing as they hang on the bush. The juice of a similar genus, *Aronia*, is used in Poland to extend black currant juice; it is tart, but not offensive, and has a deep color. Though the fruit resembles blueberries in appearance, the flavor is not as complex, and the flesh of the fruit is firmer compared to the melting texture of the blueberry.

How to Grow Amelanchiers: Planting Through Harvest

If fruit production is the goal, sites should be selected for good air drainage, since these plants flower early (May) and will fall prey to late frosts in spring. Most amelanchiers will thrive in soil with a pH from 6.0 to 7.8. Root cuttings or plants grown from root suckers can be planted at least 8 feet (2.4 m) apart. For a tighter hedgerow planting, plants can be set 5 to 6 feet (1.5–1.8 m) apart. Amelanchiers begin to bear fruit 2 to 4 years after planting, with maximum production obtained after 7 to 11 years.

Plants that readily produce suckers can be propagated by separating the root suckers from the plant during the dormant season and transplanting them. If the plant does not produce suckers, root cuttings can be taken in early spring. The root pieces should be 4 to 6 inches (10–15 cm) long and about ⅜ to ⅝ inch (1–1.5 cm) in diameter. These can be planted in a nursery row, covered with about ¼ inch (0.5 cm) of loose loamy soil, and kept watered and shaded. Some amelanchiers propagate readily from softwood cuttings. Cuttings 3 to 6 inches (7.5–15 cm) long can be taken in late spring or early summer, treated with a root promoter such as IAA (indole-3-acetic acid), and placed in an intermittent-mist bed with bottom heat.

Amelanchiers have not been extensively cultivated in North America, so we can only guess at the fertilizer requirements. A good guess is to treat them as you would elderberries, applying 2 ounces (56 grams) of ammonium nitrate per year age of the plant, up to a maximum of 1 pound (450 grams) per year.

Niches in the Landscape

Amelanchiers fit into a landscape much as highbush cranberries or elderberries do, although they are generally taller and more slender than either of those species, so plan accordingly. *Amelanchier* is particularly disease and insect free and extremely well-adapted to northern climes, making it an ideal selection where a low-maintenance but useful fruit plant is desired. Several bushes planted closely together create a nice medium-height hedge.

Pests in the Planting

A number of rusts (*Gymnosporangium* species) may attack the leaves or fruit of *Amelanchier*, causing fruit loss and defoliation. Since the alternate hosts of these organisms are red cedar, juniper, and white cedar, the best control is to try to eradicate these tree species from within a mile radius of your planting. There are no other legal controls.

Fire blight, a disease caused by a bacterium *(Erwinia amylovora)*, can also affect amelanchiers. As the name suggests, fire blight makes shoots look like they were hit with a blowtorch. Remove and burn any infected shoots as soon as you see them. It is a good idea to disinfect your pruning shears between cuts with a bleach solution (1 part bleach : 10 parts water) to prevent the spread of the disease from one cut to the next. Powdery mildew *(Uncinula necator)* can also be a problem. Unfortunately, you just have to live with this one, since no fungicides are cleared for use on *Amelanchier*.

Many borer insects *(Lepidoptera)* can infect amelanchiers. Borers tend to go after weak or diseased wood, so prune this inferior wood out of your plants and you have a good chance of avoiding a visit from these parasites. As with highbush cranberry, if you are not consuming the fruit, pesticides labeled for ornamental *Viburnum* can be used.

THE MOST MINOR OF THE MINOR BERRIES

Cranberry (*Vaccinium macrocarpon*)

Native to the United States, the cranberry is not a minor crop commercially; in fact, the commercial cranberry industry continues to grow. It is, however, minor in terms of its use in the landscape. But the plant has potential. It is an evergreen groundcover that requires acidic soil, high organic matter, and lots of water. Cranberries tolerate some shade, though they produce fruit best in full sun.

Edible Honeysuckle (*Lonicera caerulea* var. *edulis*)

A nonclimbing bush that grows to 4 to 6 feet (1.2–1.8 m), the edible honeysuckle offers fruit that is useful for jam and jelly. It is also good for attracting birds to the landscape. The seeds are small. The plant forms a dense barrier, and it leafs out very early in the spring.

Jostaberry (*Ribes nidigrolaria*)

The jostaberry is a hybrid between gooseberry and black currant. It produces black, good-flavored fruit about the size of a gooseberry (about ½ inch or 1 cm in diameter) on thornless shrubs that reach 4 to 8 feet (1.2–2.4 m) at maturity. It is extremely hardy and resistant to white pine blister rust.

Lingonberry (*Vaccinium vitis-idaea*)

From the same genus as the blueberry, lingonberry is a tart red berry grown primarily in Scandinavia. The berries are processed similarly to cranberries. The plant is a short evergreen shrub that flowers in May and again in August, with fruit ripening in two crops. Like blueberry, it requires acidic soils.

Maypop or Passionberry (*Passiflora incarnata*)

Maypop is a species of passion flower *(Passiflora)* that bears yellow to yellow-green, oval fruit on herbaceous perennial vines. Native to North America, the plants are cold hardy. The fruit is highly variable—some are delicious, some not so.

Rugosa Rose (*Rosa rugosa*)

Very thorny and very vigorous, the rugosa rose makes a great hedge and produces large, mild-flavored rose hips that make good tea, jam, jelly, and other products. It is hardy, but the thorniness may make it unsuitable for certain landscapes.

Wineberry (*Rubus phoenicoliasius*)

The wineberry is a lesser-known bramble that offers good-flavored fruit between the fruiting seasons of summer- and fall-bearing red raspberries. It will produce in somewhat shaded areas. The canes are quite prickly and the fruit is on the small side.

North American Nursery Sources for Berry Plants

This list has been compiled as a service. No endorsement of the nurseries is intended.

NURSERY SOURCES FOR STRAWBERRIES, BRAMBLES, BLUEBERRIES, AND OTHER BERRY CROPS, EXCLUDING GRAPES

The United States

A. G. Ammon Nursery, Inc.
Route 532, P.O. Box 488
Chatsworth, NJ 08019
609-726-1370 (phone)
609-726-1270 (fax)

Ag Resource, Inc.
35268 State Highway 34
Detroit Lakes, MN 56501
218-847-9351 (phone & fax)

A. I. Eppler, Ltd.
P.O. Box 16513
Seattle, WA 98116-0513
206-932-2211 (phone)

Allen Plant Co.
P.O. Box 310
Fruitland, MD 21826-0310
410-742-7122 (phone)
410-742-7120 (fax)
e-mail: rallen9084@aol.com

Bear Creek Nursery
P.O. Box 411
Northport, WA 99157
509-732-6219 (phone)
509-732-4417 (fax)
e-mail: BearCreek@plix.com
Web site:
    www.bearcreeknursery.com

Beilstein's Blueberry Patch
1285 West Hanley Road
Mansfield, OH 44904
419-884-1797 (phone)
419-526-2642 (fax)
e-mail: bpatch@richnet.net

Boston Mountain Nurseries
20189 North Highway 71
Mountainburg, AR 72946
501-369-2007 (phone and fax)

Briggs Nursery
4407 Henderson Boulevard
Olympia, WA 98501
800-999-9972 (phone)
360-352-5699 (fax)
Web site:
    www.briggsnursery.com

Brittingham Plant Farms, Inc.
P.O. Box 2538
Salisbury, MD 21802-2538
410-749-5153 (phone)
410-749-5148 (fax)

Congdon & Weller Wholesale
    Nursery, Inc.
P.O. Box 1507
Mile Block Road
North Collins, NY 14111-1507
716-337-0171 or 800-345-8305
    (phone)
716-337-0203 (fax)

Cooley's Strawberry Nursery
P.O. Box 472
Augusta, AR 72006
870-347-2026 (phone)

Daisy Farms
28355 M-152
Dowagiac, MI 49047
616-782-6321 (phone)
616-782-7131 (phone and fax)
e-mail: daisyfms@cpuinc.net

DeGrandchamp's Nursery
15575 77th Street
South Haven, MI 49090
616-637-3915 (phone)
616-637-2531 (fax)

Edible Landscaping
P.O. Box 77, 361 Spirit Ridge
    Lane
Afton, VA 22920
804-361-9134 (phone)
800-524-4156 (for orders)
804-361-1916 (fax)
e-mail: el@cstone.net
Web site: www.eat-it.com

Fall Creek Farm and Nursery,
    Inc.
39318 Jasper-Lowell Road
Lowell, OR 97452
800-538-3001 (phone)
503-937-3373 (fax)

Finch Blueberry Nursery
P.O. Box 699
Bailey, NC 27807
800-245-4662 (phone)
252-235-2411 (fax)

Hartmann Plant Co.
P.O. Box 100
Lacota, MI 49063-0100
616-253-4281 (phone)
616-253-4457 (fax)

Indiana Berry and Plant Co.
5218 West 500 South
Huntingburg, IN 47542
800-295-2226 (phone)
812-683-2004 (fax)

J. W. Jung Seed Co.
335 South High Street
Randolph, WI
53957
800-247-5864 (phone)
800-692-5864 (fax)

Kelly Nurseries
1708 Morrissey Drive
Bloomington, IL 61704
309-663-9551 (phone)

Keystone Seeds
384 Foster Road
North Versailles, PA 15137
570-966-9192 (phone)
412-672-4228 (fax)

Koppes Plants
P.O. Box 441
Watsonville, CA 95077
408-724-6009 (phone)
831-724-5123 (fax)

Krohne Plant Farms, Inc.
65295 CR-342
Hartford, MI 49057
616-424-5423 (phone)
616-424-3126 (fax)

Lawyer Nursery
950 Highway 200 West
Plains, MT 59859-9706
800-551-9875 (phone)
406-826-5700 (fax)

Lewis Nursery and Farms, Inc.
3500 NC Highway 133
Rocky Point, NC 28457
800-453-5346 (phone)
910-602-3106 (fax)

Mellinger's, Inc.
2310 West South Range Road
North Lima, OH 44452
330-549-9861 (phone)
800-321-7444 (phone)
330-549-3716 (fax)

Miller Nurseries
5060 West Lake Road
Canandaigua, NY 14424
800-836-9630 (phone)
716-396-2154 (fax)

Nor-Cal Nursery, Inc.
P.O. Box 1012
Red Bluff, CA 96080
530-527-6200 (phone)
530-527-2921 (fax)

North Star Gardens
19060 Manning Trail North
Marine on St. Croix, MN 55047-
    9723
612-433-5850 (phone)
612-227-9813 (fax)

Northwoods Wholesale
    Nursery
28696 South Cramer Road
Molalla, OR 97038
503-651-3005 (phone)
503-651-3882 (fax)

Nourse Farms, Inc.
41 River Road
South Deerfield, MA 01373
413-665-2658 (phone)
413-665-7888 (fax)

Puget Sound Kiwi Co.
1220 NE 90th Street
Seattle, WA 98115
206-523-6403 (phone and fax)

Roaring Brook Nurseries
639 Gardiner Road
Wales, ME 04280
207-375-4884 (phone)
207-375-8682 (fax)

Sakuma Bros. Farms, Inc.
P.O. Box 427
Burlington, WA 98233
360-757-6611 (phone)
360-757-3936 (fax)

Simmons Plant Farm
11542 North Highway 71
Mountainburg, AR 72946
501-369-2345 (phone and fax)

Southmeadow Fruit Gardens
P.O. Box 211
Baroda, MI 49101
616-422-2411 (phone)
616-422-1464 (fax)

Spring Hill Nurseries
110 West Elm Street
Tipp City, OH 45371
800-582-8527 (phone)
309-589-2096 (fax)

St. Lawrence Nurseries
325 State Highway 345
Potsdam, NY 13676
315-265-6739 (phone)

Stark Bros. Nurseries
P.O. Box 10
Louisiana, MO 63353-0010
800-325-4180 (phone)
800-478-2759 (phone)
800-775-6415 (for catalogs)
573-754-5290 (fax)
Web site: www.starkbros.com

Tower View Nursery
70912 CR-388
South Haven, MI 49090
616-637-1279 (phone)
616-637-6257 (fax)
e-mail: mnelson@btc-bci.com

Tripple Brook Farm
37 Middle Road
Southampton, MA 01073
413-527-4626 (phone)
413-527-9853 (fax)

Walter K. Morss & Son
R.F.D. 2
Boxford, MA 01921
978-352-2633 (phone)

Zilke Bros. Nursery
8924 Cleveland Avenue
Baroda, MI 49101
616-422-2666 (phone)

Canada

Phytosanitary certificates are required for importation of all small-fruit crops from Canada into the United States. Additional charges may be incurred. Contact individual nurseries for details.

Belamore Farm, Ltd.
RR #1, Great Village
Colchester County, NS B0M 1L0
902-668-2004 (phone)

C. O. Keddy Nursery, Inc.
982 North Bishop Road
Kentville, NS B4N 3V7
902-678-4497 (phone)
902-678-0067 (fax)

Curtis Millen
RR #1, Great Village
Colchester County, NS B0M 1L0
902-662-3820 (phone)
902-662-2891 (fax)
e-mail: acmillen@istar.ca

Ghesquiere Farms, Inc.
RR #2
Simcoe, ON N3Y 4K1
519-428-1087 (phone)
519-428-6357 (fax)

G. W. Allen Nursery Ltd.
7303 Highway 221, RR #2
Centreville, NS B0P 1J0
902-678-7519 (phone)
902-678-5924 (fax)

Strawberry Tyme Farms, Inc.
RR #2
Simcoe, ON N3Y 4K1
519-426-3099 (phone)
519-426-2573 (fax)

V. Kraus Nurseries, Ltd.
Box 180, 1380 Centre Road
Carlisle, ON L0R 1H0
905-689-4022 (phone)
905-689-8080 (fax)
Web site:
    www.krausnurseries.com

Windermere Orchards &
    Nursery
RR #1
Berwick, NS B0P 1E0
902-538-3213 (phone)
902-538-0244 (fax)

Sources of Berry Crops by Nursery

Source	Strawberries	Red Raspberries	Black Raspberries	Purple Raspberries	Gold Raspberries	Blackberries	Boysenberries	Blueberries	Currants	Gooseberries	Hardy kiwis	Elderberries	Cranberries	Other Minor Berries
A. G. Ammon								x						
Ag Resource	x	x		x				x	x				x	x
A. I. Eppler									x	x				x
Allen	x	x	x			x		x						
Bear Creek		x	x		x	x	x	x	x	x	x	x	x	x
Beilstein's		x						x						
Belamore	x													
Boston Mountain	x	x	x		x	x	x	x	x	x		x		x
Briggs								x						
Brittingham	x	x	x	x		x		x						
C. O. Keddy	x	x				x		x						
Congdon & Weller		x	x	x	x				x	x				
Cooley's	x													
Curtis Millen	x													
Daisy Farms	x	x	x	x										
DeGrandchamp's								x					x	x
Edible Landscaping	x	x	x	x	x	x		x	x	x	x	x	x	x
Fall Creek								x					x	x
Finch								x						
Ghesquiere	x	x	x	x										
G. W. Allen	x	x		x										
Hartmann*	x	x	x	x	x	x		x	x	x	x	x	x	x
Indiana Berry and Plant*	x	x	x	x	x	x		x	x	x	x	x	x	x

Source	Strawberries	Red Raspberries	Black Raspberries	Purple Raspberries	Gold Raspberries	Blackberries	Boysenberries	Blueberries	Currants	Gooseberries	Hardy kiwis	Elderberries	Cranberries	Other Minor Berries
J. W. Jung*	x	x	x	x	x	x		x	x	x	x	x		x
Kelly	x	x	x	x	x	x	x	x	x	x	x	x		x
Keystone	x	x	x					x						
Koppes	x													
Krohne	x													
Lawyer									x					
Lewis	x													
Mellinger's*	x	x	x	x	x	x	x	x	x	x	x	x	x	x
Miller*	x	x	x	x	x	x		x	x	x	x	x	x	x
Nor-Cal	x													
North Star*		x	x	x	x	x		x	x	x				x
Northwoods									x	x	x	x		x
Nourse	x	x	x	x	x	x		x	x	x				
Puget Sound Kiwi											x			
Roaring Brook		x						x						
Sakuma Bros.	x	x	x			x	x							x
Simmons	x	x	x			x	x	x		x				x
Southmeadow									x	x				x
Spring Hill	x	x	x		x	x		x						
St. Lawrence		x						x	x	x		x	x	x
Stark Bros.*	x	x	x	x	x	x	x	x	x	x	x	x		
Strawberry Tyme	x	x	x	x	x	x		x						
Tower View								x						x
Tripple Brook								x			x	x	x	x

Sources of Berry Crops by Nursery. Continued.

Source	Strawberries	Red Raspberries	Black Raspberries	Purple Raspberries	Gold Raspberries	Blackberries	Boysenberries	Blueberries	Currants	Gooseberries	Hardy kiwis	Elderberries	Cranberries	Other Minor Berries
V. Kraus	x	x						x	x	x				
Walter K. Morss	x	x		x				x						
Windermere	x													
Zilke Bros.		x												

*Carries bird-control supplies, such as netting and scare-eyes.

NURSERY SOURCES FOR GRAPES

Amberg Grafted Grape Nursery
2399 Wheat Road
Clifton Springs, NY 14432
315-462-3183 (phone)
Vitis vinifera cultivars

American Nursery
Route 1, Box 87B1
Madison, VA 22727
703-948-5064 (phone)
703-948-5150 (fax)
Vitis vinifera cultivars, selected
    Geisenheim cold-hardy
    hybrids

Bailey Nurseries, Inc.
1325 Bailey Road
St. Paul, MN 55119
800-829-8898 (phone)
native North American
    cultivars, hybrid grapes,
    seedless grapes

Bear Creek Nursery
P.O. Box 411
Northport, WA 99157
509-732-6219 (phone)
509-732-4417 (fax)
native North American
    cultivars, *Vitis vinifera*
    cultivars

Blossomberry Nursery
Rt. 2
Clarksville, AR 72830
501-754-6489 (phone)
native North American
    cultivars, seedless grapes

Boordy Nursery
Box 38
Riderwood, MD 21139
301-823-4624 (phone)
hybrid grapes

Boston Mountain Nurseries
20189 North Highway 71
Mountainburg, AR 72946
501-369-2007 (phone and fax)
native North American
    cultivars, hybrid grapes,
    seedless grapes

California Grapevine Nursery,
    Inc.
1085 Galleron Road
St. Helena, CA 94574-9790
707-963-5688 (phone)
800-344-5688 (phone)
707-963-1840 (fax)
Vitis vinifera cultivars

Carl Remkus Nursery
858 Bank Street
Painesville, OH 44077
216-354-8817 (phone)
native North American
    cultivars, hybrid grapes,
    rootstocks

Concord Nurseries
10175 Mile Block Road
North Collins, NY 14111
716-337-2485 (phone)
800-223-2211 (phone)
800-448-1267 (fax)
native North American
    cultivars, hybrid grapes, *Vitis
    vinifera* cultivars, seedless
    grapes

Congdon & Weller Wholesale
    Nursery, Inc.
P.O. Box 1507
Mile Block Road
North Collins, NY 14111-1507
716-337-0171 or 800-345-8305
    (phone)
716-337-0203 (fax)
native North American
    cultivars, seedless grapes

Cummins Nursery
18 Glass Factory Bay Road
Geneva, NY 14456
315-789-7083 (phone)
native North American
    cultivars, seedless grapes,
    hybrid grapes

David M. Taylor
Foster Concord Nurseries, Inc.
Mile Block Road
North Collins, NY 14111
native North American
    cultivars, hybrid grapes

Double A Vineyards
10275 Christy Road
Fredonia, NY 14063
716-672-8493 (phone)
716-679-3442 (fax)
native North American
    cultivars, hybrid grapes,
    seedless grapes,
    experimental selections

Dr. Konstantin Frank Nursery
9749 Middle Road
Hammondsport, NY 14840
800-320-0735 (phone)
607-868-4884 (phone)
Vitis vinifera cultivars

Edible Landscaping
P.O. Box 77, 361 Spirit Ridge
    Lane
Afton, VA 22920
804-361-9134 (phone)
800-524-4156 (for orders)
804-361-1916 (fax)
e-mail: el@cstone.net
Web site: www.eat-it.com
seedless grapes

Euro Nursery & Vineyard, Inc.
3197 Culp Road
Jordan, Ontario L0R 1S0,
    Canada
905-562-3312 (phone)
905-562-5810 (fax)
hybrid grapes, *Vitis vinifera*
    cultivars

Foundation Plant Material
    Service
University of California, Davis
Davis, CA 95616
916-752-3590 (phone)
native North American
    cultivars, *Vitis vinifera*
    cultivars, hybrids, seedless
    grapes, rootstocks, cuttings

Ge-No's Nursery
8868 Road 28
Madera, CA 93637
209-674-4752 (phone)
Vitis vinifera cultivars

Herman J. Wiemer Vineyard
P.O. Box 38, Route 14
Dundee, NY 14837
607-243-7971 (phone)
Vitis vinifera cultivars

Lake Sylvia Vineyard Nursery
Route 1, Box 149
South Haven, MN 55382
cold-hardy, Minnesota-bred
    wine and table grapes

Lon J. Rombough
P.O. Box 365
Aurora, OR 97002-0365
503-678-1410 (phone)
native North American
    cultivars, hybrid grapes, *Vitis
    vinifera* cultivars; specializes
    in unusual, rare, antique,
    and new varieties, available
    as cuttings or vines

Lorane Grapevines
80854 Territorial Road
Eugene, OR 97405
503-942-9874 (phone)
800-884-4441 (phone)
503-942-9867 (fax)
Vitis vinifera cultivars

Madera Nursery
Kendall-Jackson Winery Ltd.
421 Aviation Boulevard
Santa Rosa, CA 95403
707-544-4000 (phone)
707-544-4013 (fax)
rootstocks

Mori Nurseries
1912 Concession 4, RR #2
Niagara-On-The-Lake, Ontario
    L0S 1J0, Canada
905-468-0822 (phone)
905-468-0344 (fax)
hybrid grapes, *Vitis vinifera*
    cultivars

Omega Virginia Nursery
Rt. 4, Box 77
Leon, VA 22725
703-547-3707 (phone)
Vitis vinifera cultivars

Pense Nursery
16518 Marie Lane
Mountainburg, AR 72946
501-369-2494 (phone)
native North American
    cultivars, hybrid grapes,
    seedless grapes

Sid Butler
460 Gower Road
Nazareth, PA 18064
209-531-0351 (phone)
Vitis vinifera cultivars

Sonoma Grapevines, Inc.
1919 Dennis Lane
Santa Rosa, CA 95403
707-542-5510 (phone)
Vitis vinifera cultivars

Steve Miller Nursery
Rt. 2, Box 656
Judsonia, AR 72081
501-729-5307 (phone)
Arkansas-bred seedless grapes

Sunridge Nursery
441 Vineland Road
Bakersfield, CA 93307
805-363-8463 (phone)
Vitis vinifera cultivars,
    rootstocks

University of Texas Lands
P.O. Box 553
Midland, TX 79702
915-684-4404 (phone)
Vitis vinifera cultivars

Valone Nursery
62 Cushing Street
Fredonia, NY 14063
native North American
    cultivars, hybrid grapes

Vinifera, Inc.
8505 SW Creekside Place
Beaverton, OR 97008-7108
503-520-6250 (phone)
503-643-2781 (fax)
Vitis vinifera cultivars, grown
   from tissue culture

Vintage Nurseries
550 Highway 46
Wasco, CA 93280
800-499-9019 (phone)
805-758-4777 (phone)
805-758-4999 (fax)
Vitis vinifera cultivars, seedless
   grapes, rootstocks

Volz Vineyard & Nursery
109 Gibson Street
Bath, NY 14810
607-776-2270 (phone)
Vitis vinifera cultivars

Wortman Nursery
516 Goehmann
Fredericksburg, TX 78624
830-997-7460 (phone)
cuttings only

Glossary

abscission: the separation of a fruit or leaf from the rest of the plant. Occurs at a one-cell-thick zone, referred to as the abscission zone.

achenes: simple, dry, one-celled, one-seeded indehiscent fruit. Achenes are found on the surface of the strawberry receptacle.

adventitious: produced in an unusual or irregular position, or at an unusual time of development; used to describe plant organs such as buds, roots, or shoots.

angiosperm: a plant that has seeds borne within a matured ovary within a fruit. Broadly used as a classification for flowering plants.

berry: a simple fruit derived from one flower, in which the parts remain succulent; may be derived from an ovary or from an ovary plus receptacle tissue. More broadly used to indicate a small, soft fruit that can be eaten whole.

bramble: any plant belonging to the genus *Rubus*. Includes raspberries, blackberries, and their hybrids.

calyptra: the fused petals of a flower.

cane: the main stem of many small-fruit plants, including brambles, blueberries, and *Ribes* species. In grapes, canes are the one-year-old stems only. Also used to describe grape-training systems in which long, one-year-old shoots are replaced annually.

cordon: the horizontal or nearly horizontal stems of grape plants that are 2 or more years old. Distinguished from the vertical stems, which are called trunks. Used to describe training systems in which horizontal, semipermanent stems support short canes (spurs) for fruiting.

chlorophyll: the green pigment found in plants in which light is converted to chemical energy via photosynthesis.

chlorosis: absence of green color in the leaves.

cultivar: a cultivated variety.

cutting: a shoot or root piece used to propagate a new plant.

dicot (dicotyledon): a plant that has repeatedly branched veins. Distinguished from monocots, which have veins that are parallel through the leaf. Dicots include most broadleaved plants.

dicotyledonous: having the characteristics of dicots.

dioecious: having male and female flowers borne on separate plants; literally means "two houses."

enology: the study of wine making.

fungicide: a chemical that kills fungi.

glyphosate: a common herbicide that nonselectively removes plants. Trade name is Roundup.

gymnosperm: a plant with seeds borne on open scales, usually cones. Broadly describes confererous plants.

herbicide: a chemical that kills plants; usually used to remove weeds from cultivated areas.

horticulture: the art and science of growing plants.

ICM (IPM): Integrated Crop (Pest) Management. A system of growing crops that uses knowledge of the entire biological system (plant, insects, diseases, environment) to optimize yield.

inflorescence: a flower cluster.

inoculum: a pathogen, or its part, that can infect a plant.

insecticide: a chemical that kills insects.

macroclimate: the climate of a large area, such as of the northeastern United States.

mesoclimate: the climate of a clearly defined region, such as the southern slope of Mount Everest.

microclimate: the climate surrounding the canopy of plants in a biological system. Often used more broadly to describe the climate and conditions of a specific site, such as the field next to a house.

monocot (monocotyledon): a plant having leaves with veins that run parallel to one another. Includes all grasses.

mycorrhizae: a symbiotic (mutually beneficial), nonpathogenic association between fungi and the roots of plants. All berry plants have this association, though the nature of the association varies with the plant family.

organic matter: materials that are rich in carbon, specifically from decaying organisms. Most soils have some organic matter, however it is often added to soils to increase tilth and water/nutrient content and holding capacity.

pedicel: the small stem that attaches the fruit to the stem of the plant.

perennial: having a life span of more than 2 years.

pesticide: a chemical that kills pests. Insecticides, fungicides, and herbicides are all pesticides.

pests: organisms that injure or harm plants or their products.

photosynthesis: the production of organic substances, chiefly carbohydrates, from carbon dioxide and water. Occurs in the green leaves of plants.

phytotoxic: literally, toxic to plants. Usually used to refer to a chemically induced spot or burn on leaves.

pollination: the transfer of pollen from the anther to the stigma. May be accomplished by wind, bees, or other insects.

pomology: the study of fruit and fruit culture.

primocane: a one-year-old cane of a bramble plant.

primordia: cells, tissues, or organs in their earliest stage of differentiation.

propagation: the making of new plants, either by sexual means (seeds) or by asexual means such as cuttings, grafting, or division.

propagule: a structure that becomes separated from the parent plant and serves as a means of creating a new plant.

renovation: a process used to rejuvenate strawberry beds.

runner: a specialized above-ground stem that roots at the tip to develop a new plant.

scion: a detached stem, usually dormant, used to create a new plant via grafting.

stolon: see runner.

sucker: an adventitious shoot produced from the roots or the lower portion of a stem.

trickle irrigation: a watering system that applies water directly to the soil under the plant via tubes with holes, orifices, or emitters; contrast to overhead irrigation, which sprays water over the plants. Also called drip irrigation.

verasion: the stage of grape development when grape berries begin to turn color and/or soften.

viticulture: the art and science of grape growing.

References and Other Resources

GENERAL REFERENCES

Bailey, L. H., and E. Z. Bailey. 1976. *Hortus Third: A Concise Dictionary of Plants Cultivated in the United States and Canada.* New York: Macmillan Publishing Company.

Childers, N. F. 1983. *Modern Fruit Science.* Gainesville, Florida: Horticultural Publications.

Galletta, G., and D. Himelrick, eds. 1990. *Small Fruit Crop Management.* Englewood Cliffs, New Jersey: Prentice Hall.

Hartmann, H. T, D. E. Kester, F. T. Davies, and R. L. Geneve. 1997. *Plant Propagation: Principles and Practices.* Upper Saddle River, New Jersey: Prentice Hall.

Jackson, D. 1986. *Temperate and Subtropical Fruit Production.* Wellington, New Zealand: Butterworths.

Janick, J., and J. N. Moore. 1996. *Fruit Breeding.* Vol. II, *Vine and Small Fruits.* New York: John Wiley and Sons.

Westwood, M. N. 1993. *Temperate-Zone Pomology: Physiology and Culture.* 3rd ed. Portland, Oregon: Timber Press.

STRAWBERRIES

Childers, N. F. 1981. *The Strawberry.* Gainesville, Florida: Horticultural Publications.

Handley, D., and M. Pritts, eds. 1996. *Strawberry Production Guide.*

Ithaca, New York: Northeast Regional Agricultural Engineering Service.

Maas, J. L. 1984. *Compendium of Strawberry Diseases*. St. Paul, Minnesota: American Phytopathological Society.

Wilhelm, S., and J. E. Sagen. 1972. *A History of the Strawberry*. Berkeley: Agricultural Publications, University of California.

BRAMBLES

ADAS/MAFF Reference Book 156. 1982. *Cane Fruit*. London: Grower Books.

Ellis, M. A., R. H. Converse, R. N. Williams, and B. Williamson. 1991. *Compendium of Raspberry and Blackberry Diseases and Insects*. St. Paul, Minnesota: American Phytopathological Society.

Pritts, M., and D. Handley, eds. 1989. *Bramble Production Guide*. Ithaca, New York: Northeast Regional Agricultural Engineering Service.

BLUEBERRIES

Caruso, F. L., and D. C. Ramsdell. 1995. *Compendium of Blueberry and Cranberry Diseases*. St. Paul, Minnesota: American Phytopathological Society.

Eck, P. 1988. *Blueberry Science*. New Brunswick, New Jersey: Rutgers University Press.

Eck, P., and N. Childers, eds. 1966. *Blueberry Culture*. New Brunswick, New Jersey: Rutgers University Press.

Pritts, M., and J. Hancock, eds. 1992. *Highbush Blueberry Production Guide*. Ithaca, New York: Northeast Regional Agricultural Engineering Service.

GRAPES

Galet, P. 1979. *A Practical Ampelography: Grapevine Identification.* Ithaca, New York: Cornell University Press.

Grapes: Production, Management and Marketing. 1991. Columbus: Ohio State University Extension Bulletin 815, Agdex 231.

Morton, L. T. 1985. *Winegrowing in Eastern America: An Illustrated Guide to Viniculture East of the Rockies.* Ithaca, New York: Cornell University Press.

Mullins, M. G., A. Bouquet, and L. E. Williams. 1992. *Biology of the Grapevine.* New York: Cambridge University Press.

Oregon Winegrowers' Association. 1992. *Oregon Winegrape Grower's Guide.* Portland, Oregon: Oregon Winegrowers' Association.

Pearson, R. C., and A. C. Goheen. 1988. *Compendium of Grape Diseases.* St. Paul, Minnesota: American Phytopathological Society.

Reisch, B. I., D. V. Peterson, R. M. Pool, and M. Howell-Martens. 1993. *Table Grape Varieties for Cool Climates.* Penn Yan, New York: Cornell Cooperative Extension, Finger Lakes Grape Program, Information Bulletin 233.

Reisch, B. I., R. M. Pool, D. V. Peterson, M. Howell-Martens, and T. Henick-Kling. 1993. *Wine and Juice Grape Varieties for Cool Climates.* Penn Yan, New York: Cornell Cooperative Extension, Finger Lakes Grape Program, Information Bulletin 233.

Smart, R., and M. Robinson. 1991. *Sunlight into Wine: A Handbook for Winegrape Canopy Management.* San Rafael, California: Practical Winery and Vineyard Bookshelf.

Winkler, A. J., A. Cook, W. M. Kliewer, and L. A. Lider. 1974. *General Viticulture.* Berkeley: University of California Press.

Wolf, T., and B. Poling. 1995. *The Mid-Atlantic Winegrape Grower's Guide.* Raleigh: Department of Agricultural Communications, North Carolina State University.

Wine Making

Anderson, S. F., and D. Anderson. 1989. *Winemaking: Recipes, Equipment, and Techniques for Making Wine at Home.* Kent, England: Harcourt, Brace.

Berry, C. J. J. 1994. *First Steps in Winemaking: A Complete Month-By-Month Guide to Winemaking.* Ann Arbor, Michigan: G. W. Kent.

Garey, T. A. 1996. *The Joy of Home Winemaking.* New York: Avon Books.

Iverson, J. 1999. *Home Winemaking: Step By Step.* Seattle: Stonemark Publishing Company.

Leverett, B. 1996. *The Complete Guide to Home Winemaking.* Nashville, Tennessee: Prism Press.

Wine Making as a Hobby. 1997. University Park: College of Agricultural Sciences, Pennsylvania State University.

OTHER SMALL FRUIT CROPS

Friends of the Trees. 1992. *Kiwifruit Enthusiasts Journal.* Vol. 6. (Tonasket, Wash.)

Reich, L. 1991. *Uncommon Fruits Worthy of Attention.* Reading, Massachusetts: Addison-Wesley.

NATIONAL AND INTERNATIONAL ORGANIZATIONS

American Pomological Society
103 Tyson Building
University Park, PA 16802
This professional society produces the quarterly publication *Fruit Varieties Journal.*

The International Ribes Association (TIRA)
Executive Secretary, Ed Mashburn
707 Front Street
Northumberland, PA 17857
A wonderful organization for a little-appreciated group of fruits, specifically gooseberries and currants and related fruits.

North American Bramble Growers Association
Executive Secretary, Richard Fagan
13006 Mason Road NE
Cumberland, MD 21502
www.gfwc.com/bramble/
Primarily for commercial growers, but good information for all, with annual programs and a newsletter.

North American Fruit Explorers, Inc. (NAFEX)
1716 Apples Road
Chapin, IL 62628
www.nafex.org (a terrific Web site)
Primarily for amateurs, NAFEX is a network of individuals throughout the world devoted to developing, discovering, cultivating, evaluating, and appreciating superior varieties of fruits and nuts. Produces a great anecdotal journal written by members, called *Pomona.*

North American Strawberry Growers Association
Executive Secretary, Erin Bruzewski
2400 Beck Road
Howell, Michigan 48843
www.fvs.cornell.edu/GrowerOrganizations/NASGA/WEL-COME.HTM
Primarily for commercial growers.

In addition to these organizations, the cooperative extension system in the United States is a fertile source of local information on any agricultural pursuit. It is an educational service supported by county, state, and federal monies, with an office in nearly every county in the United States. Your local extension service can usually be found in the phone book under "Services." Most extension services also have developed web sites.

Plant Name Index

Subject Index